Andrea Palladio

The Churches of Rome

medieval & renaissance texts & studies

VOLUME 72

Andrea Palladio
The Churches of Rome

by

Eunice D. Howe

medieval & Renaissance texts & studies
Binghamton, New York
1991

Library of Congress Cataloging-in-Publication Data

Palladio, Andrea, 1508–1580.
  [Descritione de le chiese, stationi, indulgenze & reliquie
de corpi sancti, che sonno in la città de Roma. English]
  Andrea Palladio: The Churches of Rome / by Eunice D.
Howe.
        p. cm. — (Medieval & Renaissance texts & studies ;
  v. 72)
  Translation of: Descritione de le chiese, stationi, indul-
genze & reliquie de corpi sancti . . . , Le cose maravigliose di
Roma, and Schakerlay's La guida Romana per tutti i
forastieri che vengono per bedere le antichità di Roma.
  Includes bibliographical references and index.
  ISBN 0-86698-082-2
  1. Christian pilgrims and pilgrimages — Italy — Rome —
Guide-books.   2. Churches, Catholic — Italy — Rome —
Guide-books.   3. Rome (Italy) — Description — Guide-
books.   I. Howe, Eunice.   II. Schakerlay. Guida
Romana per tutti i forastieri che vengono per bedere le an-
tichità di Roma. 1990.   III. Cose maravigliose di Roma.
English. 1990.   IV. Title.   V. Series.
BX2320.5.I8P3413   1991
246'.95'0945632 — dc20   90–41061
                                                               CIP

This book is made to last.
It is set in Baskerville, smythe-sewn,
and printed on acid-free paper
to library specifications.

Printed in the United States of America

Table of Contents

List of Illustrations

Acknowledgments

I am indebted to the many individuals who offered encouragement, shared insights and directed me along the frequently tortuous path which led to the completion of this project. All were generous and unsparing in their support — Palladian scholars, experts on guidebook literature or admirers of Rome. Often friends and sometimes strangers, they know who they are. I must add my special thanks to the following: Jean D'Amato, Dorothy Metzger Habel, Victor Ingrassia, Francesca Italiano, Martin Kubelik, Douglas Lewis, Franca Nardelli, Armando Petrucci, Dana Smith, John Tedeschi, Egon Verheyen, and Paul Zygas.

I am grateful to have received grants from the American Philosophical Society and the Gladys Krieble Delmas Foundation. A Summer Institute at the Newberry Library, supported by the National Endowment for the Humanities, contributed to my understanding of textual studies. The American Association of University Women granted me a postdoctoral fellowship which launched the project. The Centro Internazionale di Studi di Andrea Palladio in Vicenza and the Royal Institute of British Architects in London offered access to their superb collections of material on Palladio. Research on guidebooks to Rome would have been unthinkable without access to the Bibliotheca Hertziana, the Biblioteca Vaticana and the Biblioteca Vittorio Emanuele. Other institutions, like the Newberry Library in Chicago, the Fowler Collection in Baltimore, the J. Paul Getty Center in Santa Monica, the British Library in London, Widener Library at Harvard University and the Biblioteca Nazionale in Florence yielded unexpected finds.

In keeping with its subject, this project was one of exploration which took me along miles of Roman pavement and into unforeseen areas of scholarly inquiry, much of it unfamiliar to an art historian. Throughout, I relied on the work of scholars who long ago tackled important issues relating to written accounts of the city. To name but the most obvious examples, Thomas Ashby, Christian Huelsen, Rodolfo Lanciani, and Ludwig Schudt all left a remarkable legacy by resurrecting literary descriptions of Renaissance Rome which inform the modern reader.

Introduction

Andrea Palladio's guide to the churches of Rome, the *Descritione de le Chiese, Stationi, Indulgenze & Reliquie de Corpi Sancti, che sonno in la Città de Roma*, was published in 1554 together with a companion volume entitled *L'Antichità di Roma*[1] (Figs. 1, 2). Both books were unabashedly popularizing in character. They were directed to the general public, visitors to Rome who had little or no knowledge of the city and its history. In light of Palladio's fascination with the building practices of ancient Rome, it seems natural that he should have undertaken a guidebook to the antiquities. Not surprisingly it met with great success and numerous editions were issued between 1554 and 1711, all prominently bearing the author's name.[2] His book on the churches, to the contrary, was never reprinted nor was the original text ever translated from the sixteenth-century Italian. Before a facsimile reprint made the work accessible to modern readers, consultation of the original guidebook was difficult. Only six copies of the work are known to survive.[3] Further complicating matters, Palladio's name appeared on the frontispiece of the guidebook of 1554, but all subsequent versions of the text, which came to be known as *Le cose maravigliose dell'alma città di Roma*, were issued as the work of an anonymous author.[4]

Ludwig Schudt, in his fundamental study of guidebooks to Rome, distinguished Palladio's literary contribution by establishing the pivotal position of *Le Chiese*. He identified Palladio's work as the source for one of the most enduring descriptions of Christian Rome, *Le cose maravigliose*.[5] Yet Schudt's conclusions about the importance of the guide and Palladio's role in its formation have never received serious consideration. Perhaps because the reputation of the author-architect promises enticements which the text does not deliver, *Le Chiese* has remained a misunderstood episode in Palladio's career.

Le Chiese is indeed a curious book. Modest in length and devout in nature, it appears uncharacteristic of the famed Renaissance architect of Vicenza and author of *I Quattro Libri dell'Architettura*. In the text Palladio ignores classical antiquity (leaving that subject for the companion guide) and addresses instead the wide but circumscribed audience of the Christian faithful. Understandably, the book easily is dismissed by architectural historians who find the contents unrelated to Palladio's own buildings, drawings or other literary projects.[6] Questions also surround Palladio's participation in the project, and his unexpected role as an authority on religious tradition. After the original publication of 1554, all traces of Palladio's authorship vanished. His name disappeared from the frontispiece and his preface to the readers was dropped in later, revised editions; concurrently, the title of the work was changed to *Le cose maravigliose di Roma*. Such idiosyncracies have served to obscure Palladio's contribution as the author of one of the most influential guidebooks to Roman churches written during the Renaissance.

Palladio's first books, the two guides to Rome, are distinct from his subsequent literary ventures. His later works, published after 1570, were directed to a different audience and dedicated to distinguished patrons or dignitaries. Polished and erudite, these treatises are a testimony to Palladio's intellectual independence, critical judgment and humanistic training. No theory of architecture has endured longer than that espoused by Palladio in *I Quattro Libri dell'Architettura*.[7] Research for the project was well underway as early as 1555, although the books were published only in 1570. Palladio revised the text several times before the final version with woodcut illustrations was published by Domenico de' Franceschi of Venice. The concise language, painstaking research and didactic images contributed to the resounding success of the *Quattro Libri*, a treatise which appealed to the intellect while promising tangible rewards to the architect and patron. Throughout the text of the *Quattro Libri*, Palladio refers to his long-standing and first-hand familiarity with the remains of the Roman world. In the dedicatory preface published in 1570, the author establishes his authority in characteristically succinct prose when

he relates that he saw ancient monuments with his own eyes and measured them with his own hands.[8] In the introduction to Book 1, Palladio brings his research on the project into contemporary focus by
acknowledging his friends and colleagues of Venice and Vicenza. The
work had evolved over the course of the architect's career, and in its entirety represented the consummation of his studies. Rather than the general public, Palladio aimed the treatise at an educated readership in an
effort to communicate fundamental principals and closely-held beliefs.

Palladio remains most renowned as the author of the *Quattro Libri*, but
he also produced erudite studies on historical subjects from the ancient
world. Although *I Commentari di C. Giulio Cesare* originated in the early
stages of Palladio's career, the book was printed five years after the *Quattro Libri* by the same Venetian publishing house. The Venetian Senate
issued a decree on 2 March 1575 which granted Palladio publication
privileges for a new edition of the translation of the *Commentari*, a preface
and drawings.[9] Palladio was prompted to bring the project to fruition
by the sudden deaths of his two sons, Leonida and Orazio, who illustrated the work and whom he wanted to commemorate.[10] The text was
based on an Italian translation of 1554, with Palladio's sons modelling
their maps and some diagrams after the illustrations published in earlier editions as well. Palladio composed an introduction to the work which
acknowledged the influence of his mentor Giangiorgio Trissino but he
ended with a dedication to Giacomo Boncompagno, the natural son of
Pope Gregory XIII and leader of the army of the Catholic Church. The
Commentari was a distinguished military treatise growing out of an age-
old literary tradition which glorified the practice of warfare as an art.[11]
Such scholarly efforts not only indicated Palladio's absorption with antiquity but also demonstrated his belief in the authority of earlier texts.

Palladio's published works provide but a partial picture of his studies
of antiquity. It is well-established that he intended to add another chapter on the subject of Roman bath structures to the *Quattro Libri*. The drawings for this section of the treatise were not published until 1730 by Lord
Burlington who had discovered them at the Villa Barbaro in Maser. But
the drawings also were known to Palladio's contemporaries.[12] A second
project left unfinished at Palladio's death was a study of the Greek historian
Polybius dedicated to Francesco de' Medici, Grand Duke of Tuscany.[13]
Historical inquiries in collaboration with Giangiorgio Trissino and Daniele
Barbaro enabled Palladio to amass other scholarly material. During the
early 1550s, he engaged in research and executed illustrations for Daniele

Barbaro's edition of Vitruvius: *I Dieci libri dell'architettura di M. Vitruvius* (Venice, 1556). An architect steeped in the classical tradition, Palladio entertained a life-long preoccupation with historical and literary sources. His unfinished, collaborative projects undoubtedly attracted the attention of his contemporaries and were instrumental in establishing Palladio's preeminence.

The subject of Palladio's *Le Chiese* thus occupies a singular place among his literary works. Because Palladio composed the book for the Christian pilgrim, the narrative combines an account of relics and indulgences with historical background on the churches of Rome. Despite his disclaimers, Palladio borrowed material from earlier guidebooks, relying in particular on the 1550 edition of *Le cose maravigliose*. His writing is devoid of literary flourishes and flights of imagination. Only rarely does the author digress from his stated objectives of accuracy and practicality by including observations about recent renovations or artistic commissions. *Le Chiese* was directed to the first-time visitor to Rome who was motivated by the desire to venerate the relics and visit the sites of Christian Rome.

Palladio prefaces his work with a statement of his intentions to produce a revised description of sacred "things" as a supplement to his recent book on the antiquities. He perceived his contribution to the guidebook tradition as twofold — to correct inaccuracies then circulating in printed books and to construct a new itinerary. For each church he lists pertinent facts about the foundation, relics, indulgences and stations. In this respect, it is significant that Palladio emphasizes personal contact with sites instead of reliance on written sources. He dismisses literary accounts as outdated, instead preferring the authority of writings on stone tablets — papal bulls and sacred histories — conserved in the churches themselves.[14] He admonishes readers of the complexity of the subject by reminding them that Rome was said once to possess more than 3,000 churches. Finally, and significantly, Palladio makes a favorable comparison between sixteenth-century Rome and antiquity. He cites, as evidence of her enduring attraction, those "sacred things which are still hers" (Trans., p. 72).

The most important innovation which Palladio made in *Le Chiese* was to establish a sequential list of churches comprising a route through Christian Rome for the pilgrim to follow. Palladio begins with the standard history of the origins of the Roman church and then turns to a description of the seven major churches: San Giovanni in Laterano, San Pietro in Vaticano, San Paolo, Santa Maria Maggiore, San Lorenzo, San Se-bastiano, Santa Croce in Gerusalemme. However, the heart of the guide-book consists of an itinerary divided into four circuits (Fig. 5). The first route covered the two churches on the Tiber Island as well as nine in Trastevere and nine in the Vatican Borgo. The northern entrance to Rome, the Porta del Popolo, marks the beginning of the next sequence which ended at the Capitoline Hill. This was the longest circuit, including fifty-two churches along the way. The Capitoline was the starting point for the final two itineraries—one which headed north toward the "moun-tains" and the other, south in the direction of the "ancient" city. Earlier guidebooks listed churches in a haphazard order whereas Palladio or-ganized effectively a logical method of visiting the sacred sites of Rome. His reference to the considerable effort entailed reflects perhaps the strain of the undertaking—which involved the ordering of one hundred and twenty-one churches: "Thus, when everyone is informed, they will have no small amount of praise for this effort of mine" (Trans., p. 72). It turned out to provide a legacy of uncertain value for Palladio. Although later authors of guidebooks to Roman churches conformed to the configura-tion of the itinerary, they never acknowledged Palladio's *Le Chiese* as their source.

The present study examines issues which had an impact on the gene-sis and dissemination of *Le Chiese*. The first chapter reconstructs Palla-dio's youthful experiences in Rome and, in evoking the inquisitive spirit of those years, speculates on his involvement with the topography, ar-chitecture and traditions of the city. The second chapter assesses Palla-dio's motives for composing *Le Chiese*. Attention is directed to the practical and scholarly concerns of the young architect, the debt he felt to his pa-trons and lastly the religious climate of mid-sixteenth-century Italy. The final chapter considers the text of *Le Chiese* by suggesting sources for Pal-ladio's guidebook as well as reconstructing the process whereby it was transformed into successive editions of *Le cose maravigliose*.

Note on the Translation of *Le Chiese* and *La guida romana*

Palladio's original text of 1554 has been translated into English. Only the list of *Le Stationi, Indulgentie & Gratie spirituali*, which may be found in Murray (1972), has been omitted from *Le Chiese*.

The earliest alterations of Palladio's text discovered to date appear in a 1561 edition of *Le cose maravigliose*, but these revisions were slight compared to those introduced in the edition of 1563 where sentences or short passages were attached to the end of many paragraphs. The result was an updated text which offered current, and occasionally more detailed, information to the reader. In the English translation, the lines of text added by the anonymous editor of 1563 have been italicized, affording for the first time a comparison with Palladio's original book. In those instances where Palladio's text was altered, the new lines — always italicized — appear in brackets. (It should also be borne in mind that Palladio's preface to the readers was dropped from all later editions, as explained in chapter three.)

A survey of later editions of the guidebook reveals the steps in its transformation. (See *Le cose maravigliose*: List of Editions Consulted). The evidence is necessarily fragmentary because revisions in surviving copies of *Le Chiese* may not reflect the actual date of their introduction. Nevertheless, the juxtaposition of the editions of 1554 and 1563 shows the changes effected in Roman churches during the intervening years, and the foundation which Palladio's book laid for all editions of *Le cose maravigliose* of

the later sixteenth century. Despite the inevitable corrections and am-
plifications, his account remained integral and indispensable.

I have deferred to Palladio throughout the translation in respect to word-
ing and grammar. In so far as possible an identical pattern of phrasing
has been maintained even when it presents a certain awkwardness to
the modern reader. Some descriptions therefore lapse into cumbersome
discourses or employ antiquated figures of speech — probably true as well
in Palladio's own era. Nevertheless, the cadence of his prose frequently
reveals his opinions or biases and for this reason it seemed preferable
to preserve the original form. I have indicated *lacunae* or illegible char-
acters in the guidebook by inserting [?] in the text. Churches and sites
retain their Italian titles. The names of saints, popes and patrons are
anglicized, if an equivalent exists. If not, the Italian form has been employed.

The appendix consists of a short guide to Roman antiquities, *Trattato
delle Antichità, chiamato La guida romana*. This account was composed by an
Englishman called Schakerlay who, residing in Rome, compiled an itinerary of two and a half days' duration for tourists who wanted to visit ancient monuments. *La guida romana* was introduced in the 1557 edition of
Le cose maravigliose, the first to be published after Palladio's *Le Chiese*. It
became a fixture of all subsequent editions, the most ubiquitous and surely
the most popular guide to ancient Rome. Yet, *La guida romana* has never
been translated, nor has the first edition, that of 1557, appeared in its
entirety. Here, the original text of *La guida romana* has been collated with
the earliest revisions, also printed in *Le cose maravigliose* of 1563. A comparison reveals the painstaking care with which editorial changes were
made, with the goals of clarity, succinctness and accuracy.

The guidelines for the translation are similar to those for *Le Chiese*.
Unlike Palladio however, the author of *La guida romana* used colloquial
figures of speech. I have refrained from making substantive changes, but
have attempted consistent spelling where the author fails. The italicized
text comes from the edition of 1563; it is enclosed in brackets when replac-
ing the original.

In an effort to limit commentary, I have directed notes to the following observations: corrections of outright mistakes, clarifications where
the meaning might be unclear (and especially when the monument in
question has been destroyed, moved or is otherwise unrecognizable) and
occasional remarks on the juxtaposition between the original text and
the additions in *Le cose maravigliose*. I leave larger conclusions to the reader —
"Allaquale augurando felicità vivete liete."

Part I

Commentary

Chapter One

Palladio's Roman Experience

In contrast to the notoriety of his other written works, *Le Chiese* attracted little attention from the admirers, scholars and followers of Palladio.
Palladio's authorship of a guidebook to the churches of Rome went largely
unnoticed by his contemporaries—to judge from surviving evidence.
There is no documentation of the attendant historical facts nor any record
of his own role in its composition. Palladio's early biographers ignored
the book completely. Writing in 1616, Paolo Gualdo recalls only that the
author travelled to Rome for the fifth time and produced a small volume
on the antiquities, often matched and sold with the *Mirabilia Romae*. As
later authors were to do after him, Gualdo ignored *Le Chiese* in favor of
its more conspicuous companion volume, *L'Antichità di Roma.*[1]

Palladio's experiences in Rome belonged to his formative years and
defined the course of his intellectual development. By the time of his fifth
and last trip in 1554, Palladio's commitment to the study of ancient Rome
had shaped his perception of the theory and practice of architecture. He
had interspersed his visits to Rome with architectural commissions in
and around his adopted city of Vicenza, buildings and projects which
displayed his debt to antiquity. In this context, his motivations for
publishing *Le Chiese* are difficult to comprehend, as the production of a
traditional guidebook for the Christian pilgrim to Rome appears an uncharacteristic and unusual undertaking. Yet his involvement with the

project may be understood as the result of the architect's personal contacts and scholarly pursuits at a particular, and seldom examined, phase in his career.

Rome in the 1540s with Giangiorgio Trissino

Andrea di Pietro della Gondola was born in Padua in 1508, most likely on 30 November. Apprenticed to a local stonecutter he moved permanently to Vicenza in 1524. There he immediately enrolled in the guild of the masons and stonecutters, and joined the shop of Giovanni di Giacomo da Porlezza of Pedemuro and Girolamo Pittoni. He married a decade later, and the first of his five children was born the following year.[2] Although still called a stonecutter in the documents, Palladio was working on his first architectural commission, the Villa Godi (now Malinverni) at Lonedo di Lugo Vicentino (Vicenza) from c. 1537–1542. He already had formed what was to become a lasting bond with Giangiorgio Trissino who was building a villa at Cricoli. His first certain encounter with Trissino dates to 1537, but he may have known the Vicentine humanist since 1531.[3] Trissino was the first patron to champion the young architect, and he supervised Palladio's humanistic education and professional training (Fig. 7). At Trissino's urging, Palladio adopted his new name out of admiration for the wisdom of the ancients, and Pallas Athena in particular. The eponym also alluded to a guardian angel in Trissino's epic poem, *L'Italia Liberata dai Goti*.[4] Trissino's sponsorship provided opportunities to visit Rome, and Palladio departed on his first trip in 1541.

Knowledge about the dates of Palladio's journeys to Rome arises from circumstantial evidence. Gualdo, Palladio's earliest known biographer, writes only that Trissino took Palladio to Rome on three separate occasions so that the young architect could measure and draw the monuments of antiquity.[5] On the basis of Trissino's documented residence in the city, this first trip must have taken place during the summer of 1541.[6] Palladio's initial contact with the city surely elicited an immediate and enthusiastic response. He began to collect drawings of ancient buildings at this early stage, perhaps with an eye to applying motifs to his own work, but more likely as part of a general desire to absorb the lessons of antiquity.[7] A knowledge of Vitruvius, fostered by Trissino, provided the foundation for Palladio's study of the ancient world as did his earlier exposure to Roman monuments in northern Italy.[8] His drawings of antique structures originating from the first Roman sojourn demonstrate a sure grasp of the classical orders and monumental building types. Modern Rome too left its imprint on the young architect who for the first time confronted works by Bramante, Peruzzi, Antonio da Sangallo, Raphael and Giulio Romano. Palladio documented for posterity his study of these buildings, some of which were already known to him through Sebastiano Serlio's drawings for his *Treatise on Architecture*, with on-site sketches executed during his stay in 1541.[9]

Palladio's early endeavors were encouraged, if not orchestrated, by his influential protector, Giangiorgio Trissino. The sixty-three-year-old patron had invited the young architect to join his entourage in Vicenza, and upon arrival in Rome, surely introduced Palladio to a wider circle of acquaintances including artists, scholars and dignitaries at the papal court. It was natural that Trissino should use his contacts to open doors for Palladio who must have enjoyed access to the leading intellectuals of his day, gaining exposure to their philosophical and religious leanings.

Few individuals were better suited to the role of mentor than Giangiorgio Trissino. Born in Vicenza, he originally visited Rome as a twenty-two-year-old humanist in 1500.[10] He returned after the election of Leo X with whom he maintained close relations, first as an intimate of the papal court and then as ambassador. Trissino published his early works in the Rome of Clement VII where he lived from 1523–1525. The following decade saw yet another period of residence in the city and, when Trissino arrived with Palladio in the summer of 1541, he received a cordial welcome from Pope Paul III (1534–1549).

Trissino excelled at composing short verses which he dedicated to artists, friends, humanists and historical figures. On the occasion of this trip to Rome, he presented an epigram to Paul III which introduced a manuscript copy of Ptolemy's *Libri harmonicarum*.[11] The personal ties between the Vicentine humanist and the Farnese family must have created an hospitable environment, offering new experiences to the young Palladio. As Trissino's companion, he may have witnessed scholarly discourse on the subject of music as well as antiquity. He would have travelled with Trissino to outlying Roman sites, such as Viterbo and Bagnaia. Finally, the assistance offered to Palladio by the reigning pope insured Palladio access to the great architectural projects of sixteenth-century Rome.[12]

Elected pope on 12 October 1534 at the age of sixty-seven, Cardinal Alessandro Farnese brought to the papacy a zeal for ambitious building schemes and a natural inclination for scholarly discourse. As Paul III, he fostered the work of a circle of humanists, in particular musicians and writers. He assumed an active role in the Counter-Reformation, and pushed in vain for a meeting of the Council in Vicenza in 1537. Although he had never joined a religious order, he espoused the causes of the Capuchins and Jesuits. But it was as a patron of the arts that Paul III left his most enduring mark. Upon his succession to the papacy he took an immediate interest in completing the decoration of the Sistine Chapel, continuing the rebuilding of San Pietro and renovating the Belvedere and its gardens—projects which were all underway by 1541.[13]

Other undertakings which had changed the urban landscape of Rome included the additions at San Marco and the Aracoeli, the design of the piazza on the Capitoline and the fortifications of the city. Antonio da Sangallo, who was then papal architect, supervised the building at San Pietro; he resumed work at the Farnese Palace during the very year that Palladio first arrived in Rome. It is quite likely that the younger architect inspected these projects before Sangallo's death in 1546.[14]

Palladio departed from Rome after the summer of 1541 but spent little time in Vicenza during the years which immediately followed. Finally he returned to Rome in September, 1545 and except for a brief absence in February and early March of the following year, he remained in the city until July, 1547. He made the initial trip back to Rome in the company of Trissino, Marc'Antonio Thiene and Giovanni Battista Maganza but he seems to have absented himself independently in order to return to Vicenza.[15] Although two trips to Rome are credited to Palladio during this period, it is more accurate to assume that the city served as his home base for nearly two years. This interpretation of the evidence is supported by the report that Trissino travelled to Rome only twice with Palladio before a final expedition in 1549.[16] Thus this protracted stay represented Palladio's most significant contact with the city.

After sharing rental property, Trissino bought a house near the Pantheon in Campo Marzio which accommodated his young friends.[17] Palladio was already acquainted with Marc'Antonio Thiene who had commissioned a house in the contrada of Santo Stefano (Vicenza) from the architect.[18] Thiene, however, became more than a patron; he formed an intimate friendship with Palladio. The Vicentine noble was a wealthy landowner who cultivated an interest in the arts, and Palladio later lauded his "cultura architettonica."[19] While he stayed in Rome, Thiene apparently dedicated himself to a systematic study of antiquity. These pursuits included Maganza and Palladio, and probably formed the core of what Thiene called the "accademia nostra."[20]

Giovanni Battista Maganza was both a painter and a poet who specialized in the Vicentine dialect. He was a prominent member of the tightly-knit group which surrounded Trissino in Rome. His close association with Marc'Antonio Thiene and Palladio developed into a lifelong friendship.[21] Years later, when Maganza had become an accomplished master, he produced a portrait of Palladio which was to become the most widely replicated image of the architect. Painted in 1576 for the Marchese Capra, it hung in his collection at the Villa Rotonda where it served as the model for numerous engravings[22] (Fig. 6). The artist employed conventions to identify the subject as an architect. Palladio holds the attribute of his profession, the compass, and an scroll inscribed with his name and the date. Although Palladio's scholarly credentials were well-established by this date, and in fact the *Commentarii* had been published during the previous year, no reference to his literary pursuits exists. The scroll, even if it lacked the inscription which exists at present, served to recall his architectural designs, not his investigations of antiquity. Despite his long contact with the subject, Maganza did not introduce a personal characterization of the architect, unless it is the sense of modesty which the restrained image projects. Maganza remained a close friend until Palladio's death in 1580.

During his Roman sojourn, Maganza received several portrait commissions. It is ironic that he may well have arrived in Rome just after the departure of his fellow northerner, Titian, who had resided in Rome from April to July 1545 while working on a papal portrait. The great Venetian master rose above any competitors in contrast to Maganza who must have faced the challenge of finding work in a city already crowded with artists seeking a livelihood. At the same time Maganza continued his studies with members of Trissino's circle, in accord with their philosophy that scholarly activities should serve as a complement to the practice of the arts.[23] Indeed, the convictions which they held in common make it understandable that the painter Maganza should continue to write poetry throughout his career.

It is tempting to speculate that the Vicentine group frequented an academy in Rome organized by Giangiorgio Trissino and patterned after the activities at Cricoli. The elder humanist already had created a scholarly program or, as it came to be known, an "Accademia Trissiniana" situated at his Villa at Cricoli. There, participants followed a rigorous regime of study, focusing on ancient languages and philosophy, as well as rules governing personal conduct. Trissino attributed moral and intellectual value to the scholarship conducted at Cricoli which already had steered Palladio toward a deepening of his knowledge of the ancient world.[24] In Rome, Trissino's circle delved into the material at hand, which meant for Palladio not only a more intense exposure to Vitruvius and Roman remains, but also the continuation of his education as a man of letters. Although impossible to reconstruct, the program of study may have resembled that of the contemporary "Accademia dei Virtuosi," a group of Vitruvian scholars who met on the Palatine. The scholarly activities of Claudio Tolomei were sponsored by the Farnese family. Tolomei maintained contact with noted architects such as Sebastiano Serlio, Pirro Ligorio and Giacomo Barozzi da Vignola — all of whom were known to Trissino and his group including, of course, Palladio who shared their interest in Vitruvius and Polybius.[25] The two academies may have coexisted; no evidence links the two scholarly programs which were fostered by a common thirst for knowledge of the ancient world and its application to contemporary culture.

While participating in the "Accademia" sponsored by Trissino, Palladio made trips on horseback to Tivoli, Palestrina, the Port at Ostia and Albano where he sketched antique structures. As a dedicated scholar, Palladio also travelled on foot when he was unable to borrow a mule from Trissino. During his Roman stay of 1545–1547, he must have visited sites in southern Italy: the Phlegraean Fields, Capua and Naples.[26] It is likely that he spent as much time measuring buildings as drawing them, for he frequently calls attention to these early experiences in his later writing.[27] His Fourth Book on architecture provides evidence of those ancient monuments which fascinated him, and those within Rome and to the south which he studied first-hand: the Temple of Hadrian, the Tempietto at Clitunno, the Pantheon, the Temple of Vesta at Tivoli, the Temple of the Dioscuri in Naples and the Temple (Basilica) of Maxentius in Rome. Copious notes accompany his surviving drawings of antiquity, demonstrating Palladio's tendency to thoroughly document a building for the purpose of future reinterpretation. During these early years in Rome, Palladio must have started collecting architectural drawings executed by other draftsmen. He also consulted descriptions of the city in the works of ancient authors as well as in guidebooks to contemporary Rome. These written sources provided the architect with historical background which would later emerge in his own literary production just as he would rely upon architectural drawings as models for his own renderings.[28]

Thus Palladio explored the literary and physical remains of the ancient city with the support of Trissino and his "Accademia." The architect's ever-deepening involvement with the study of antiquity surfaced in the designs for the Basilica which he presented in Vicenza in February–March of 1546. Palladio had modified an earlier plan in the hopes of resolving the quandary about the design of Vicenza's city hall. Like the previous proposal for the facade, Palladio's new plan relied on northern Italian models but now demonstrated an infusion of archaeological detail.[29] Although his ideas seem not to have been solicited by the Deputies of the Basilica, Palladio travelled back to Vicenza specifically for the purpose of unveiling his new project for which an experimental bay was constructed in wood. The fact that he returned expeditiously to Rome suggests either that he had intended only to deliver a type of progress report or that his ideas did not meet with unanimous approval. At any rate, the architectural problem continued to be of deep concern to him, and possibly to the whole of Trissino's entourage.[30] The long-standing dispute about the design of the city hall continued in Vicenza until the end of the decade when Palladio, then recognized as a mature architect, received the commission. But in mid-March, 1546, he renewed his studies in Rome.

Palladio returned to Vicenza at the behest of Trissino in July, 1547. The apparent motive for the trip was to deliver some printed copies of Trissino's latest work, *Italia liberata dai Goti*, to his son Ciro. Trissino sent not only Palladio on this secret mission, but also another associate named Terpandro and, probably, Maganza.[31] This time Palladio stayed in Vicenza for the next two years, gathering architectural commissions and bringing to a conclusion his designs for the Basilica. Submitted by Palladio in association with Pedemuro, the proposal which finally won the favor of the Deputies utilized the Serlian motif on the two levels of the facade.[32] On 5 May 1549, an honorary citizenship was bestowed on Palladio as a result of his project for the loggia of the Basilica.

With Palladio's reputation as an architect established, a summons to Rome followed several months later. Gualdo writes that Palladio was enlisted to work on the new church of San Pietro but never began, due to the death of the pope shortly thereafter.[33] Paul III died on 10 November 1549 and Palladio returned to Vicenza the following month, never again to find in Rome a papal court supportive of his scholarly interests. The successors to the Farnese pope—Julius III, Marcellus II and Paul IV—were less concerned with the study of ancient monuments while Pius IV (1559–1569) delegated the study of antiquities to his preferred architect, Pirro Ligorio.

Despite the brevity of his visit in 1549, the opportunity arose for Palladio to seek out old friends in Rome, review the lessons of antiquity and visit new architectural projects. Once more Palladio found himself in the company of Giangiorgio Trissino and certainly Marc'Antonio Thiene who was then living in Rome. It is unclear whether Palladio and Trissino travelled together, for the elder humanist, who was now seventy-two years old, had returned to Venice in October of 1549. In Rome, he first lived with Fabio di Augubio, the Auditor of the Rota, or Felice Accoramboni, before moving into the lodgings of Marc'Antonio Thiene.[34] If during this period he introduced Palladio to his close friend Michelangelo, the younger architect could only have responded with enthusiasm.[35] After the death of Antonio da Sangallo in 1546, no architect commanded more respect nor exercised greater authority than Michelangelo.

Throughout these months Palladio was able to scrutinize the architectural projects of contemporary Rome. Although Gualdo asserts that Palladio turned his attention to ancient building types in and around Rome, this type of systematic study should be associated with his prior and more lengthy period of residence in the city. Similarly, his last visit to the city in 1554 was brief and motivated by other concerns. Instead, in 1549, Palladio could familiarize himself with recent work on San Pietro, including the frescoes of the Sistine and Pauline chapels. Michelangelo's design of the cornice for the Farnese Palace and the plans for the Capitoline Palaces had been realized. While Palladio was able to study Michelangelo's later works from engravings, those projects which he viewed first-hand had an immediate and lasting impact on his artistic development.[36] Moreover, Gualdo's assertion — and there is no reason to doubt him — that Palladio was to be involved with the building of San Pietro lends credence to the idea that Palladio was actively engaged in planning architectural projects at this point in his career.

Daniele Barbaro and the Trip of 1554

Palladio's final trip to Rome occurred five years later and, according to Gualdo's report, under circumstances different from any of his previous stays.[37] In the first place, he was accompanied by a new group of friends which included Daniele Barbaro, as is well known, and other Venetian gentlemen as well. Secondly, Palladio and his entourage appear to have focused on archaeological research. Finally, this last Roman sojourn resulted in the publication of Palladio's *L'Antichità di Roma* and, although

Gualdo omits it, *Le Chiese*. The trip commenced in February and ended before 29 May 1554 when Palladio was back in Vicenza.[38]

Daniele Barbaro played a decisive role in Palladio's Roman activities of 1554 (Fig. 8). He had become a protector and confidante of the architect, filling the void created by Giangiorgio's death in 1550. The three men shared friends and intellectual pursuits, and must have met when Barbaro was a student in Padua in 1538–1540.[39] It is indicative of their mutual sympathies that Palladio's close friend, the painter-poet Maganza, eventually entered Barbaro's circle as well. Barbaro's intense interest in humanistic studies and, in particular, the history of ancient architecture made him an ideal fellow traveller.

The Roman trip of 1554 may well have been prompted by research for the commentary on a new edition of Vitruvius, a project undertaken by Daniele Barbaro in collaboration with Palladio some years earlier, probably in 1547 before Barbaro moved to England as a Venetian ambassador.[40] In his enthusiasm for the ancient treatise on architecture, Barbaro sought first-hand exposure to the world of antiquity. He visited excavation sites with his entourage, surveyed ancient buildings and discussed methods of construction. Palladio recorded the fruits of these investigations in a series of woodcut engravings which were published as illustrations to Barbaro's *I Dieci libri dell'architettura di M. Vitruvio*, printed in Venice in 1556. Palladio's creations were original and, unlike those used for his own treatise, the woodcut images were representations of ideal concepts.

As an ecclesiastic, Daniele Barbaro enjoyed connections with leading members of the church hierarchy while, as a scholar, he was familiar with humanist circles in Rome. Both interests explain his contact with Pirro Ligorio, the archaeologist-architect in the employ of the papal court. Ligorio accompanied the Venetian prelate, and presumably his associates, on expeditions to ancient monuments.[41] However, Palladio's own acquaintance with Ligorio must have dated back to his earlier Roman trips. Palladio had used Ligorio's drawings as models and visited such sites as the Port of Trajan, near Ostia, and the Tempietto at Clitunno to study them first-hand.[42]

It is likely that Ligorio's own architectural designs held a strong attraction for Palladio. Ligorio had moved to Rome from his native Naples around 1534 and had pursued a career as a painter. By the end of the next decade, he had entered the employ of Cardinal Ippolito II d'Este of Ferrara, working as a painter, architect and archaeologist.[43] When

Cardinal d'Este became governor of Tivoli in 1550, Ligorio presumably directed the design, if not the construction, of the family villa and gardens. He also began excavations for antiquities at Hadrian's Villa in Tivoli which he described in three written accounts. Palladio, in the company of Daniele Barbaro, would have been able to visit both sites before work was temporarily halted in 1555. Cardinal d'Este himself was absent from Rome, but the party of Venetian visitors was surely entrusted to Pirro Ligorio whose plans for the villa gained the admiration of Daniele Barbaro, the scholar of Vitruvius, who had a natural interest in the design of the villa.[44] In addition, they must have seen the d'Este property in Rome, the villa and gardens studded with antiquities on the Quirinal Hill.

Ligorio's activities for the d'Este only partially explain the renown which would have brought him to the attention of Palladio. Furthermore his fame as a practicing architect came in later years when he became papal architect for Paul IV and Pius IV. Pirro Ligorio's real distinction lay in the profound knowledge of antiquities which he had already acquired, although he was only a few years older than Palladio. By the time of Palladio's last visit to Rome, Ligorio had prepared about forty volumes on Roman antiquities. These never went to press but were related to two shorter works: a study of the Baths of Diocletian, published by Tramezzini in Rome in 1558, and the *Libro di Pyrrho Ligorio Napoletano delle antichità di Roma*, published by Tramezzini in 1553.

The latter book was important for Palladio and may even have inspired him to compose his own guide to antiquities, *L'Antichità di Roma*, published in Rome and Venice the following year. Ligorio's account of the circuses, theatres and amphitheaters of ancient Rome represented but a portion of his larger project which listed monuments *sui generis*. Ligorio, while maintaining the standard format used since the *Mirabilia*, appended corrected identifications of Roman sites in the same spirit of antiquarian accuracy which Palladio espoused in the introduction to his own short guide. Like Palladio, Ligorio included no illustrations with his text. However, the first of his reconstructions of the ancient city had been issued the year before, in 1552, reproducing a panoramic view of antique monuments interspersed with ancient buildings[45] (Fig. 14). Both the book and the maps may have been available to Palladio in northern Italy, allowing him to study the organization of the ancient and modern city. Upon his return to Rome, Palladio must have consulted the leading antiquarian who was in the process of forging that mix of humanistic and artistic traditions which enlivened mid-sixteenth-century culture.

Palladio's Architectural Activities

It was inevitable that Palladio should make the most of each of his Roman sojourns to broaden his understanding of the city and its traditions, including its architectural marvels. His contact with practicing architects, never the primary motivation for his trips, was probably incidental and limited to exceptional luminaries like Michelangelo or fellow archaeological enthusiasts like Pirro Ligorio.[46] Palladio's own activity as a architect remains an unknown and undocumented dimension of this Roman experience. His earliest biographer is silent on the subject of architectural projects undertaken by Palladio during his stays in Rome. Gualdo, indeed, seems to emphasize that Palladio practiced architecture only after his return to northern Italy when he received numerous and significant commissions. The range of projects specified by Gualdo illustrates the diffusion of Palladio's fame: a palace in Trent, a palace in Turin, the cathedral facade in Bologna, the town hall of Brescia, many buildings in Venice and finally his works in Vicenza.[47] Yet a long-standing tradition, at least as old as Gualdo's account, attributes two works to Palladio, while later authors have credited him with two other Roman projects.

Palladio's name is linked with the altars of the Church and Hospital of *Santo Spirito*. Gaspare Celio in *Memorie delli nomi dell'artefici delle pitture*, published in 1639, attributes the design of the ciborium of the high altar of the church (now lost) and the altar tabernacle in the central chapel of the Corsia Sistina (extant but greatly altered) to Palladio.[48] Celio composed his guidebook eighteen years before its publication making his description roughly contemporary with Gualdo's biography. To judge from their diverse viewpoints and subjects, there is no reason to suspect that the authors were aware of each other's works or consulted the same sources. This is the earliest reference, discovered to date, of commissions undertaken by the architect during his trips to Rome, and among the Roman works attributed to Palladio, the Santo Spirito projects possess the strongest connections to his architectural activity in the city from 1545 to 1547. Two seventeenth-century engravings in combination with literary descriptions provide a general idea of the altars' earlier, though not necessarily original, appearances[49] (Figs. 9, 10). The classicizing design and decoration of both works, like Bramante's architecture, derive from antique prototypes and represent a solution suggestive of Palladio's antiquarian interests and familiarity with contemporary architectural design.

Of the two works, the ciborium formerly over the high altar of the Church of *Santo Spirito* displayed the stronger affinity to Palladio's own architecture. The small, free-standing ciborium was crowned by a triangular tympanum intersecting an octagonal drum and a cupola. The use of a centralized, free-standing structure reflects Palladio's interest in antique monuments. The design of the ciborium also suggests the influence of Michelangelo's projects for the design of San Pietro and Bramante's design of the *Tempietto*.[50] In its present state, the tabernacle in the Corsia Sistina possesses a more problematic relationship to Palladio's architecture (Fig. 11). The ocular windows in the drum and the ornamentation of the frieze have been identified as discordant elements in a Palladian design.[51] In addition, the lower part of the tabernacle supporting the frieze utilizes heavy supports of awkward proportion and colored marble, which clash with the canons of classical restraint espoused by Palladio.

Both the ciborium of the church and the altar of the hospital originated during an extensive building campaign at *Santo Spirito* which coincided with the very period when Palladio resided in Rome from 1545 to 1547. Major renovations were carried out at *Santo Spirito* under the direction of Francesco de Landis (1536–1546) and Alessandro Guidiccione (1546–1552), preceptors of the institution.[52] Construction of a new church began in 1538; the interior was embellished with funerary monuments and an organ in 1547. In that same year, a new coffered ceiling was installed in the Corsia Sistina which had been enlarged by the addition of a third wing. Guidiccione, who oversaw the continuing improvements at the institution, was a papal *familiare* and Paul III named him to head the hospital and its order in 1546.[53] In fact, it is likely that Paul III instigated the projects at *Santo Spirito* and witnessed their completion before his death in 1549.

As papal architect, Antonio da Sangallo had designed the new Church of *Santo Spirito* and, probably, the modifications to the Corsia Sistina. He was working as well on the program of fortifications of the Vatican Borgo, including the Porta Santo Spirito, up until the month before his death in August, 1546.[54] Sangallo many have intended a baldachin for the high altar of the church, especially as such a design tended to emphasize rather than obstruct the tall apse and impressive barrel vault terminating the nave (Fig. ;0). He already had fashioned a ciborium for the Pauline Chapel in the Vatican.[55] But the possibility also arises that the recently appointed preceptor of the hospital, Guidiccione, assigned the projects to a successor. Indeed the new administrator may have turned to Palladio, availing himself of an architect who, although inexperienced, had come to the attention of Paul III and surely the late Antonio da Sangallo.[56]

The earliest reproduction of the freestanding altar in the hospital, the engraving published in 1649, most likely represents the monument in an altered form (Fig. 9). During the sixteenth century, the altar of the SS. Sacramento, where daily mass was conducted at the center of the hospital, was composed of four white marble columns, a gold tabernacle and a tribune.[57] It offered an unobstructed view of the sacraments so that services could be witnessed by patients on three sides, in the Corsia Sistina as well as in the third wing. At some point, probably in the early seventeenth century, remodelling took place which added a vertical altar tabernacle and substituted unmatched supports of aggregate material for the four columns. But modern restoration of the hospital tabernacle has revealed the residuals of decoration from the sixteenth century(Fig. 11). The interior of the small cupola is painted with classicizing motifs and the exterior displays lilies which recall the insignia of Paul III.[58]

The absence of documentation coupled with the damage to the altars make an attribution to Palladio tenuous. Nevertheless the possibility persists of his intervention in the design of both altars during his Roman residence of 1545–1547. The emergence of an early seventeenth century reference to works at Santo Spirito by Palladio lends new weight to the attributions. It also is significant that later in his career Palladio designed a ciborium for the altar of the Ospedaletto of *Santi Giovanni e Paolo* in Venice, a project begun in 1574/75 and completed in 1580. As in the Church and perhaps the Hospital at *Santo Spirito*, the altar consisted of four fluted pilasters, or columns, elevated on steps, with a stone parapet. The surviving contract of 1575 reveals that the work was to be executed by stone carvers after his design.[59] As a mature architect, Palladio revived the form of an altar tabernacle which he had already used many years earlier for a comparable space within the Hospital of *Santo Spirito*.

The attribution of another work, a two-story loggia in the garden facade of the Palace of the Dukes of Tuscany, had gained currency as early as the mid-seventeenth century when Giovanni Battista Mola mentioned Palladio's name in connection with that part of that palace in the Campo Marzio.[60] With the publication of Temanza's authoritative biography, the project entered the repertory of Palladio's works. Yet, when pointing to the Roman commission as evidence of the architect's ability to compete with other luminaries active in the city, Temanza's words suggest less than certain conviction about the attribution of the *Palazzo di Firenze* to Palladio.[61] Moreover by the seventeenth century, a tradition had already gained currency that Jacopo Barozzi, il Vignola, was the architect responsible for the early palace renovations, including the inner court and the garden facade.[62]

The Roman residence of the Medici Dukes after 1562, the *Palazzo di Firenze* was designed around an interior courtyard, with a garden to the back. The plan of the entire palace evolved in stages as the property changed hands in the mid-sixteenth century.[63] In 1550–1551, Pope Julius III acquired the Cardelli family palace which he renovated, reputedly with funds from the Apostolic Treasury, before bestowing the building on his brother, Balduino del Monte. The Florentine architect, Bartolomeo Ammannati, who was already engaged by the pope at his villa, worked intermittently on the *Palazzo di Firenze* from 1552 to 1555. With the death of Julius III in 1555, the palace was sequestered by Paul IV. The property passed to the Medici family in 1562, and Ammannati returned at regular intervals to work on the palace.[64]

A two-story loggia constructed of marble was inserted in the masonry wall which faced the garden, providing an open portico at the center of the rear facade in the tradition of the Renaissance villa (Fig. 12). The loggia attributed by Temanza to Palladio has engaged columns of the Ionic and Corinthian orders, and shelters rooms decorated with frescoes in the "grottesque" style and sculptural relief. The truncated form of the loggia and the mannered architectural features of its interior invalidate the attribution to Palladio. Moreover, Palladio's only opportunity for direct intervention in these projects would have been limited to his brief Roman sojourn of 1554, because his earlier visits preceded the building activity at the *Palazzo di Firenze*.

It is similarly difficult to link Palladio with the facade of *Santa Marta* at the Collegio Romano. The Church of *Santa Marta*, at the south-west side of the piazza, belonged to a religious company founded in 1543 by Sant'Ignazio of Loyola. The foundation stone was laid in 1546, which legitimizes the possibility of Palladio's supervision on the basis of his residence in Rome during that year. However, construction progressed slowly, and in 1561 the property passed to an order of Augustinian nuns who oversaw the consecration of the church in 1570. Later remodelling by Carlo Fontana apparently did not affect the entrance portal belonging to the original fabric[65] (Fig. 13). The classicizing motifs, engaged columns and balanced proportions explain the traditional, but undocumented, attribution to Palladio.[66]

Adding to the uncertainty about these commissions is the absence of working drawings from Palladio's hand which might substantiate involvement with building projects during his trips to Rome. The drawings of his Roman periods are concerned almost exclusively with the study of ancient monuments.[67] When Palladio did sketch sixteenth-century buildings, he focused on the works of Bramante and his generation. He has left us drawings of Bramante's *Tempietto* (Vic D26v) and *San Biagio* (Vic D11v), and of Raphael's *Villa Madama* (RIBA X 18).[68] During the period when Palladio frequented scholarly and artistic circles in Rome, the genius of Bramante had become universally acknowledged; even Michelangelo, by 1546–1547, was lauding Bramante's plans for *San Pietro*. Palladio seems to have sought out these early plans, integrating the ideas of Bramante and his circle into his own architectural vocabulary. They later would prove influential in his designs for Venetian churches.[69]

There is little doubt about Palladio's sincere admiration for Bramante's architecture which, to him, was a logical outgrowth of the architect's immersion in the culture of the ancient world. In the *Quattro Libri*, Palladio noted that Bramante was an enthusiastic student of ancient buildings, that he erected some of the most beautiful buildings in Rome and that he was the first to bring back good and beautiful architecture hidden since the ancients.[70] Just as he studied ancient structures, Palladio must have spent considerable time analyzing Bramante's architecture. He demonstrated his ability to identify the antique origins of Bramante's designs when he cited the source of the Belvedere staircase as the Portico of Pompei.[71] Through his second-hand knowledge of Bramante's designs, thanks to the studies of Sebastiano Serlio, Palladio already had applied some of Bramante's ideas to his own building projects. So profound was Palladio's respect for his predecessor that he even may have modelled his own Roman experience after Bramante's example. It was believed by Palladio's contemporaries that Bramante had tried to live independently—free from the encumbrance of commissions—so that he could travel and take measurements of ancient architecture in Rome, Campania, Naples and Tivoli.[72] The same all-encompassing quest for knowledge about the ancients characterized Palladio's activities in Rome. The legendary genius of Bramante had legitimized the value of such pursuits, thereby expanding Palladio's vision of architecture beyond his immediate historical circumstances.

Palladio provides a clue in the text of *Le Chiese* to his interest in the architecture of Vignola, a contemporary who shared his respect for Bramante as well as antiquity.[73] In describing *Sant'Andrea* outside the

Porta del Popolo as a "round chapel of great art and beauty built by the Lord of our Lords, Pope Julius III" (Trans., p. 89), Palladio calls attention to Vignola's recently completed project for the Del Monte family. The construction of the church took place from June 1552 to August 1553 on a strip of land along the Via Flaminia, acquired for the purpose of fronting the family properties of the *Villa Giulia*.[74] It is not surprising that the small church gained Palladio's admiration at the time of his final visit to Rome. Vignola's design of a centralized structure with an elliptical, raised drum and attached temple front arose out of familiarity with classical building types. Moreover, this scheme had been applied to a small yet prominent pilgrimage church, attracting visitors to Rome who stopped at the site along Via Flaminia outside the northern entrance to the city for the indulgences granted on the Feast of Sant'Andrea. Palladio must have been well aware of the importance of Vignola's small building which resulted from a papal commission and represented the continuity with Christian as well as antique traditions.

Palladio's investigations of antiquity did not prevent him from experiencing contemporary Rome. At the time of his last visit to the city in 1554, he was aware not only of the latest architectural project in Rome, *Sant'Andrea*, but also of the slightly earlier churches of *Santo Spirito, Santa Maria di Loreto, San Giovanni dei Fiorentini* and *San Biagio della Pagnotta*.[75] During these four months, Palladio was involved with historical research for the illustrations for Barbaro's edition of Vitruvius. Then, presumably, he also was preparing the texts of *Le Chiese* and *L'Antichità di Roma* both of which necessitated, according to the author, first-hand experience of the monuments. As well, at the time of this last visit, he was able to renew his contacts with fellow architects still working in Rome — Ligorio, Michelangelo and Vignola — and to refresh his memory of Bramante. Palladio departed at the end of May 1554, never to return to Rome. However, he had succeeded in establishing ties to the culture and intellectual life of the city which would endure throughout his career.

It is as difficult to measure the impact of Rome on Palladio's development as to imagine what kind of architecture he would have designed had he never travelled there. Significantly, when Palladio first visited Rome in 1541 at thirty-three years of age, he arrived fresh with enthusiasm for his new ventures. He had prepared at Trissino's Academy in Vicenza where he had obtained a deep and abiding appreciation for antiquity, even before he confronted the monuments of the city. Furthermore, he was already well-versed in the architecture of his own century. He had studied the designs and absorbed the advice of Sanmicheli, Serlio and Sansovino just as he was familiar, albeit second-hand, with the major works of Bramante and Raphael. Lastly, his training as a stone mason in the Veneto assured him of a grasp of the practical aspects of building which few other architects of his generation, if not his century, were to acquire. An instinct for the material, tangible qualities of architectural structure propelled Palladio to the study of extant monuments of Roman history.

Palladio came to Rome neither for direction nor for inspiration, but to seek contact with the sources of good building which he certainly had identified earlier in his career. The surviving evidence shows that he investigated the form of ancient architecture, the methods of construction and the "revival" of admirable building design in his own age. Palladio's architectural designs were characterized by a fusion of the abstract with the material, but his own approach was always grounded in history.

Thus Palladio used his opportunities in Rome to broaden the humanistic education which he saw as essential to the practice of good architecture. His literary projects, although most were completed later in his career, grew out of these experiences: *L'Antichità di Roma* and *Le Chiese*, the *Quattro Libri*, the *Commentari di C. Giulio Cesare*, the study of Polybius and his research for Barbaro's edition of Vitruvius. He clearly wanted to make each of these works understandable and to reveal guiding principles, or virtues recommended by the ancients. As such, his style of writing remained eloquent but lucid, and true to the original source. For Palladio, his guidebook to churches—*Le Chiese*—was a logical outgrowth of his interest in building traditions. In both his writing and his architectural projects, he strove for clarity of form and historical accuracy.

Chapter Two

The Publication of the *Descritione* de le *Chiese di Roma*

Palladio wrote the guidebooks, the *Descritione de le Chiese di Roma* and *L'Antichità di Roma*, out of respect for tradition as well as conviction in the authority of history. In his preface to the latter work, Palladio revealed his plan of correcting the many falsehoods circulating in the standard chronicles.[1] Zealous declarations of intent were hardly original with Palladio; Flavio Biondo and Pirro Ligorio had been critical about earlier sources in their own descriptive accounts of antiquity.[2] However, Palladio placed greater emphasis on the practical nature of his books, for he envisioned them as tools useful to the visitor to Rome.

Palladio was correct in anticipating the demand for a new description of Roman monuments. The Jubilee year of 1550 had turned the public's attention to literary descriptions of the city, or more precisely to the availability of guidebooks. With his updated account of the churches of Rome, Palladio reached a ready market which must have responded immediately. The book became so successful that publishers reissued it regularly under the title of *Le cose maravigliose di Roma*. Oddly enough though, Palladio never received credit for these subsequent editions, and the extent to which he and his publisher, Vincenzo Lucrino, stood to gain from even the original venture remains unclear.

Nevertheless financial reward is only a partial explanation of Palladio's motives in producing *Le Chiese*. Other factors influenced his decision to begin his writing career as the author of two guidebooks for the general public. His interest in the genre of the guidebook was a natural outgrowth of contact with early patrons—Giangiorgio Trissino and Daniele Barbaro. Moreover, the religious climate in mid-sixteenth-century Rome encouraged a revival of interest in the traditional practices of the Catholic church. Palladio's authorship of *Le Chiese* demonstrates a willingness to promote these values at a time when some of his fellow Vicentines adopted the opposing position espoused by the Protestant reformers. In the preface to his book, Palladio aligns himself with papal Rome by relating how the city retained her preeminence because of the presence of sacred things through which "she has become the head and real seat of the true Christian religion. To which I add wishes of sincere and enduring felicity" (Trans., p. 72).

Scholarly Concerns

When Giangiorgio Trissino introduced Palladio to the world of antiquity, he determined the course of the young architect's development. Trissino's study of Vitruvian architecture, left unpublished at his death, paved the way for Palladio's subsequent work.[3] Similarly Trissino's knowledge of the guidebook tradition must have stimulated Palladio's interest. On 5 March 1537, Trissino sent a description of Cocolo di Costoza, a territory of Vicenza, to Leandro Alberti who included the passage in his important guidebook, *Descrittione di tutta l'Italia*, published in 1550.[4] While conducting research for *Italia liberata dai Goti* in 1545–1547, Trissino had occasion to reconstruct the topography of the ancient city. A map of Rome appears in his book published by Valerio and Luigi Dorico of Rome in May of 1547—the first of three editions.[5] Trissino's inquiries coincided with the very period when Palladio was consulting classical and modern descriptions of Rome cited in the introduction to *L'Antichità di Roma*.[6] Not only were contemporary guidebooks and descriptions of antique Rome known to Trissino, but his library included the ever-popular "Jubilee book," or pilgrim's book to Rome of 1550.[7]

Palladio gained exposure to the literature of the church as well as that of antiquity through his close relationship with Daniele Barbaro, commentator and translator of the 1556 edition of Vitruvius. Returning to Venice from England in 1551 (the year after Trissino's death), Barbaro found in Palladio an able and knowledgeable illustrator for his treatise.[8]

The architect also collaborated with Barbaro on his treatise on perspective, another Vitruvian study, as well as designing his villa at Maser.[9] Barbaro possessed an impressive personal library with books and manuscripts on art and history, and he nurtured a lifelong fascination with the classics. Later he turned also to theological studies, a branch of inquiry sustained by his religious office.

Barbaro was recalled as the Venetian ambassador to the English court and appointed bishop-elect to Aquileia. While the post did not require Barbaro to exercise religious authority nor even to join an order, it did allow him to serve as a papal emissary. He was immediately dispatched to the Council of Trent, convened for the second time by Julius III in 1551. But only the third council under Pius IV (1559–1565) resulted in Barbaro's long-term residence in Trent from 14 January 1562 to 4 December 1563.[10] On this occasion, Barbaro participated in setting policy for the church's *Index of Prohibited Books*.

Whatever Barbaro's personal religious views, his career had placed him at the center of major controversies. While a resident in England, Barbaro found himself surrounded by Protestants who had little patience with Catholic views.[11] At the next stage of his career as bishop-elect of Aquileia, Barbaro maintained close connections with the clergy and was well-informed about current attitudes and practices endorsed by the Catholic church. His belief that Christian burial monuments were more suitable to a public space than to the interior of a church parallels a view expressed in Carlo Borromeo's *Instructiones*.[12] Although his influence as an ecclesiastic was modest compared to that as a humanist, Barbaro undoubtedly saw no competition or conflict between these two spheres of activity. His last will and testament includes an act of extraordinary Christian faith in calling for the simple burial rites of a commoner.[13]

Just as Giangiorgio Trissino must have stimulated Palladio's interest in guidebook literature, so Daniele Barbaro would have found compatible the juxtaposition of the secular and sacred in Palladio's *L'Antichità di Roma* and *Le Chiese*. The two guidebooks maintain the distinction between the history of ancient monuments and current religious practice. When balanced against his antiquarian studies, Palladio's motivation in describing relics and indulgences for the Christian pilgrim becomes understandable. A thoroughly traditional guidebook such as *Le Chiese* implicitly reenforced the Counter-Reformatory position of the Catholic church, an institution with origins which Palladio traced back to antiquity.

The Religious Climate

Recognizing the challenge posed by the Protestant Reformation, progressive laymen and clergy had urged reform early in the century. By the time the First Council of Trent convened in 1545–1547, a wave of evangelism had been replaced by the more stringent policies endorsed by the Jesuits and the Roman Inquisition. Strict measures were sought to outlaw the dissemination of heretical ideas and enforce the ascendancy of Catholicism. The authority of the church influenced the publishing activities of the Venetian press which shortly before had produced books on profane subjects. It now tended toward devotional works although antiquarian studies as well as the history of the early church remained acceptable subjects.[14] Barbaro, who was intimately involved with these decisions, had counseled moderation as well as an historical perspective in revising the *Index of Prohibited Books*.[15]

Disputes over the prolific veneration of saints and relics as well as the practice of granting indulgences to Christian pilgrims had been gestating long before the decrees promulgated by the final Council of Trent in 1563.[16] These clerical prerogatives had aroused vehement criticism not only in the Protestant north but also among some Catholic constituencies. The church periodically revised the manner in which indulgences were offered and placed limitations on their use. Yet, at the Council of Trent, the conservative forces which argued for the system prevailed. While abuses of the system were deplored, the proclamations of 1563 upheld the practice of dispensing indulgences. Similarly, the veneration of relics and memorials to saints were endorsed as a significant part of the Christian ritual. Churches were urged to maintain decorum in the worship of sacred images.[17]

Palladio's two guidebooks fit into the mainstream of Catholic policy as made manifest subsequently at the Council of Trent in 1563. A new version of the *Mirabilia urbis Romae*, allegedly purged of its historical inaccuracies, promised an objective view of the ancient world. Similarly, an updated account of the indulgences and relics of Rome — known previously as the *Libri Indulgentiarum* — was likely to endorse their veneration and confirm their authority. Issued at a time when controversy reigned within the church, *L'Antichità di Roma* and *Le Chiese* perpetuated traditional Catholic values and practices.

Palladio must have been aware of the sensitive position which Barbaro occupied in respect to the authority of the church. During their Roman visit of 1554, Barbaro was beset by personal difficulties on account of accusations that he had abused the system of church benefices.[18] Furthermore, it is likely that Palladio's Venetian patron was suspected of having communicated with reformers who espoused a cause antithetical to established church doctrine. In Venice, Barbaro stayed at the palace of Giacomo Contarini, active in radical circles of religious reformers. The papacy had long recognized and condemned the Protestant ideas infiltrating humanist groups in Venice and Vicenza. Yet the popes of the Counter-Reformation also recognized the importance of maintaining close relations with these northern cities, and as early as 1537 Paul III had accepted the Venetians' offer of Vicenza as the proposed site of the Council, although Trent finally was selected in 1542.[19]

Throughout his career Palladio maintained friendships with the intellectual elite of Vicenza who included in their ranks leading reformers denounced as heretics by the church.[20] After Palladio became established as an architect, he numbered among his close associates Odoardo Thiene, Mario Repeta and Giacomo Angaran — all patrons as well as intimate friends. The companions of his early years also demonstrated connections to the Protestant Reformation, albeit in an indirect fashion. Giangiorgio Trissino was painfully aware of the Lutheran influences on his son Giulio (1504–1576), the archpriest of Vicenza, who later became a leader of the Calvinist movement in Vicenza.[21] One of the city's most notorious reformers to be convicted of heresy was Giangiorgio's nephew, Alessandro Trissino (1523–1609).[22] Marco Thiene, whose sister married Giangiorgio Trissino's son by a second marriage, was a cousin of the Thiene family whose palace in Vicenza undoubtedly sheltered many a Protestant sympathizer. Giovanni Battista Maganza, the painter and poet, moved in the same circles. He decorated the Villa Repeta with frescoes (destroyed in 1672) which may have incorporated an Anabaptist message. Maganza outlived his close friend, but pursued associations with scholars who espoused Protestant ideas.[23]

The evidence suggests that Palladio was familiar, if not in sympathy, with heretical beliefs which circulated in Venice and Vicenza. Palladio's identification with his countrymen was strong and, during his trips to Rome, he remained close to fellow northerners who gravitated toward his mentors, first Trissino and then Barbaro. Nevertheless his activities with Marco Thiene and Maganza seem to have focused exclusively on the rediscovery of the ancient world. Palladio's sense of loyalty to his associates, even later in his life, should not be misconstrued as an endorsement of their sometimes controversial religious convictions. His patrons, who regularly became his friends, pursued rigorous intellectual inquiry into multiple areas of humanistic study. Palladio lauded them for their "nobility and excellent learning," and they in turn remembered Palladio for his revival of ancient ideals.[24]

It is difficult to ascertain the extent to which Palladio was personally affected by the controversy which engulfed the Catholic Church at mid-century. Late in his career, when he was designing churches in Venice, he must have considered the prescriptions of the Council of Trent regarding the decoration and plans for places of worship. *San Giorgio* (1564–1580) and *Il Redentore* (1576–1580) were conceived with austere, white interiors and broad, well-illuminated naves allowing a clear view of the altar. The longitudinal orientation of these church plans recalls *Il Gesù*, the prototypic Counter-Reformation church of Rome, which Palladio had never studied first-hand but which came to symbolize the regeneration of Catholicism.[25]

Palladio took pains to publicly affirm his religious faith, professing his piety in conformity with the will of God. He closed the preface to the *Quattro Libri* with an expression of hope for the success of the work, conditional to the will of God, before acknowledging his belief in the principles of ancient architecture. Scattered throughout the text are references to the wisdom of our "Blessed Creator" culminating in an invocation of God as a model for the plan of the church.[26] Palladio's writings generally reveal that the author was guided by firm principles — whether his loyalty to friends, his religious beliefs or his profound confidence in the lessons of antiquity. In dedicating the *Commentari* to the commander of the military forces of Catholicism, Palladio endorsed the pope and his natural son, conspicuous representatives of Catholic militancy. But it is in *Le Chiese* that Palladio reveals an unexpected aspect of his religious faith. His scholarly approach toward Christian tradition not only emerges as an expression of support for the practices and policy of the Catholic Church, but as an attempt to renew the public's appreciation of her sacred sites.

The Publisher

Thus, assorted motives led Palladio to compose companion guides to Rome and, ultimately in 1554, to the city where they would be published.

It is likely that he travelled directly from Venice to Rome, for he was in the company of Daniele Barbaro as well as other Venetian gentlemen.[27] He remained in the city for less than four months, and before he returned to Vicenza he had delivered the text of *L'Antichità di Roma* and *Le Chiese* to the Roman publisher, Vincenzo Lucrino. Due to his prior familiarity with the subject at hand, Palladio may have initiated his guidebooks before returning to Rome. His practice of consulting literary sources made this a feasible method. However, he certainly completed the projects with reference to the actual sites, as he needed to scrutinize texts recorded in the churches and survey current architectural projects.

The title page of the *Descritione de le Chiese, Stationi, Indulgenze & Reliquie de Corpi Sancti, che sonno in la Città di Roma* divulged the essential facts of its 1554 publication (Fig. 1). The identities of the author and publisher were revealed: "Brevemente raccolta da M. Andrea Palladio & novamente posta in luce." The publisher provided a statement of his rights, his emblem and his signature: "Con Gratia e Privilegio per anni dieci; FORTES, FORTUNA ADIUVVAT IN ROMA Appresso Vincentio Lucrino, 1554." Vincenzo Lucrino seems never to have printed another edition of the guide, and Palladio's preface, which clearly reveals the author's intentions, does not appear in other versions. Here, Palladio refers to another book in which he described "l'antiquità de la Città di Roma, con quella diligenza & brevità" (Fig. 3). The passage implies a definite sequence to Palladio's writings, demonstrating that the author envisioned the two guides as complementary.

L'Antichità di Roma di M. Andrea Palladio raccolte brevemente da gli autori antichi e moderni. Nuovamente poste in luce was published in Rome by Vincenzo Lucrino in 1554, but also in Venice by Matteo Pagan "in Frezeria all'insegna della Fede" in the same[28] Palladio allegedly transported the manuscript to Venice, after its publication in Rome, as his presence in the north is documented in July, 1554.[29] The timing of the publication in Venice need not depend on the whereabouts of Palladio because his text may have travelled independently between Roman and Venetian publishers. A reference exists to yet a third copy published in 1554, this one by the press of Antonio Blado, which has not survived.[30] Whatever the chronology of the various copies of *L'Antichità di Roma*, Lucrino's two books were surely issued in the sequence established in Palladio's preface to *Le Chiese*, with the account of Christian Rome following that of the pagan city.

In selecting Vincenzo Lucrino as the Roman publisher of his first literary works, Palladio passed over better-established presses. The decision can not have been arbitrary, for Palladio must have recognized the stature of printing as a commercial and scholarly activity in sixteenth-century Rome. Palladio's countryman, Ludovico degli Arrighi, operated a press famous in the early decades, which produced the first edition of Calvo's *Antiquae urbis* of 1527, a work certainly familiar to Palladio. Although Arrighi was no longer active as a printer by the time Palladio reached Rome, his reputation in Vicentine circles was insured by the 1524 publication of Giangiorgio Trissino's treatise on spelling and grammar.[31] Michele and Francesco Tramezzino, printers with offices in Venice and Rome, also produced respected scholarly studies of Roman history.[32] Through exposure to these early examples of the typographer's art as well as advice from Trissino and Barbaro, Palladio had the opportunity to assess the capability of the printers established in Rome and Venice.

Yet Palladio ended up collaborating with a relatively obscure printer rather than either of the two prominent publishing houses of mid-sixteenth-century Rome. It is curious that he did not engage the press of Antonio Blado who had assumed an important role in the publication of church-sponsored material including the second edition of the *Index Auctorum et Librorum* in 1558. Because they disseminated such sensitive material, booksellers and printers of the mid-sixteenth century like Blado were often at the center of controversy.[33] But Blado also continued the production of standard and popular books such as the *Mirabilia urbis Romae* in 1522, 1524, and 1550. Scholarly works too were issued by his press, including Marliani's *Le Antichità di Roma* of 1548 and Labacco's *Libro . . . all'Architettura* of 1552. The other major Roman press was that of the Dorico Brothers who issued editions of the two previous works as well as Trissino's poem, *Italia liberata dai Goti* in 1547 and Calvo's *Antiquae urbis* in 1532.[34] As leading figures in the field, Blado and Dorico headed publishing concerns which occasionally produced translations and editions of identical texts. Both printers issued editions of *Le cose maravigliose* shortly after Palladio introduced *Le Chiese* in 1554.

Vincenzo Lucrino, the publisher of Palladio's guidebooks, was a relatively obscure figure in the world of Roman printing although he was associated intermittently with both major presses until 1562. It is likely that for reasons of financial expediency, Vincenzo Lucrino entered into a partnership with Valerio Dorico in 1550 and with Antonio Blado in 1557.[35] In several editions of the classical authors, Lucrino's name is affiliated with the Dorico's, introduced by terms like "ad instantiam," "in officina" or "apud." Then, from 1552 to 1560, six works carried Lucrino's name alone despite the evidence that the Dorico Brothers actually printed the books. In still other examples of blatant piracy, Lucrino seems to have replaced the frontispiece of another press with his own insignia. He employed unscrupulous business practices with Blado and Paolo Manuzio as well.[36]

Further examination of Vincenzo Lucrino's production suggests that he collaborated with an established press in publishing *Le Chiese*. The roles of printer, publisher, engraver and bookseller merged frequently in sixteenth-century Rome, and Vincenzo Lucrino seems to have pursued actively each of these occupations.[37] Two Roman views and one map, issued as prints, may be associated with Lucrino during the decades of the 1550s and 1560s. Lucrino did not invent these scenes; instead, he disseminated famous views, most likely to appreciative tourists, by publishing later states. In 1558, he reissued a scene of "La Festa del Tostaccio [*sic*] fatta in Roma" with Du Pérac. He published an engraved elevation of Michelangelo's design of the apse of San Pietro in 1564, an indication of his possible contacts with architects and his cordial relations with Pope Pius IV. In 1558, he issued an important print of "Italia Nuova" which reproduced an older map of the peninsula.[38] Such projects demonstrate his acumen for selecting subjects with popular appeal and the promise of commercial success.

Even on the basis of what meager documentation survives, Vincenzo Lucrino emerges as a figure with far-reaching contacts and considerable entrepreneurial skills. As a merchant, Lucrino obtained permission from Pius IV to organize a paper shop for the city in 1559, although the project never materialized.[39] On 27 January 1559, he is mentioned in connection with the wool trade, in which he may have speculated for financial gain. Later, in 1567, he appears as a property owner, perhaps a landlord, in the neighborhood of San Marcello. The following year he had acquired the title of dispenser of lead seals and bibliophile. His business acumen must have been well-known, for a fellow printer named Facchi nominated Lucrino as the procurator of his property on 2 May 1569, in one of the final known notary acts which mentions his name. During the same year he was also active in the *Compagnia dei Bresciani*, a society which promoted the careers of his fellow countrymen, including important printers like Girolamo Francini and Marco Amadori.[40] He probably died shortly thereafter.

Books bearing Vincenzo Lucrino's insignia appeared from 1552 to

1566.[41] His emblem consisted of a crown and serpent, at times embellished with other devices. In Palladio's guide, the frontispiece shows a serpent framed by a wreath (Fig. 1). The crest appears again, surmounted by a dove with a ring, before the list of stations of the church. The motto of "FORTES FORTUNA ADIUVAT" also identifies Lucrino's press.[42] He maintained an office at the Campo dei Fiori and, later, on Via del Pellegrino — addresses which recall the location of the presses of the Dorico Brothers.[43] The relationship is hardly incidental. The typography used by the Dorico Press resembles the chancery cursive of Lucrino's editions of *Le Chiese* and *L'Antichità di Roma*. The typeset as well as the historiated capitals taken from woodcut impressions belong to their repertoire. Three years later the Dorico Press would publish an edition of *Le cose maravigliose* with the same woodcut initial "A" opening the text. It recurs in the Dorico edition of 1558, although both images differ in the details of the background.[44] The frequency of borrowed motifs as well as the documented nature of Lucrino's complicated professional affiliations raise the distinct possibility that the Dorico Brothers were involved with the printing of Palladio's text. Vincenzo Lucrino, however, claimed responsibility for its distribution by placing his own name on the frontispiece.

The connection between the author and Vincenzo Lucrino remains obscure unless the publisher's wider associations are taken into account. Lucrino also appears to have enjoyed close contact with the Jesuits. When Sant'Ignazio of Loyola sought to establish a printing press in Rome, Lucrino acted as arbiter. He served as intermediary between the head of the Jesuits and a book dealer in Venice who offered type for sale in 1556. Only two years earlier, and concurrent with the publication of Palladio's *Le Chiese* and *L'Antichità di Roma*, he had printed a work by Martino Polanco, at his own expense, for the order.[45] Lucrino's dealings with the Jesuits reflect the pressures of the Counter-Reformation in Rome. A publisher like Lucrino who produced works of classical authors needed also to maintain ties to the hierarchy of the church. Other booksellers, less astute in calculating the political climate, became targets of persecution as a result of their relations with Calvinist and Lutheran forces from the north. Palladio had the good fortune, and perhaps the shrewdness, to collaborate with a printer who was associated with a leading press — the Dorico Brothers — and with prominent arbiters of church policy.

Lucrino's documented role in the Jesuit purchase of 1556 further suggests that he had connections with printers in Venice who produced numerous editions of *Le cose maravigliose*. In 1560, Lucrino obtained publishing rights for ten years from the Venetian Senate to print the *Opiniones in Jure Communes*.[46] Although it was common practice for publishers outside of Venice to seek protection for their material, the initiative taken by Lucrino is an indication of his connections with the authority of the Republic. In 1564, while maintaining his press in Rome, Lucrino printed two books "apud Jo. Variscum et socios" in Venice. Other publishing enterprises were divided similarly between the two centers of printing in the sixteenth century. Vincenzo Valgrisi, a Frenchman, oversaw printing presses contemporaneously in Venice and Rome from at least 1549 to 1551.[47] While no link is known to have existed between Lucrino and Valgrisi, the resemblance of their emblems — two fists clutching intertwined serpents — may be more than coincidental. Due to his wide-ranging professional ties, Vincenzo Lucrino emerges as a crucial figure who may have been instrumental in negotiating between the better established Dorico Press and Venetian printers, and even in insuring the sanction of the church for Palladio's two guidebooks.

Chapter Three

The *Descritione de le Chiese*
and *Le cose maravigliose dell'alma città di Roma*

The *Descritione de le Chiese di Roma* was issued in an unpaginated octavo
(15.5 cm) edition, fifty folios in length. The configuration of the publication was so simple that many editions of the earlier *Libri indulgentiarum*
and *Mirabilia urbis Romae* seemed elaborate in comparison. No illustrations accompanied Palladio's text. The sole embellishment consisted of
two historiated capitals, the "H" of the preface and the "R" of the first
chapter. These were inserted into squares which framed, respectively,
a landscape motif and a satyr with sleeping nymph in the background
(Figs. 3, 4). Even after its transformation into *Le cose maravigliose dell'alma
città di Roma*, the description of Roman churches never acquired the more
artistic illustrations of contemporary works on archaeology or topography. The compact size and plain format met the basic needs of the Christian pilgrim, and the guidebook remained a portable reference-work,
unpretentious in appearance. It was inexpensive to produce and, to judge
from the frequency of printing, in considerable demand.

There is little known about the circumstances leading to the publication of Palladio's guide, but the surviving copies of the book, however
rare, give some indication of its commercial success. It is likely that numerous copies of the book were lost immediately following its initial circula-
tion. No record of the first printing survives, and the book escaped the
attention of Palladio's early biographers as well as later authorities on

the Roman press during the sixteenth century.[1] The first census did not appear until 1930 when Schudt identified two copies: Vatican and Rome (Hertziana A).[2] Four additional examples may now be added: London, Vienna, Rome (Hertziana B) and Madison, Wisconsin.[3] Some are well-worn and inscribed with marginalia correcting the text or updating the chronology of the stations. In two examples (the Hertziana A and the Vatican), fly-leaves bear signatures of owners.[4] Evidence of continuous and casual use shows that Palladio's book was utilized as a companion guide rather than conserved in a library.

It is ironic that the success of *Le Chiese* as a pilgrim's guidebook contributed to the physical destruction of the text. The practice of tearing out leaves to study a text in transit and the markings of constant reference gradually took their toll, and relatively few examples remain to substantiate the reputation of the book.[5] In contrast, numerous copies of *L'Antichità di Roma* of 1554 are conserved in modern libraries.[6] Palladio's description of the ancient city was not necessarily more popular, but rather subject to a different kind of use. Its more scholarly subject matter— better suited perhaps to a collector's library than to his travel pouch— led to its preservation. Curiously the two books which Palladio wrote in 1554, *Le Chiese* and *L'Antichità di Roma*, do not appear together today. Only one of the six surviving copies of *Le Chiese* is bound with his guide to antiquities, and the latter appears in an edition of 1566 (Hertziana A). Similarly, one copy of *Le Chiese* is bound with an edition of the *Mirabilia urbis Romae* of 1550 (Hertziana B), indicating that all these booklets were issued separately, to be paired in various combinations according to demand.

Literary Models

The idea of composing companion guides to the ancient and modern city did not originate with Palladio. A well-known guidebook of the Renaissance, the *Opusculum de Mirabilibus novae et veteris urbis Romae* (1510), juxtaposed descriptions of old and new Rome. The author, Francesco Albertini, considered his work original although the first two books on ancient buildings and spaces are derivative of earlier accounts.[7] Albertini's third book, however, described the contemporary city—the papal Rome of Julius II. This section introduced the reader to a first-hand account of private palaces, collections and urban projects. Albertini originally wrote his guidebook in 1506–1509 for Galeotto della Rovere but, after the cardinal's death, rededicated it to Pope Julius II. The *Opusculum* was issued four times between 1510 and 1523, the latter a lavish production with woodcut illustrations.[8]

Albertini directed his guidebook to a select and educated audience, quite distinct from the general public Palladio was later to address. Furthermore the earlier author attempted to synchronize the monuments of the Renaissance city with their counterparts in antiquity. Albertini was not concerned with informing the Christian pilgrim but with constructing a comprehensive, analytic overview of Roman topography. Yet, even despite his different objectives, the Florentine author must have influenced Palladio. In the preface to the *Opusculum*, Albertini identified the scholarly sources for his report on ancient Rome; he cited the contributions of the early humanists, Giovanni Tortelli, Flavio Biondo and Pomponeo Leto.[9] His description of the ancient city followed the traditional format, also adopted by Palladio, of categorizing monuments under generic headings. The scholarly bias distinguished the account of antiquities from the medieval *Mirabilia urbis Romae* because Albertini, like Palladio, claimed to have expunged unfounded traditions. In a dedicatory letter, the author recalled that Galeotto della Rovere prompted him to correct the fables of the *Mirabilia*.[10] More revealing, however, is Albertini's reference to an earlier book which had attracted the attention of his current patron. Albertini composed *De stationibus et reliquiis urbis* for the emperor Maximilian I. Now lost, this work must have consisted of a guide to the churches of Rome, with the Latin text and royal dedication indicating that it was intended for limited distribution. As if to confirm its exclusivity, the author promised an Italian translation—*Le stationi di Roma*—for the unlettered devout.[11]

It is not known if Albertini ever brought the project to fruition nor is it possible to ascertain the precise contents of the guidebook. In the third book of the *Opusculum*, however, Albertini abbreviates his description of the major Roman basilicas and the Hospital of Santo Spirito by citing his book on the stations of the churches, just as he frequently refers to his collection of inscriptions, the *Epigrammata*, only published—and then incompletely—in 1521.[12] Thus the guide to the stations and relics of Rome assumed an important place in the author's consciousness, if not in the public's, and its resemblance to Palladio's *Le Chiese* is instructive. Both authors, knowledgeable about literary tradition, produced practical guides for a Christian audience. More specifically, Palladio may have found a model in Francesco Albertini's *De stationibus et reliquiis urbis* as a reliable alternative to the *Libri indulgentiarum*.[13]

The scholarly accounts of ancient Rome must have fired Palladio's imagination and stimulated his intellectual curiosity. Guidebooks to antiquities had gained favor since their introduction in the early fifteenth century. Poggio Bracciolini, a Florentine humanist, was among the first to produce a topographical description of ancient Rome.[14] Leon Battista Alberti followed with another account of Roman antiquities in his *Descriptio urbis Romae* and a map of the lost city.[15] These narratives were superseded by *Roma instaurata*, composed in 1444 by Flavio Biondo who was the only author of the quattrocento mentioned by Palladio in the preface to his own *L'Antichità di Roma*. Published in 1481, the widely-read text provided the first analytical guide to Roman monuments.[16] Biondo's work depended on the *Mirabilia urbis Romae* for the organization of the text, but utilized modern scholarship by incorporating inscriptions, literary texts and the first-hand observation of monuments. The *Antiquitates urbis* by Andrea Fulvio, published first in 1513, developed out of the same tradition and, like Biondo's guide, took into consideration some of the oldest churches in Rome.[17] These early antiquarians stressed the implicit connection between ancient and modern Rome — a parallel which must have intrigued Palladio. Palladio was familiar as well with Bartolomeo Marliano's *Topographia antiquae Romae*, issued in 1534, and he also acknowledged the antiquarian studies of Lucio Fauno and Giorgio Fabricius in his preface. These authors not only provided background material for Palladio's research on antiquities, but prefigured the attitude of scholarly objectivity claimed by Palladio in his own work on *L'Antichità di Roma*.

Textual Sources

Palladio professed a comparable attachment to documented history in his preface to *Le Chiese* when he promised to record the correct foundation date, relics and privileges associated with each church. He dismissed other written sources as outdated in a manner recalling the disparaging reference to the *Mirabilia* in his preface to *L'Antichità di Roma*. Yet, despite his low opinion of its reliability, Palladio often relied on the *Mirabilia urbis Romae*. The text did claim to represent the survival of ancient traditions even though it had twelfth-century origins and, after all, it was the earliest guidebook to sites in ancient Rome.[18] The first section concentrated on historical background while the second recorded fantastic legends associated with famous sites. The narrative also included an itinerary for the tourist along a continuous route through the city which began at the Vatican and ended in Trastevere. Most redactions of the text share this tripartite organization. The practical format and appealing information made it one of the most popular books in Europe.

Yet, especially after the Holy Year of 1300, the Christian pilgrim required additional instructions, and thus, lists of relics, stations, and indulgences were appended to the texts of the *Mirabilia urbis Romae*. Some of these short treatises retained the same title, but others assumed a separate identity, taking the title of *Libri indulgentiarum*.[19] The contents of these guidebooks fluctuated as the number of churches shifted over the course of the fifteenth century, and the historical components were expanded. Still, pagan legends continued to mingle with the lists of Roman churches and their indulgences. A typical product of this epoch was the guidebook of the British pilgrim, John Capgrave, who divided his text into three sections dealing with antiquities, churches and, lastly, relics and indulgences. His work of 1450–1453 records personal observations but owes the greater debt to the *Mirabilia urbis Romae* and the *Libri indulgentiarum et reliquarum*. Capgrave's section on the churches of Rome remained unfinished, although he recorded the seven principle basilicas, thirty-four churches for the Lenten stations and eleven churches dedicated to the Virgin. The author relied on literary sources and a map to spark his memory, as he composed the book after his return to England.[20] Two decades later, William Brewyn used comparable sources for his guidebook to Roman churches and produced a different sequence of churches to be visited.[21]

Some printed *Libri indulgentiarum* were limited to a few pages of text listing the indulgences granted to the pilgrim at the seven basilicas. Others included discursive excerpts from the *Mirabilia*, sections on the history of Rome and accounts of relics.[22] Woodcut engravings frequently illustrated these works which took the titles of the *Indulgentiae, Mirabilia et indulgentiae, Indulgentiae ecclesiarum urbis Romae* and *Mirabilia urbis Romae nove.* When translated into the vernacular, *Le cose maravigliose della città di Roma* appeared around 1540.[23] The text acquired a more elaborate but standardized form which covered the founding of Rome, a genealogy of Roman emperors, a history of the age of Constantine the Great, the indulgences available at churches, a list of stations and, lastly, the names of the popes, emperors and doges.[24]

As learned authors did before him, Palladio drew from traditions vali-
dated by the acceptance of past generations. He used the *Libri indulgentiarum* (*Le cose maravigliose*) as a standard source for *Le Chiese*. He lifted entire
passages from the section on the age of Constantine and inserted them
word for word in his opening chapter. His reference to Platina's *Lives
of the Popes* resulted from the replication of a passage from an earlier source
and does not mean that he actually consulted the text (Trans., p. 78).
Moreover, the historical introduction of *Le Chiese* repeats the text on Constantine and Helena from the 1550 edition of *Le cose maravigliose*. Palladio
reproduced some sources and abridged others, a research technique which
was common practice in the sixteenth century.[25] The description of the
major basilicas in *Le Chiese* also owes much to earlier compilations of *Le
cose maravigliose*. Such dependence indicates deference on the part of the
author to the authority of his predecessors, much as artists of his generation were apt to copy drawings of older masters. He relied on earlier
tradition where modern research or records were lacking. Yet Palladio
also contributed original insights in the expanded section on Roman
churches and offered the pilgrim an updated account of foundations and
privileges. While eighty-four churches had appeared in *Le cose maravigliose*
of 1550, Palladio described one hundred and twenty-one. Rather than
naming sanctuaries on a single circuit like that of the early *Mirabilia*, he
constructed distinct and realistic itineraries for the pilgrim.

Palladio may have derived his knowledge of Roman topography as much
from the study of urban plans as from personal experience. Just as he
consulted guidebook literature, so he must have referred to the numerous maps of the city issued at mid-century. In 1552, the Roman publisher Tramezzino issued Pirro Ligorio's map of modern Rome incorporating
views of reconstructed antique monuments (Fig. 14). The scholarly nature of the plan, which preserved the Latin titles of ancient buildings,
extended to an accurate rendering of the contemporary Roman terrain.[26] Bufalini's map of 1551 represented antiquities as well as churches
in the earliest attempt at geometric projection.[27] Giovanni Antonio Dosio sketched a bird's eye view of the city from the vantage point of the
eastern hills (Fig. 15). In a sweeping panorama, the Dosio view of 1562
reflects a careful study of Roman topography including her famous monuments and the network of streets crossing the urban center. In addition
to views of single Roman landmarks, Dosio also was responsible for the
discovery of a map of ancient Rome, the "Forma urbis," fragments of
which entered the Farnese household.[28] Undoubtedly, Palladio shared

in this enthusiasm for the recreation of the ancient city, and the documentation of its remains. City views offered him a range of information — from archaeological reconstruction to an overview of the terrain.

Contemporary topographical studies may have facilitated Palladio in creating new itineraries through the city, because the routes which he traced for the pilgrim dissected the city into quadrants (Fig. 5). The itineraries cut through the urban center at equal intervals, leading to four divergent points at the outer limits, the walls of Rome. He devised one circuit which connected a sequence of sites in Trastevere with those in the Vatican Borgo, and then he presented three additional routes. The second originated at the customary entry to the city from the north and ended at the Capitoline Hill which in turn provided the beginning of the third and fourth itineraries leading to the distant hills. In designating the Capitoline Hill as the hub of the system, Palladio thus acknowledged its geographical and symbolic importance, while the churches of the outlying areas, "to the left" and "to the right," drew the pilgrim toward distinct destinations along separate axes. Like three spokes of a wheel, these itineraries allowed the pilgrim to circulate between the sacred sites of Rome without the repetition or confusion engendered by earlier guidebooks. Older maps of Rome were oriented in a similar fashion with the north at the top of the plan (the beginning of Palladio's second route) and the heart of the secular city (the Capitoline Hill) at the center. This kind of logical symmetry also surfaced in Palladio's literary account which directed the pilgrim to all four corners of Rome. But the ideal plan coexisted with the practical needs of the visitor to Rome. Palladio, ignoring the remains of ancient Rome, concentrated on a logical progression of churches which required a first-hand knowledge of contemporary Roman topography and put the reader in contact with the sites. His guidebook did not include a map, but it prepared the way for later graphic representations of Rome. Palladio's directives amounted to a literary map of the city. It was but a simple step for authors of succeeding generations to produce diagrams of the pilgrimage routes.[29]

Palladio invented a new type of guidebook, one which discarded the legendary *Mirabilia* and proposed a realistic method of visiting the city's churches. A separate guidebook, *L'Antichità di Roma*, became the repository for some of the pagan history, albeit revised and abbreviated, which had appeared in medieval accounts. For *Le Chiese*, he expanded information about indulgences by creating a calendar and adding a list of stations at the end of his guide. Finally, the itineraries of Roman churches offered an expedient alternative to the cumbersome lists in the *Libri indulgentiarum*. The publication of *Le Chiese* in 1554 made Rome accessible to the faithful who then were able to assess systematically the historical importance of the city's churches.

The Transformation of the Text

Only three years after its publication, Palladio's *Le Chiese* was reissued without his name and with a different title (*Le cose maravigliose dell'alma città di Roma dove si tratta delle chiese, stationi, indulgenze & reliquie de i corpi santi che sonno in esse*)[30] (See *Le cose maravigliose*: List of Editions Consulted). The guidebook omitted the author's preface (*Alli lettori*) but reprinted Palladio's text to the letter, including the list of stations and indulgences at the end. The publishers retained the simple format and limited ornamentation to an historiated "R" to introduce the history of Rome, and block capitols to differentiate between topographical districts. The historiated capital, different from the "R" in the original Palladio edition, depicted a man driving a stake into the ground. Inexplicably, the frontispiece of this new edition identified the text as the work of an anonymous author, rather than a variant of Palladio's text.

The title continued with reference to a short guide to antiquities: *Con un breve trattato della antichità, chiamato La guida romana*. This was the earliest intrusion of *La guida romana* into Roman descriptive tradition, indicating the gradual evolution of Palladio's *Le Chiese* into a full-fledged guidebook illuminating multiple aspects of the city. In his capacity as *Cicerone*, the author of *La guida romana* outlined a two and a half day tour of Roman antiquities designed for the tourist who had limited time to spend sightseeing (see Appendix). Neither a scholarly account nor even particularly accurate, the text nevertheless offered practical, first-hand advice on how to visit the famous ruins of the city. As such, *La guida romana* enabled the traveller to supplement visits to churches with a tour of the celebrated sites of antiquity. The 1557 edition closes by listing the sovereigns of Europe: "Et i nomi de i Sommi Pontifici, de gl'Imperatori, de i Re di Francia, Re di Napoli, de i Dogi di Venezia & Duchi di Milano." These genealogies, which required periodic updating, provided the reader with a system of reference to historical as well as contemporary events.

In printing the first known edition of *Le cose maravigliose* to follow Palladio's *Le Chiese*, the Roman firm of Valerio Dorico "alla Chiavica di S. Lucia" initiated a literary genre which would endure for decades.[31] A guide-book for the pilgrim-tourist required the simplest of formats, allowing for minimal revisions over the years. The small (octavo) volumes were pocket-sized and unembellished so that modest production costs could ensure a low price. The major Roman presses found that these guide-books, still called *Mirabilia Romae* in popular parlance, were a mainstay. Moreover, the printers of the early Dorico editions were able to reuse the woodcut illustrations which introduced the sections on the seven basil-icas. These consisted of small figures, busts or symbols of the saints as-sociated with the respective churches.[32]

The success of the 1557 edition is confirmed by its reissue the follow-ing year and again in 1561, always by Dorico. All shared the identical combination of the texts of *Le Chiese*, *La guida romana* and the *Nomi de i sommi pontifici*. However, the 1561 edition diverged from the original ver-sion in including editorial revisions to Palladio's text, thereby anticipating some changes found in following years. It incorporated new informa-tion about church foundations and a revised sequence in the itinerary.[33] Yet, it also preserved the original version of *La guida romana* intact, together with the preface by the author Schakerlay. During these same years the only other typographer known to have entered the same market was Antonio Blado who, in 1562, printed an edition of *Le cose maravigliose*. Although the description of churches is missing from the sole surviving copy, evidence suggests that the text adhered to the previous version.[34] The fragment begins with the last page from Palladio's compilation of indulgences and contains *La guida romana* in its entirety, including the author's preface.

Dorico issued a new edition of *Le cose maravigliose* in 1563 in which both Palladio's account of *Le Chiese* and *La guida romana* underwent substantive editing. This was surely the most significant elaboration on the original text of 1554, for it endured until 1588, long after church construction had rendered some information in the guide obsolete. The guidebook conserved the simple woodcut engravings and the list of stations and indulgences. It also admonished the reader that the text had been "ultimamente cor-rette, ampliate e ristampate," terms which, however, were applied liberally to many reprints. Antonio Blado printed a copy of *Le cose maravigliose* in the same year, apparently in conjunction with Palladio's *L'Antichità di Roma*.[35] Palladio's *Le Chiese* was thus expanded and altered, as was *La guida romana*. The necessity for handy reference to the sites had resulted in the addition of an index to churches, now numbering one hundred and forty.[36]

The anonymous editor of Palladio's *Le Chiese* avoided substantive changes and concentrated instead on bringing material up to date by appending one or two sentences to the descriptions of selected churches. The historical introduction remained unaltered, as did the description of the basilicas. The editor rewrote the passage about the pine cone in the courtyard of the Vatican, corrected some information regarding indulgences and added information about church renovations, both old and new. Papal patronage, particularly that of Pius IV, was duly noted in respect to the basilicas as well as the other churches. Paul IV (1555–1559) was mentioned only twice, in connection with a station for a Sunday in Lent at *San Martino* and a station at *San Pietro* on 18 January. Works undertaken by renowned cardinals, such as Carafa at *San Martino* and de Cesis at *Santa Caterina dei Funari*, entered the literary tradition. Eleven churches in the area of the Campo dei Fiori and Via Giulia appeared for the first time; various other churches also found their way into the itinerary. The editor intervened where Palladio's text was outmoded (especially in reference to relics) or simply wrong. The change in the Trastevere itinerary, which resulted in *San Crisogono* preceding *Santa Maria in Trastevere*, obviously insured a more logical route; it had occurred already in the edition of 1561. The edition of 1563 added a reference to Raphael's altar in *San Pietro in Montorio*. Palladio had omitted this noteworthy item, instead calling attention to the work of his countryman Sebastiano del Piombo. Aside from these revisions, a new feature of *Le cose maravigliose* of 1563 concerns the titular and collegiate churches which appear for the first time, and the frequent references to lay companies attached to other churches. In keeping with the contemporary nature of the updated text of *Le Chiese*, the guide to antiquities in the appendix acquired a more current outlook. The text of *La guida romana* was edited by a scholarly hand and the preface (*Alli lettori*) was dropped for good.

In 1565, two Venetian presses issued the same revised version of *Le cose maravigliose* and *La guida romana*. Pelegrino Amador and Giovanni Varisco both printed handsome volumes with distinctive woodcut illustrations and stylized ornamentation.[37] That they used a common source, however, is clear from the similarity of the two texts, down to pagination and conventions in spelling. Only Palladio's index to Stations and Indulgences changed as new churches entered the list. Finally a significant innovation occurred in the chronology of popes, when Onofrio Panvinio (1529–1568) updated the list to the reign of Pius IV.[38] The contribution of the famous Augustinian theologian and librarian of the Vatican lent the imprimatur of scholarly authority to the guidebook.

The next decade saw no changes in the text of *Le cose maravigliose*. However, the field of competing presses expanded to include Giulio Bonano degli Accolti (Accolto) of Rome and Osmarino Gigliotto of Rome who both appended a treatise on the acquisition of indulgences to the guide. The pamphlet, numbering about five pages, first appeared in the Accolto edition of 1566: "Trattato over modo d'acquistar l'indulgentie alli stationi," by A. M. Castore Durante D. G.; it remained in most copies through the Holy Year of 1575. The historical section on the building of Rome, which introduced *Le Chiese*, seems to have been eliminated first by the printer Accolto in 1574. Thereafter, and for the Holy Year of 1575 in particular, the text of *Le cose maravigliose* took on a uniformly Christian character as it became paired with Palladio's description of antiquities. Although Palladio's works had been combined earlier, the format became standardized only at this point. The guidebook now, in all its constituent parts, provided a comprehensive overview of the sacred and secular remains of the city.

In acquiring any edition of 1575, the pilgrim or traveller might find an account of the churches (*Le cose maravigliose*), a short treatise on the acquisition of indulgences (*Con un trattato d'acquistar l'indulgentie*), an abbreviated tour of ancient ruins (*La guida romana*), a genealogy of European sovereigns (*I nomi dei sommi pontefici*), a description of ancient Rome (*L'Antichità di Roma* by Palladio) sometimes with a discourse on the fires of the ancients (*Et un discorso sopra i fuochi degli antichi*) wrongly attributed to Palladio but written by an anonymous author, and, in conclusion, a pastoral letter composed by Cardinal Borromeo for the Jubilee of 1575. This combined material was squeezed into a small edition, apparently introduced by the firm of Antonio Blado, of not more than fifty folios and narrow enough to fit into a pocket. The guidebook had become standardized and the constituent parts remained consistent as late as 1587, when the Venetian firm of Zoppini was still printing the version with Borromeo's letter.

Finally, in 1588, two important developments affected the evolution of *Le cose maravigliose*. First, variants of the text appeared simultaneously, bringing an end to the uniformity which had allowed the text to be circulated among publishers and passed down through generations. Secondly, didactic illustrations appeared in selected editions. Both innovations reflected the character of Rome under Sixtus V (1585–1590) whose papacy had ushered in a new era for the city. Any contemporary visitor to Rome would have been struck by the physical changes in the urban topography, changes which were intended to mark the rejuvenation of Christian

Rome. As the popular guidebook of its day, *Le cose maravigliose* commemo-
rated those urban projects undertaken by Sixtus V—specifically the installation of obelisks and the renovation of aqueducts. In general, the
text was expanded to include further insights into the monuments of the
city, providing not only names of patrons, but of artists and architects
as well. The form of churches and chapels, represented in woodcut illustrations, took precedence over their liturgical significance. Relics and indulgences, while still a matter of concern for the pilgrim, gradually became
subordinate to the history of the foundation and construction of each
church.

Girolamo Francini printed a luxury edition of *Le cose maravigliose* which
was issued in Venice in 1588 with a special dedication to Pope Sixtus
V.[39] A frontispiece printed in color displayed elaborate emblematic
devices, and a composite image of the architectural projects undertaken
by the pope (Fig. 16). The title referred to the installation of obelisks
and the Acqua Felice as well as illustrations of churches. Thus the first
guidebook to be fully illustrated emerged from Francini's press. His woodcut engravings offered simple, generally frontal, views of sacred buildings visited by the contemporary pilgrim. The plates provided rare, and
in some cases unique, glimpses of the original design of recently constructed churches, the same buildings which frequently underwent al-
teration during the next century. The engraver recorded in detail the
appearance of the sixteenth-century facades of *Santa Maria dell'Orto*, *Santa
Trinità*, *Santa Maria Maddalena*, *San Bartolomeo* and *San Luigi*. Dedicatory inscriptions appear along the facades of *San Giacomo in Augusta*, *Sant'Anastasia*, *Il Gesù* and *Santa Caterina dei Funari*. The text discussed other
architectural commissions and the woodcut views documented projects
at *Santo Spirito in Sassia*, *Sant'Angelo in Burgo*, *Santa Maria Traspontina*, *Santa
Maria dei Monti* and *L'Annunziata del Gesù*. In addition, the Francini edition
of 1588 included a section on the obelisks erected by Sixtus V. Illustrations and descriptions of the monuments, paired with the appropriate
basilicas, appeared at the front of the book, introducing the pilgrim to
a contemporary portrait of Rome as it had been refashioned under Sixtus V.[40]

The woodcut engravings produced by Girolamo Francini, then by
Giovanni Antonio and his other heirs, enjoyed wide circulation from the
time of their inception in 1588, when different examples appeared simultaneously in editions of Bartolomeo Marliano's *Urbis Romae topographia*,
Andrea Fulvio's *Antichità di Roma* and the *Stationes quadragesimae*.[41] There-

after publishers of successive editions of *Le cose maravigliose* expanded the number of illustrations. New images joined the text as churches were constructed or building projects were altered in order to make each edition of the guidebook current. Views of ancient monuments, which had first appeared also in 1588, multiplied and representations of the facades of Renaissance palaces enriched the guidebook tradition in 1596.[42]

The influential edition of 1588 differed from its predecessors in respect to content as well as form. The title page attributed the textual innovations to Fra Santi, an Augustinian friar and professor of theology who had compiled the *Stationi delle Chiese di Roma* in the same year.[43] The four itineraries followed the traditional route, ending as always with *Santa Maria in Via* after *Santa Maria Annunciata*, so that the original sequence of churches established by Palladio formed the framework, but the descriptive accounts of the individual churches underwent extensive revision. The entries on older churches were abbreviated while newly constructed churches received careful attention. Moreover, the parishes and companies affiliated with Roman churches were listed at the end of each entry. Tradition dictated that the first section be dedicated to the major basilicas. Fra Santi added a history of their respective obelisks and ended with an account of *Santa Maria del Popolo* which had replaced *San Sebastiano* as a major pilgrimage church.[44] In another instance of keeping up to date, Fra Santi inserted *Santa Maria dei Monti*, founded in 1580, after *Santa Maria di Loreto* and he expanded the history of the construction of *Il Gesù* (thus named for the first time). *Le cose maravigliose* of 1588 mentioned the decoration of church interiors, important sixteenth-century works heretofore ignored. Fra Santi called attention to the paintings by Raphael, Salviati, Peruzzi, Sebastiano del Piombo and Sermoneta (Girolamo Siciolante) in *Santa Maria della Pace*; he dwelled on the newly decorated choir of *Santo Spirito* (1584–1585). A woodcut illustration of the statue of the *Risen Christ* in *Santa Maria sopra Minerva* appeared, albeit without the name of the artist, Michelangelo, which was not to surface until the 1595 edition of *Le cose maravigliose* published by Facciotto.[45] The text of *La guida romana* of the 1588 edition was brought up to date for the third time. The contemporary tourist could still find references to sixteenth-century patrons and collectors, but also information about the works of Sixtus V scattered about the city—from the obelisk at *San Pietro* to the papal *vigna* at *Santa Maria Maggiore*.

A second and divergent version of *Le cose maravigliose* appeared concurrently with the Francini edition. In 1589, the Roman firms of Giovanni

Martinelli and Vincenzo Accolti printed concise editions of the guide-book with updated accounts of the churches of Rome but without wood-cut illustrations. The title omitted the dedicatory letter to Sixtus V while references to the pope appeared only sporadically. Yet the descriptions of the churches demonstrated that the editor was aware of contemporary papal projects like the Sixtine obelisks and Lateran Palace. The title page did not disclose the identity of the editor, but the 1594 Zannetti copy gives credit to a certain "Flaminio Primo da Colle" who may also have been responsible for the important revisions originating five years be-fore. Although Francini's edition of the previous year contained more discursive observations on sixteenth-century art and architecture, this version of *Le cose maravigliose*, like its companion text of *La guida romana*, revealed unexpected insights. For example, the description of *San Paolo fuori le Mura* ended with an observation, not found in Fra Santi's descrip-tion, about the beauty of the new ceiling.[46]

The only illustrations in the Martinelli edition of 1589 were small wood-cuts representing the saints and symbols associated with the major basil-icas. A Spanish translation of the same year, printed by the Diani Press in Rome, repeated a similar iconography, which in turn was modeled after the earliest copies of *Le cose maravigliose*. Since Francini produced a Spanish translation of his version in the same year, the two literary traditions may have developed in direct competition. Both found favor with the general public who consulted these editions for years to come with both types continuing into the seventeenth century as the firms of the Accolti, Zannetti, Mutii, Fei and Mascardi all issued similar volumes over the next two decades. It is likely that these printers collaborated on occasion, for identical woodcuts, frontispieces and joint credits suggest various partnerships and cooperative ventures.[47] Evidence shows that the volumes printed in the late sixteenth century remained in circula-tion for years to come when, even though outdated, visitors to Rome still consulted these early editions for advice on visiting sacred sites.[48]

In 1600, Giovanni Antonio Francini, "herede di Girolamo Franzini," printed an edition updated by Prospero Parisio which represented an offshoot of the Martinelli text despite the presence of woodcuts stem-ming from his predecessor Girolamo Francini. In particular, Parisio in-serted observations in reference to selected churches decorated by Pope Clement VIII — an effort undoubtedly endorsed by the pope for the Jubilee year of 1600.[49] He also composed a section on "All'Antichità dell'Alma città di Roma," and added updated information to the text of *La guida romana.* The compilation of material includes a version of *L'Antichità di Roma* without reference to Palladio and the discourse on the fires of the ancients. At least four other editions of *Le cose maravigliose* appeared in 1600, all with varying degrees of conformity to the original text.

The renovations and decorative programs initiated by Pope Paul V (1605–1621) emerged in the 1609 edition printed by Mascardi. The frontispiece attributed the new commentary to Giovanni Battista Cherubini who recorded pertinent works of art and building programs at each site. The projects undertaken by the Borghese pope were also documented in a French translation of 1612 which, curiously, is the only edition of *Le cose maravigliose,* discovered to date, which names Palladio as the author.[50] The most radical changes to the internal structure of *Le cose maravigliose* were effected by Pietro Martire Felini. His book, issued from 1610 until 1615 in an identical format, presented material on no fewer than 303 churches. The *Trattato nuovo delle cose maravigliose di Roma* united the traditional components: an updated account of the churches with a list of stations, *La guida romana* and Palladio's *L'Antichità di Roma.*[51] However, in keeping with the increasing emphasis on illustrations, the text was cut down with the result that images — many descending from the Francini editions — dominated each page. Descriptions of artistic commissions gained new prominence as they overshadowed accounts of relics and pardons. The itinerary for the tour of churches underwent revisions producing a more coherent method of circulating around seventeenth-century Rome. Finally, illustrations proliferated as sacred and secular buildings appeared together with ancient and modern monuments.

The innovations of Felini's edition made *Le cose maravigliose* a useful and comprehensive reference work which, as always, had to fulfill the needs of a diverse audience. The general format of the guidebook persisted, with some variations, through the eighteenth century. No longer a simple pilgrim's guide to the relics and stations of the churches, *Le cose maravigliose* had become an essential resource for any first-time visitor to the monuments of Rome. It was a worthy descendant of *Le Chiese,* the practical yet scholarly book which Palladio had composed in 1554. While Palladio's work incorporated some information about current church building, his most significant contribution was his insistence on personal contact with the monuments. He stressed his direct experience of Roman churches in the preface to the guidebook when he acknowledged the authority of commemorative tablets, necrologies and papal bulls conserved on the walls — inscriptions which recorded foundation dates, patrons and sacred history[52] (Trans., p. 72). The author was guided by his faith in first-hand observation and contact with actual sites, and he expected his readers to follow his example. His was a book which never was intended to reside in a library, but rather to remain in the pockets of travellers.

DESCRITIONE

DE LE CHIESE

Stationi , Indulgenze & Reliquie
de Corpi Sancti,che fonno in la
Citta de Roma.

B R E V E M E N T E   R A C C O L T A

da M. Andrea Palladio & noua=
mente posta in Luce.

Con gratia & Priuilegio per anni diece.

IN ROMA

Appresso Vincentio Lucrino.

1554.

Fig. 1. Frontispiece of Palladio's *Descritione de le Chiese di Roma,* Rome, Lucrino, 1554 (Photo: author)

LANTICHITA

DI ROMA

DI M. ANDREA PALLADIO.

RACOLTA BREVEMENTE
da gli Auttori Antichi, & Moderni.
Nouamente posta in Luce.

Con gratia & Preuilegio per anni diece

IN ROMA
Appresso Vincenzo Lucrino.
1554.

Fig. 2. Frontispiece of Palladio's *L'Antichità di Roma,* Rome, Lucrino, 1554 (Photo: author)

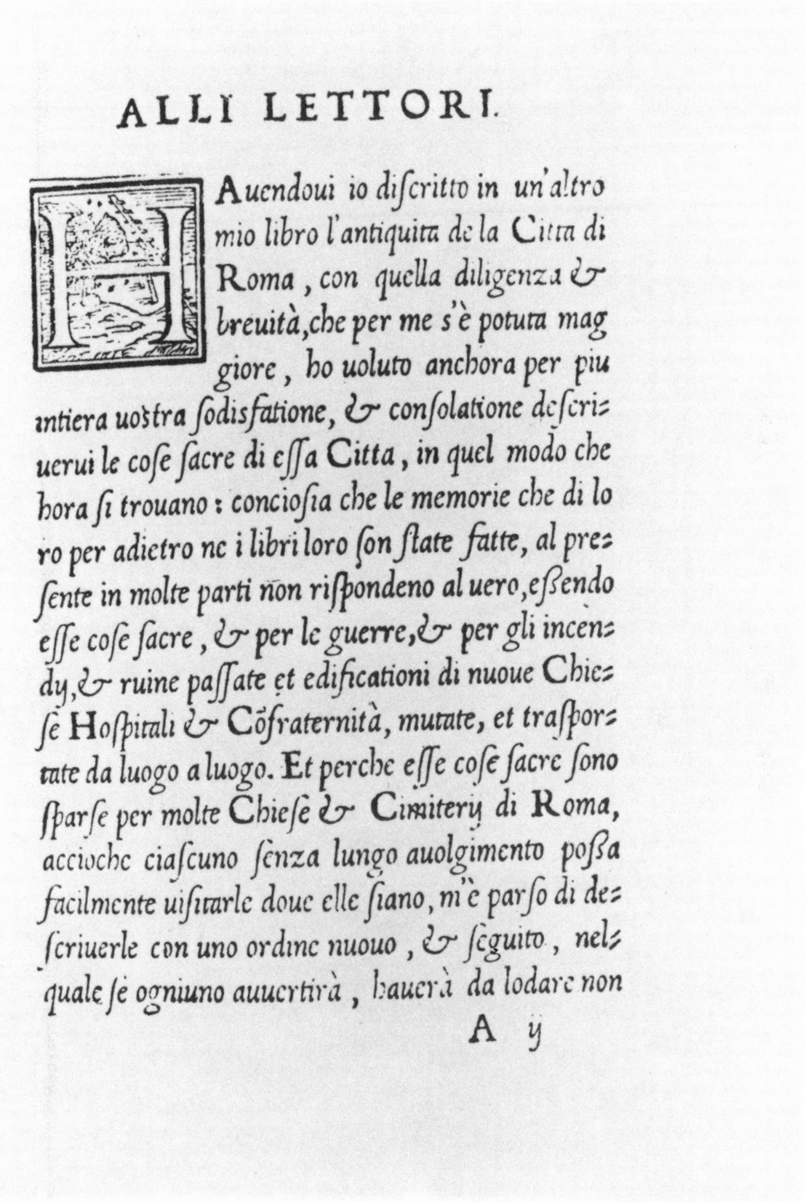

ALLI LETTORI.

Auendoui io diſcritto in un'altro mio libro l'antiquita de la Citta di Roma , con quella diligenza & breuità,che per me s'è potuta mag giore , ho uoluto anchora per piu intiera uoſtra ſodisfatione, & conſolatione deſcri; uerui le coſe ſacre di eſſa Citta, in quel modo che hora ſi trouano : concioſia che le memorie che di lo ro per adietro ne i libri loro ſon ſtate fatte, al pre; ſente in molte parti non riſpondeno al uero,eſſendo eſſe coſe ſacre , & per le guerre,& per gli incen; dy,& ruine paſſate et edificationi di nuoue Chie; ſe Hoſpitali & Côfraternità, mutate, et traſpor; tate da luogo a luogo. Et perche eſſe coſe ſacre ſono ſparſe per molte Chieſe & Cimiterij di Roma, accioche ciaſcuno ſenza lungo auolgimento poſſa facilmente uiſitarle doue elle ſiano, m'è parſo di de; ſcriuerle con uno ordine nuouo , & ſeguito , nel; quale ſe ogniuno auuertirà , hauerà da lodare non

A ij

Fig. 3. First page of Preface to Palladio's *Descritione de le Chiese di Roma,* Rome, Lucrino, 1554 (Photo: author)

DELLA EDIFICATIONE

di Roma, & fuccesso fino alla cõuersio=
ne di Constantino Magno Impera=
tore, & de la donatione fatta alli
Sommi Pontifici de la
S. R. Ecclesia.

OMOLO primo Re
e fondatore di la Citta
di Roma , la edifico
gl'anni del mondo.
4333. adi 21. de Apri=
le, fopra la riua del Te
uere. 15. miglia longi
al Mare Tirreno, do=
poi del quale ne fuc=
cesse fei altri Re e lultimo fu Tarquinio fuper=
bo , il quale fu fcacciato da Roma perche Se=
fto fuo figliuolo violo di notte Lucretia mo=
glie di Collatino : & regnorno detti fette Re,
anni. 243. l'Imperio de li quali nõ fi diftende=
ua fe non miglia quindeci. Scacciati li Re poi
ordinorno il viuere politico,& ciuile, La qual
forma di gouerno duro anni. 465. nel qual
tempo con. 43. battaglie acquiftorno quafi il
principato del mondo,& vi furno. 877. Con=
foli, dui anni gouerno li dieci huomeni &. 43
li tribuni de foldati con potefta confolare, &

A iiii

Fig. 4. First page of the text of Palladio's *Descritione de le Chiese di
Roma,* Rome, Lucrino, 1554 (Photo: author)

Fig. 5. Itineraries proposed by Palladio in the *Descritione de le Chiese di Roma* superimposed on Nolli's map of Rome (1748) (Photo: author)

Fig. 6. Giovanni Battista Maganza, *Portrait of Andrea Palladio,* oil on canvas (Photo: Count Angelo di Valmarana, Villa Valmarana ai Nani, Vicenza)

Fig. 7. Giuseppe Zocchi, *Portrait of Giangiorgio Trissino,* engraving from Castelli (1753) (Photo: author)

Fig. 8. Paolo Veronese, *Portrait of Daniele Barbaro,* oil on canvas (Photo: Rijksmuseum, Amsterdam)

prospectus mediae partis maior aulae Nosocomii

Fig. 9. Ciborium of Hospital of Santo Spirito, Rome, engraving from Saulnier, *Dissertatio Sacri Ordinis S. Spirito,* 1649 (Photo: Biblioteca Apostolica Vaticana)

Fig. 10. Altar of Church of Santo Spirito (destroyed), Rome, engraving from Saulnier, *Dissertatio Sacri Ordinis S. Spirito,* 1649 (Photo: Biblioteca Apostolica Vaticana)

Fig. 11. Ciborium of Hospital of Santo Spirito, Rome (Photo: author, after Lavagnino, 1962)

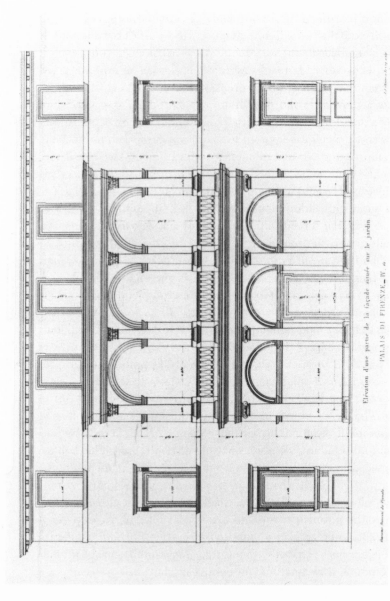

Fig. 12. Garden Facade of Palazzo di Firenze, Rome, engraving from Létarouilly, Édifices de Rome moderne, 1849-66 (Photo: author)

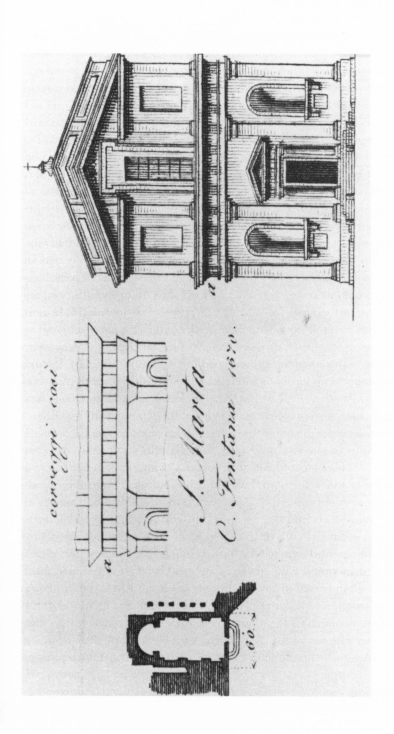

Fig. 13. Facade of Santa Marta, Rome, engraving from Cipriani, Itinerario figurato, 1835–37 (Photo: author)

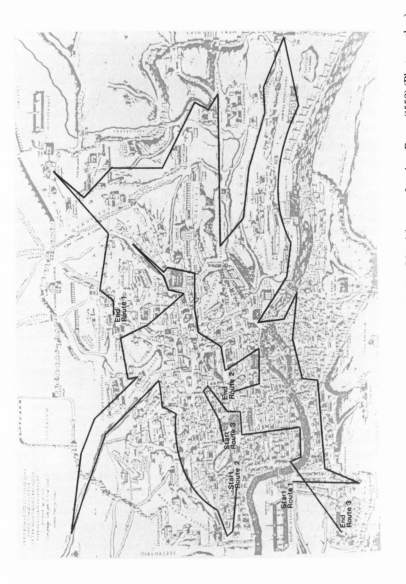

Fig. 14. Itineraries proposed in *La guida romana* superimposed on Ligorio's map of ancient Rome (1552) (Photo: author)

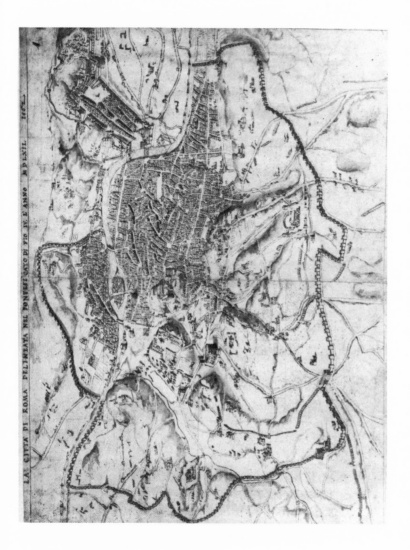

Fig. 15. Giovanni Antonio Dosio, attrib., *Map of Rome* (1562), London (Photo: The British Architectural Library, RIBA, London)

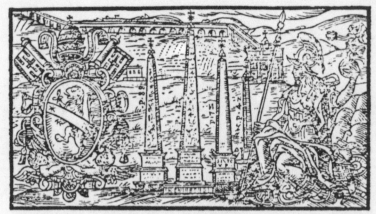

LE COSE

MARAVIGLIOSE
DELL'ALMA CITTA'
D I   R O M A,
DOVE SI VEGGONO IL MOVIMENTO
delle Guglie, & gli Acquedutti per condurre
l' Acqua Felice,

*Le ample , & commode strade , fatte à beneficio publico,
dal Santissimo* S I S T O *V. P. O. M.*

Et si tratta delle Chiese , rappresentate in disegno da Gieronimo
Francino , con le Stationi , & Reliquie de' Corpi
Santi che vi sono .

Et vn Trattato del medo d'acquistare l'Indulgenze.

La Guida Romana, che insegna facilmente à i Forastieri à ritrouare le
più notabili cose di Roma .
Li nomi de i S O M M I P O N T E F I C I , I M P E R A T O R I , & altri
Principi Chistiani .
Il numero delle Parrocchie , & Compagnie che sono in Roma .
L'A N T I C H I T A' di R o m a , breuemente raccolta; & vn discorso
sopra li fuochi de gli antichi .

Nuouamente corretu, & purgati da molti errori, & ampliate dal
Reuerendo Padre Fra Santi de Sant'Agostino .

Con Priuilegio del S U M M O P O N T E F I C E .

IN V E N E T I A , Per Girolamo Francino , Libraro in Roma ,
al segno della Fonte . M D L X X X V I I I ·

Fig. 16. Frontispiece of *Le cose maravigliose dell'alma città di Roma,*
Venice, Girolamo Francini, 1588 (Photo: author)

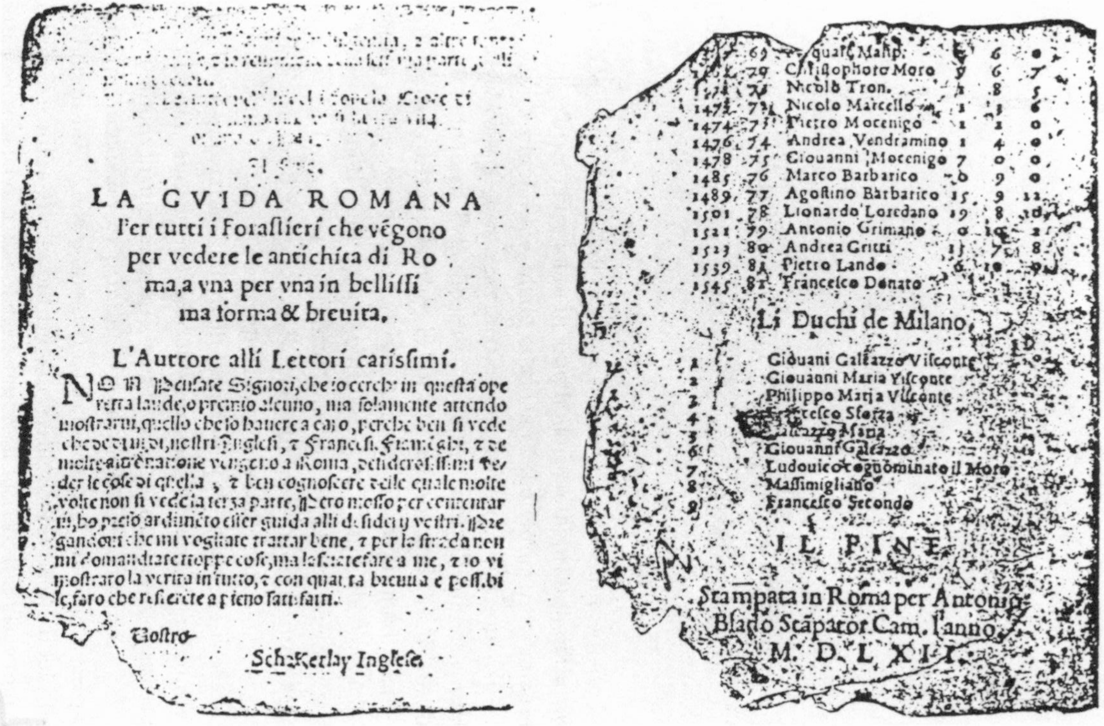

LA GVIDA ROMANA
Per tutti i Forastieri che vēgono
per vedere le antichita di Ro
ma, a vna per vna in bellissi
ma forma & breuita.

L'Auttore alli Lettori carissimi.

Schakerlay Inglese

Li Duchi de Milano

Giouani Galeazzo Visconte
Giouanni Maria Visconte
Philippo Maria Visconte
Francesco Sforza
Galeazzo Maria
Giouanni Galeazzo
Ludouico cognominato il Moro
Massimigliano
Francesco Secondo

IL FINE

Stampata in Roma per Antonio
Blado Scapator Cam. l'anno
M. D. L X I I.

Fig. 17. First and last pages of *La guida romana,* Rome, Blado, 1562; London, British Library (Photo: author)

Part II

Descritione de le Chiese di Roma

List of Churches in Palladio's *Le Chiese*

Of the Seven Principal Churches

San Giovanni in Laterano
San Pietro in Vaticano
San Paolo
Santa Maria Maggiore
San Lorenzo fuori le Mura
San Sebastiano
Santa Croce in Gerusalemme

On the Island

San Giovanni Calabita
San Bartolomeo

In Trastevere

Santa Maria dell'Orto
Santa Cecilia
Santa Maria in Trastevere
San Crisogono
San Francesco

San Cosimato
San Pietro in Montorio
San Pancrazio
Sant'Onofrio

In the Borgo

Santo Spirito in Sassia
Sant'Angelo
Santa Maria in Camposanto
Santo Stefano degli Indiani
Sant'Egidio Abbate
Santi Lazzaro, Marta e Maddalena
Santa Caterina
San Giacomo Scossacavallo
Santa Maria in Traspontina

From the Flaminian Gate

Sant'Andrea
Santa Maria del Popolo
Santa Maria dei Miracoli
Santa Trinità
San Giacomo in Augusta
Sant'Ambrogio
San Rocco
San Girolamo degli Schiavoni
San Lorenzo in Lucina
San Silvestro
Le Convertite
Santi Apostoli
San Marcello
Santa Maria in Via Lata
San Marco
Santa Maria di Loreto
Santa Marta
Santa Maria della Strada
Santa Maria sopra Minerva
Santa Maria Rotonda
Santa Maria Maddalena

Santa Maria in Campo Marzio
Santa Elisabeta
San Macuto
Sant'Eustachio
San Luigi
Sant'Agostino
San Trifone
Sant'Antonio dei Portoghesi
Sant'Apollinare
San Giacomo degli Spagnoli
Santa Maria dell'Anima
Santa Maria della Pace
San Tommaso in Parione
San Salvatore in Lauro
San Giovanni dei Fiorentini
San Biagio della Pagnotta
Santa Lucia
San Giovanni in Agina
San Girolamo
La Casa Santa
San Lorenzo in Damaso
Santa Barbara
San Martinello
San Salvatore in Campo
Santa Maria in Monticelli
*Santi Vincenzo e Anastasio
*San Tommaso
*Santa Caterina
*San Tommaso
*Sant'Andrea
*Santa Brigida
*Santa Caterina da Siena
*Santa Maria di Monserrato
*Sant'Eligio
*Santo Stefano alla Chiavica
*Santi Celso e Giuliano
San Biagio
Santa Maria del Pianto
Santa Caterina dei Funari

Sant'Angelo
San Nicola in Carcere
Santa Maria in Aracoeli

From the Capitoline to the Left

San Pietro nel Carcere Tulliano
Sant'Adriano
*San Lorenzo
Santi Cosma e Damiano
Santa Maria Nuova
San Clemente
Santa Maria Imperatrice
Santi Quattro Incoronati
Santi Pietro e Marcellino
San Matteo in Merulana
San Pietro in Vincoli
San Lorenzo in Panisperna
Sant'Agata
San Lorenzo in Fonte
Santa Potenziana
San Vito in Macello
San Giuliano
San Eusebio
*San Luca
Santa Bibiana
San Martino
Santa Prassede
*Sant'Antonio
San Quirico
Santa Susanna
San Vitale
Santa Costanza
Sant'Agnese
*Santa Maria degli Angeli

From the Capitoline to the Right

Santa Maria Liberatrice
Santa Maria della Consolazione

*San Giovanni Decollato
*Sant'Alo
Sant'Anastasia
Santa Maria in Portico
San Gregorio
Santi Giovanni e Paolo
Santa Maria della Navicella
Santo Stefano Rotondo
*San Giorgio
San Sisto
Santa Sabina
Sant'Alessio
Santa Prisca
Santa Saba Abbate
Santa Balbina
San Giovanni
Sant'Anastasio
*Santa Celi
Santa Maria Annunciata
*Santa Maria in Via

* In *Le cose maravigliose* of 1563

To the Readers —

Having already described in another of my books the antiquities of the city of Rome with the most diligence and brevity possible, I wanted still for your complete satisfaction and consolation to describe for you the sacred things of the city, in the manner in which they now appear.[1] Keep in mind that past assertions made about them in books do not now correspond to reality in many cases because these sacred things, due to wars, fires, past destruction and the construction of new churches, hospitals and confraternities, have been changed and transported from place to place. Because these sacred things are dispersed throughout many churches and cemeteries of Rome, I have decided to describe them in a new order and sequence so that each person without extensive digression may visit them easily. Thus, when everyone is informed, they will have no small amount of praise for this effort of mine. First, therefore, I will write in this book about the seven principal churches of Rome beginning at the Island and proceeding directly to Trastevere and the Borgo, which together form one section. Then one progresses in sequence from the Porta del Popolo, formerly called Flaminia, directly through the city as it is now populated until reaching the Tiber, and finally turning at the Capitoline toward the location of the seven hills and old Rome. About these churches you will find out (1) who founded them and (2) how many relics of holy bodies adorn them, which holy popes granted them privileges and how many indulgences and stations they have. Thus in Lent, as in each and every day of the year. (And all this I have taken from the bulls which in many of these churches can be read at the choir or are elsewhere displayed, from sacred histories and from ancient tablets.) You should be advised that in Rome there used to be more than three thousand churches, among which four hundred were consecrated in honor of the Virgin Mary, and most of these are in ruins, but it has happened that others have been rebuilt again and many hospitals and confraternities have been founded which every day perform many pious works for the Virgin, the poor and pilgrims — as you will readily be able to understand once you read further. Therefore, you will recognize that whereas Rome once was feared and esteemed by the whole world for the great things brought about by the ancients, that it is now even worthier of admiration on account of so many and such sacred things which are still hers, and for which she has become the head and real seat of the true Christian religion. To which I add wishes of sincere and enduring felicity.

On the Building of Rome
and the Era Which Followed
Until the Conversion
of Emperor Constantine the Great
and on the Donation Made to the Holy Popes
of the Holy Roman Church.

❧

Romulus, the first king and founder of the city of Rome, built it in the year of the world 4333 on 21 April along the Tiber River and fifteen miles distant from the Tyrrhenian Sea. Six other kings followed and the last was Tarquin the Proud, who was chased out of Rome because Sestus, his son, violated Lucretia, the wife of Colatinus, at night. Those seven kings ruled for 243 years during which time their power extended no more than fifteen miles. After the kings were expelled, political and civil life was determined by a form of government which lasted for 465 years. During this time there were forty-three battles by which Rome came to rule nearly the whole world. There were 877 consuls. For two years ten men governed, and for forty-three years, tribunes of soldiers with consular power. For four years Rome remained without a ruler, and later Julius Caesar, under the title of Perpetual Leader, simultaneously took control of the empire and its freedom. Thus, the Roman Empire lasted for 360 years from the time of the emperor Caesar until the holy Christian popes. The emperor Constantine the Great then converted it to the Faith of Christ as it is written in the chronicles.

Constantine, like his predecessors, persecuted the Christians. The Blessed Silvester, who was the pope in that period, hid with other clerics at Monte Soratto, twenty miles distant from Rome. In that time God afflicted Constantine with incurable leprosy and since he did not benefit from the aid of medicine, as the ultimate remedy suggested by the doctors, he was counseled to wash in the warm blood of infants.[2] Hence, having made preparations and seeing over twenty-thousand children and their mothers tearing their hair, crying miserably and mourning, he was moved by tender pity and thus he said to the afflicted women: "Do not fear because I decided rather to die than to live as a result of the murder of so many innocent children." Having said this, he ordered that all those infants be returned to their own mothers with designated gifts. On account of this act of mercy, the glorious Apostles Peter and Paul appeared on the following night to him and said: "Because you have determined that the letting of blood of these innocent creatures is odious, our Lord Jesus Christ has sent us to tell you that to improve your health you should make use of Pope Silvester who is hiding at Monte Soratto." Because the emperor was warned by the vision, he sent for St. Silvester who persuaded him to dress immediately in the whitest of robes and to order constitutions for seven consecutive days in honor of Jesus Christ and of all Christians. On the eighth he came to the holy confession, all the imperial emblems having been tossed away. With his arms lowered to the ground and with tears, he threw himself into the holy baptismal font and no sooner than he was positioned in the holy font than he saw with his own eyes a hand sent down from heaven which cured him of leprosy. Having been quickly baptized, he decreed with a public proclamation that the temples to the pagan idols be closed throughout the Roman Empire and that the churches of Christ should be built and that the sepulchres and relics of martyrs should be honored and revered with great veneration.

In this period, Helena, mother of Constantine, who lived in Britain, was persuaded by the Jews to take part in their rites and to leave the cult of the idols and not follow the Christian religion about which she wrote to her son in Rome. To this Constantine answered that he wanted the Jewish and Christian priests to debate in his presence. All the wisest men in the Roman Empire took part in the disputation. Convening in Rome were seventy-five Christian bishops and 290 Hebrew priests excluding the twelve scribes whom Isacar [?] their holy pontiff ordered there, all of them men gifted in Hebrew, Greek and Latin. The judges and arbitrators of this contest were two philosophers who were neither Christians nor Jews. One was called Cratone. It was not ever possible to persuade him to receive gifts, nor to have personal possessions, nor to set aside anything for the future for he said that he enjoyed the greatest security by denying wealth. The other philosopher was named Zenofilo, a steady and very prudent man. They were so highly esteemed, these two men, that without any doubt on anyone's part, everything they said was accepted as the truth and all decisions as binding. When all gathered together in front of the emperor Constantine and his mother Helena, a very important debate took place between St. Silvester and those scribes. In the end, the most blessed pope so clearly convinced them that everyone unanimously demanded the expulsion of those from Rome who did not accept the fact that Christ was the Son of the true God; for this reason still others of the Jews who had come to impugn the holy faith converted. And the philosopher-judges of the disputation were also baptized. One of the scribes who wanted to show the power of his faith did this in the presence of everyone; he brought a bull of such ferocity that barely one hundred men were able to lead it. Then he whispered certain words in its ears so that it fell dead immediately. The scribe was not able to resuscitate it through the power of his words. Therefore, all the Jews promised that if he were able to revive it in the name of Jesus Christ, they would be baptized. And thus St. Silvester did so. In that time he dispelled, with the sign of the cross, the pernicious power from a dragon which was contaminating all of Rome with an incurable plague. It was then that Helena, the mother of Constantine, together with everyone else kissed the feet of the Blessed Silvester. Having been confirmed in his faith on account of these miracles, Constantine addressed the Roman Senate so wisely that all were baptized. Through their own will and devotion, they decided to exalt the faith of the Blessed Peter Prince of the Apostles so that the Roman seat should remain dominant over all the churches in the world and ordered that all successive popes of this church be considered the highest princes of the world, that they should be able to oversee as superiors and arbitrators the divine cult, as well as the Christian faith since they occupied the principality and the throne of the Apostolate where Jesus Christ had commanded the Blessed Peter to locate it and where the Apostle savored the chalice of his martyrdom. And so that the pontifical dignity would not suffer because of poverty, but instead would grow through the glory and dignity of the Roman See, he gave to the Blessed Silvester and to all his successors: his Lateran palace, the city of Rome, all of Italy, all the western provinces, the regions, the urban lands and the islands which surround Italy. He then departed from Rome, and transferred the Empire to the East to the city of Byzantium which then he had called Constantinople after his own name. He left in his Roman palace at the Lateran a church of gold, silver and precious stones in honor of

our Saviour Jesus Christ. In addition, he built the church of the Blessed
Apostles Peter and Paul along with other churches. He had Father St.
Silvester collect with his own hands the relics of the martyrs and he installed them in honor of Jesus Christ, our Lord and Saviour, as we will
see in this book.

Of the Seven Principal Churches

The first church, which is the seat of the papacy, is San Giovanni in
Laterano at Monte Celio which was built by Constantine the Great at
his palace and endowed with grand bequests since it had been damaged
and ruined by the heretics. Nicholas IV had it rebuilt, and Martin V
began to have it painted and to have the pavement laid. Eugenius IV
had it finished. *In our times, Pius IV decorated it with a beautiful ceiling and levelled
the square of the same church.* It was consecrated in honor of the Saviour, St.
John the Baptist and the Evangelist by St. Silvester on the ninth of November. During the consecration an image of the Saviour appeared, which
still today can be seen above the tribune of the high altar, and has never
burned although this same church caught fire twice. There is a station
here on the first Sunday of Lent, Palm Sunday, Holy Thursday and Saturday, the Saturday before the eighth of Easter, and the eve of Pentecost.
On the Day of St. John in front of the Porta Latina, there is a plenary
remission of sins and the release of a soul from Purgatory. On the Day
of St. Bernardino, which is the twentieth of May, until the first of August,
every day has a plenary remission of sins. And on the Day of St. John the
Baptist, of the transfiguration of the Lord, of the beheading of St. John
and on the dedication of the Saviour, there is a plenary remission of sins.
On the Day of St. John the Evangelist, there are twenty-eight thousand
years of indulgences and as many quarantines and the plenary remission of sins.[3] And every day there are 6048 years of indulgences and as
many quarantines and the remission of a third part of sins. Whoever
celebrates or holds services in the chapel next to the sacristy will liberate
a soul from the punishment of Purgatory. There are still infinite indulgences which mean in particular that there is no need to go to the Holy
Sepulchre of Christ or to St. James Campostella. In that church, there
are the following relics which are shown on Easter day after vespers. In
the tabernacle which is above the altar of the Magdalene: the kingdom
with which Constantine crowned Silvester; the head of St. Zachary the

father of St. John the Baptist; the head of St. Pancratius Martyr from which blood issued for three continuous days when this church was burned down by the heretics; some relics of St. Mary Magdalene; a shoulder of St. Lawrence; a tooth of St. Peter the Apostle; the chalice from which St. John the Apostle and Evangelist drank the poison at the command of the holy emperor and which did not harm him; the chain with which he was tied when he was led from Ephesus to Rome and one of his tunics which, when placed over three corpses suddenly brought them back to life; some ashes and the hair-shirt of St. John the Baptist; some milk, hair, and clothing from the glorious Virgin Mary; the shirt which she made for Jesus Christ; the cloth with which our Saviour dried the feet of his disciples; the cane with which the head of our Saviour was beaten; the red robe put on him by Pilate which is stained with his most precious blood; some wood from the cross; the veil of the glorious virgin which covered the private parts of Jesus Christ on the cross; the shroud which was placed over his face in the sepulchre and some water and blood which issued from his side. Above the papal altar, in those iron gratings are the heads of the most glorious Apostles Peter and Paul. Whenever they are shown, there is an indulgence of three thousand years for the inhabitants of Rome who are present, of six thousand years for those from nearby towns and of twelve thousand years for those who came from distant lands. Then there are as many quarantines of indulgences and a remission from a third part of the sins. Beneath this altar is the oratory of St. John the Evangelist when, as a prisoner, he was led to Rome. Those four pillars of the bronze railing which are in front of that altar, are filled with holy earth carried from Jerusalem, and were made by Augustus from the prows of the galleys which he captured in the naval battle of Egypt and placed together.[4] In the chapel which is next to the large door, there is the altar which St. John the Baptist had while in the desert, the Ark of the Covenant, the Rod of Aaron and of Moses and the table on which our Saviour had the Last Supper with his disciples. These things were brought to Rome from Jerusalem by Titus. Above, at one end of the hall where the last Lateran Council was held, there is a stone slab on top of four columns on which the dice were thrown for the robes of our Saviour. The distance from the stone to the ground is said to measure his height. At the other end of the hall there are three marble doors which were in the palace of Pilate at Jerusalem and it is said that our Saviour was led through these to Pilate. Those two porphyry seats which are outside the Chapel of St. Silvester, it is said, were ordered after that woman was made pope in order to confirm the testicles of new popes. The latest deacon performs this office. But Platina in the Lives of the Popes [*in the life of Pope John VIII*] says otherwise.[5] The marble window which is over the door leading to that chapel was once in the house of the Virgin Mary in Judea and they say that the angel Gabriel entered through here when announcing the Incarnation of the Son of God. That staircase of twenty-eight steps, which is next to that chapel, comes from the palace of Pilate. There our Lord fell and spilled his most precious blood—the traces of which are still visible today. Whoever climbs on his knees with great devotion will have nine years for each step as well as forty more of indulgence and the remission of a third part of his sins. That column in two parts was in Jerusalem and split apart with the death of our Saviour. The chapel called the Sancta Sanctorum, where women are never allowed to enter, was consecrated by Nicholas III in honor of St. Lawrence Martyr.[6] Among other relics, it houses an image of the Saviour at twelve years which is decorated with silver and gems. It is believed that this was designed by St. Luke and finished by the angel. As Leo IV commanded, on the fourteenth of August after vespers nearly every year, it is carried in the manner of an ancient triumph—that is on the mutual shoulders of the most honorable citizens—to Santa Maria Maggiore, where people gather from all of Rome and nearby cities. The following day after a choral mass, it is carried back to the Lateran with equal pomp. On the same day, fourteen men who had life sentences are freed from prison. The washing of the feet of the Saviour at Santa Maria Nuova is observed in memory of the washing performed by the priests every year on the first day of April, the feast of the goddess Cibele in that little river which flows from beyond the Porta San Sebastiano near this church and toward the hospital. There, the place where Constantine the Great was baptized is still standing. It is round in shape, covered with a lead roof and surrounded by porphyry columns. It was decorated in this manner: the top was of porphyry and the part which held the water was of silver. A porphyry column, in the middle, held a lamp of gold weighing fifty pounds on top which burned balsam instead of oil on Easter night. At the outer edge of the font was a golden angel and a silver statue of the Saviour weighing ten pounds with an inscription: "Behold the angel of the Lord who lifts up the sins of the world." Yet still there were seven deer which spewed water, and each one weighed eighty pounds. Those three chapels which are nearby were consecrated by Hilarius III. One was dedicated to the cross where wood from the cross, covered with gems, was placed.[7] The two columns encased in wood in that chapel come from the house of the Blessed Virgin. The other chapel, where women never enter, was once Constantine's room; it was consecrated to St. John the Baptist and held many relics. The third was dedicated to St. John the Evangelist. The Hospital of the Saviour, today known as San Giovanni in Laterano, was built by the very famous Colonna family and enlarged by various Roman barons, cardinals and others. Once the following things were in that church and are no longer there today: Constantine the Great installed a Saviour which weighed three hundred and thirty pounds, twelve apostles which measured five feet each and weighed [?] pounds, another Saviour weighing one hundred and forty pounds and four angels, each weighing one hundred and five pounds. These things were of silver. In addition, there were four gold crowns with dolphins weighing twenty pounds and seven altars of two hundred pounds. Pope Hormisdas donated a silver crown of twenty pounds and six vases.

San Pietro in Vaticano. This church was built and endowed by Constantine the Great. It was consecrated by St. Silvester on the eighteenth of November. There are stations on the Feast of Epiphany, the first and fifth Sunday of Lent, the Saturdays after the aforementioned first Sundays, the Monday after Easter, the Feast of the Ascension of our Lord, the Feast of Pentecost, the Saturday after Pentecost, the Saturdays of all the four periods and the third Sunday of Advent, the Feast of St. Mark, the first and fourth Sunday of Advent and the Feast of Corpus Christi. From the Holy See there is a plenary indulgence on the Sunday of Pentecost, a plenary indulgence and twenty-eight thousand years and as many quarantines. On the Feast of St. Gregory there is a plenary indulgence. On the Feast of the Annunciation of our Lady there are a thousand years of indulgence, and from that day until the first of August, there are twelve thousand years of indulgence for each day and as many quarantines and the remission of a third part of all sins. On the eve and the Feast of St. Peter, the second Sunday in July, the Feast of SS. Simon and Jude and the day of the dedication of that church, the Feasts of SS. Martin and Andrew there is a plenary remission of sins. Every day there are 6048 years of indulgence, as many quarantines and the remission of a third part of all sins. On the Feast of St. Peter, of the seven principal altars of that church and all the feasts therein, the aforesaid indulgences are doubled. Every day there is a plenary indulgence in the Sistine Chapel.

Whoever climbs with devotion the stairs in front of this church and the Chapel of St. Peter will have seven years of indulgence for each step. On Fridays during March there are innumerable indulgences. This church has the bodies of SS. Simon and Jude Apostles; St. John Chrysostom; SS. Processo and Martiniano; St. Gregory Pope and St. Petronilla. There is the head of St. Andrew which was brought to Rome by the Prince of the Marches at the time of Pius II and was carried all the way from the Ponte Molle, as well as those of St. Luke the Evangelist, St. Sebastian, St. James the Less, St. Thomas the Bishop of Conturba and Martyr and St. Amando. There is a shoulder of St. Christopher and St. Stephen as well as other bodies and relics of saints whose names are recorded in the Book of Life. Under the high altar is the mitre of the bodies of SS. Peter and Paul. In the tabernacle to the right of the principal entrance is the Veronica, called the Holy Face, and the iron of the lance which passed through the rib cage of our Saviour which was sent by the Great Turk to Innocent VIII. Whenever this is shown, the inhabitants of Rome who are present gain an indulgence of three thousand years. Those who come from nearby gain six thousand and anyone who comes from distant lands, twelve thousand and as many quarantines and the remission of a third part of all sins. There is still a small painting with the figures of SS. Peter and Paul which is displayed on the feast days of the church over the high altar. This belonged to St. Silvester. It is the one which he showed to Constantine when he asked who were Peter and Paul who had appeared to him. Whoever so desires may read about this story in the life of St. Silvester. The columns which are in the Chapel of St. Peter and that which is encased in iron in the church — against which our Saviour leaned as he preached and from which he suddenly liberated the demons — come from the Temple of Solomon in Jerusalem. Honorius I had this church covered with gilt bronze tiles taken from the Temple of Jupiter Capitolinus.[8] Eugenius IV had the exterior doors made by Antonio of Florence in memory of the nations which were reconciled to the church in his own time. The bronze St. Peter which is under the organ was formerly a statue of Jupiter Capitolinus. The pine cone in the courtyard, which is made of bronze and measures five and two-fifths arms in height, comes, they say, from the top of the cupola of the Pantheon [*used to be on the top of the Tomb of Hadrian where the Castel Sant'Angelo now stands*]. A flash of lightning knocked it down and [*from there*] it was brought to San Pietro. The peacocks formerly decorated the Tomb of the Scipioni.[9] The emperor Otto II is buried in that porphyry tomb.[10] He transported the body of St. Bartholomew from Benevento to Rome. The following ornaments used to be in the church, but have disappeared due to the ravages of time. First, over the tomb of St. Peter, Constantine the Great placed a golden cross weighing one hundred and fifty pounds, four silver candelabra decorated with sculptures of the years of the Apostles, three golden chalices weighing ten pounds apiece, four silver vases weighing fifty pounds apiece, a patent and a golden censor weighing thirty pounds and decorated with a blue dove. The gate of the altar of St. Peter is gold and silver, decorated with many precious stones. Pope Hormisdas donated ten vases and plates of silver. The emperor Justinian the Elder gave a golden chalice of five pounds, encrusted with gems as well as his patent of twenty pounds. The emperor Justinian donated a golden vase covered with gems weighing six pounds, two silver vases weighing twelve pounds apiece and two silver chalices weighing fifteen pounds apiece. Charlemagne bequeathed a silver tablet which was sculpted with the city of Constantinople. King Theodoric decorated [the church] with a silver beam weighing 1,020 pounds and two silver candle fixtures weighing thirty-five pounds apiece. From the spoils of Vitiges, Bellisarius offered a golden cross weighing a hundred pounds and decorated with precious stones and two costly candle fixtures. Michele, the son of Emperor Theophilus of Constantinople, donated a chalice and patent of gold, decorated with gems of great value.

San Paolo. This church is located on the Via Ostia about one mile outside of Rome. It was built, endowed and decorated — as was San Pietro — by Constantine the Great on the spot where the head of St. Paul the Apostle was miraculously discovered. It is adorned with great columns and very high architraves. Honorius IV had it decorated with a variety of marbles which were splendidly carved. It was consecrated by St. Silvester. The stations are on Wednesday after the fourth Sunday of Lent, the third Feast of Easter, the second Sunday before Lent and the Feast of the Innocents. Then, there is an indulgence of a hundred years on the Day of the Conversion of St. Paul with as many quarantines and a plenary remission from all sins. On the commemoration day there is a plenary remission from sins; on the dedication day there are a thousand years of indulgence, as many quarantines and a plenary remission from sins. Whoever visits this church on every Sunday during the year will obtain as many indulgences as at the Holy Sepulchre of Christ, or St. James Campostella. Every day there are 6048 years and as many quarantines of indulgence as well as remission from a third part of all sins. There are the bodies of St. Timothy, the disciple of St. Paul; SS. Celso, Julian, and Basilissa, as well as many Innocents; an arm of St. Ann, the mother of the Virgin Mary; the chain with which St. Paul was shackled; the head of the Samaritan; a finger of St. Nicholas and many other relics. Beneath the high altar is the mitre of the bodies of SS. Peter and Paul. To the right of the altar is the image of the Crucifixion which spoke to St. Bridget, Queen of Sweden, when she prayed on that spot. *There are seven altars with privileges and whoever visits them earns as many indulgences as at the seven altars of San Pietro.*

Santa Maria Maggiore. This was the first church dedicated to the Virgin Mary in Rome. It was built during the time of Pope Liberius by Giovanni, a Roman noble, and his wife. As they had no children, they wished to spend their riches in his honor. Thus, on the night of August fifth, a vision instructed them to go the following morning to the Esquiline and, where the ground was covered with snow, to build a temple. The pope had the same vision as well and that morning he went with his whole court to the spot. Having found the snow, he began to dig with his own hands. Thus the church was founded. There is a station every Wednesday of the four, Holy Wednesday, Easter Day, the first Sunday of Advent, Christmas Eve and Day, the first of the year, the Feast of the Madonna of the Snow, the Feast of St. Jerome and his translation which is celebrated on the eve of the Ascension, with a plenary remission from sins. And on the Feast of the Purification, the Ascension, the Nativity, the Presentation and the Conception of the Virgin Mary, there are a thousand years of indulgence and the plenary remission of sins. From the Day of her Assumption until her Nativity, other than the daily indulgences, there are twelve thousand years of indulgence. Each day of these are worth 6048 years of indulgence and as many quarantines, as well as remission from a third part of all sins. Whoever celebrates or has celebrated for him a mass in the Chapel of the Manger will free a soul from the punishment of Purgatory. In this church are the bodies of St. Matthew the Apostle; SS. Romula and Redenta; St. Jerome; the manger where Christ lay in Bethlehem; the drapery with which the Blessed Virgin wrapped him; the stole of St. Jerome; the tunic, stole and maniple of St. Thomas, Bishop of Conturbia which is stained with his blood; the head of St. Bibiana and of St. Marcellinus Pope; an arm of St. Matthew the Apostle and Evangelist, of St. Luke the Evangelist, of St. Thomas the Bishop and of St. Bibiana and many other relics which are shown on Easter Day after vespers. There were the following ornaments. Sixtus III donated a silver altar weighing four hundred pounds, three silver patents weighing forty pounds each, five silver vases, twenty-eight silver crowns, three silver candelabra, a burner of fifteen pounds, a silver deer above the baptistery. Pope Simaco had made a silver ark of fifteen pounds and Gregory III donated a picture in gold of the Virgin Mary holding the Christ Child. *Alexander VI adorned the church with a beautiful ceiling. During our day, Cardinal de Cesis ornamented the church with a very beautiful chapel and another was decorated by Cardinal Santa Fiore who is the present-day archpriest of that church. The canons have remodelled the choir in a better way.*

San Lorenzo fuori le Mura *is the fifth church.* This church is situated about one mile outside of Rome along the Via Tiburtina. It was built by Constantine the Great who donated a gold lamp of twenty pounds and ten silver lamps of fifteen pounds apiece. Cardinal Oliviero Carafa then decorated it with various marbles and a very beautiful golden ceiling.[11] There are stations on the ninth Sunday before Easter, the third Sunday of Lent, the Wednesday between the eighth of Easter and the Thursday of Pentecost. Then on the Day of St. Lawrence and St. Stephen and for the whole octave, there are one hundred years, as many quarantines of indulgence and remission from a third part of sins. On the Day of the Invention of St. Stephen and of his feast, and on the stations in that church, aside from the aforementioned indulgences, there is a plenary remission from sins. Whoever confesses and enters as a repentant through the door from the courtyard of the church and moves from the crucifix which is beneath the portico to that which is over the altar opposite that door will receive a plenary indulgence from sins. Whoever visits this church every Wednesday for a year will free a soul from the punishment of Purgatory and the same is true for whoever celebrates, or has celebrated for him, a mass in that small subterranean chapel on the site of the cemetery of Cyriaca. Every day there are 6048 years of indulgence, as many quarantines of indulgence and remission from a third part of all sins. There are the bodies of SS. Lawrence and Stephen Protomartyrs; one of the stones with which he was persecuted; the slab on which St. Lawrence was placed after his death — stained with his flesh and blood; the vase with which he baptized St. Lucillo when in prison; a piece of the grating on which he was burned and many other relics.

San Sebastiano. This church is located along the Via Appia *about a mile* outside of Rome. It was built by the Blessed Lucina. On the Day of St. Sebastian and on all Sundays in May, there is plenary remission from sins. There are as many indulgences as in the churches of San Pietro and San Paolo for entering the catacombs, the site of the well where the bodies of SS. Peter and Paul were once hidden. Every day there are 6048 years and as many quarantines of indulgence and the remission of a third part of all sins. Whoever celebrates or has celebrated for him a mass at the altar of St. Sebastian will free one soul from the punishment of Purgatory. In the cemetery of Calisto, which is under this church, there is a plenary remission of sins. One hundred and seventy four thousand martyrs are there, among which are numbered eighteen popes. In the church are the bodies of St. Sebastian, St. Lucina Virgin, *and of St. Stephen Pope and Martyr* and the stone which used to be in the Chapel of "Domine Quo Vadis" where Christ left traces of a footprint when he appeared to St. Peter who was fleeing Rome. *And there are an infinite number of relics.*

Santa Croce in Gerusalemme. This church was built by Constantine, the son of Constantine the Great, at the behest of St. Helena. It was consecrated by the Blessed Silvester on the twenty-second of March. As it subsequently went to ruin, Gregory II restored it. Cardinal Peter de Mendoza renovated it and at that time the title from the cross was discovered above the tribune of the high altar. It is a titular cardinalate church. Stations are there on the fourth Sunday of Lent, Holy Friday and the second Sunday of Advent. On the Feast of the Invention and Exhaltation of the Cross, and its octave, there is a plenary remission from sins in the chapel which is below the high altar where women never enter, if not on this day. There are three hundred years and as many quarantines of indulgence as well as remission from a third part of sins on all the Sundays of the year. Every day there are also 6048 and as many quarantines of indulgence and remission from a third part of all sins. There are the bodies of SS. Anastasio and Cesareo; an ampulla full of the most precious blood of our Lord; the sponge with which he was given vinegar and salt to drink; two thorns from the crown which was placed on his head; one of the nails which were used to affix the title to the cross which was placed above by Pilate; some wood from the very holy cross which was installed by Helena and covered with silver and decorated with gold and gems; one of the thirty coins which were sold; the mitre of the cross of the good thief and many other relics which are shown on

Good Friday. There were the following ornaments. Constantine donated four silver candelabra and four vases, ten golden chalices, a gilt and silver patent weighing fifty pounds and one of silver weighing two hundred and fifty.

On the Island

San Giovanni Calabita on the Island *has a convent for women.*[12] In this church there is an image of the Virgin Mary which, after it had sunk in the Tiber, did not show any damage whatsoever nor did the water extinguish the lamps burning in front of it.

San Bartolomeo on the Island *has a monastery for Franciscan friars.* This church was built by Pope Gelasius II.[13] On the Feast of St. Bartholomew there is a plenary remission of sins and on Palm Sunday there is an indulgence of two hundred years. There are the bodies of St. Paulinus, St. Superante, St. Albert and St. Marcellus which were found in that well in front of the high altar, and the body of St. Bartholomew which was brought from Benevento to Rome by the emperor Otto. There are many relics which are displayed on the Feast of St. Bartholomew and Palm Sunday. *The church was damaged by the flooding of the Tiber in 1557.*[14] It is a titular cardinalate church.

In Trastevere

Santa Maria dell'Orto near the Ripa is a hospital for sick sailors [*for the sick of that company*].[15] Their Madonna is an object of great devotion and grants plenary indulgence to the butchers, greengrocers and artisans of Rome who form her company.

Santa Cecilia is also in Trastevere. The church is located on the site of the very house and dwelling place of St. Cecilia which Pope Paschal consecrated in honor of God, St. Mary, the Apostles Peter and Paul and St. Cecilia. It is a titular cardinalate church. There are stations on the Wednesday after the second Sunday of Lent. On the Feast of St. Cecilia there is a plenary indulgence. There are the bodies of St. Cecilia, St. Valerian her husband, St. Tiburtius, St. Lucius I Pope, and St. Massimo as well as *the veil of St. Cecilia and* many other relics. *The oratory of St. Cecilia still exists. Whoever celebrates, or has celebrated for him a mass on the altar of the Blessed Sacrament in this church will free a soul from the punishment of Purgatory. As is written to the side of the altar, this privilege was conceded by Pope Julius III. At the same place there is a convent for venerable Roman women who serve God with good works and a holy life.*

Santa Maria in Trastevere. The Taberna Meritoria of Trastevere was located on the site of the present church. Here board was given by the Senate for the duration of the lives of those Roman soldiers who could no longer serve in the military due to old age. In the place near the choir where there are now two windows with iron grating, a fountain of abundant oil arose miraculously from the earth on the night when our Saviour was born. In the space of a day it flowed in a great stream as far as the Tiber. Calixtus I built a small church there to commemorate this miracle. As it subsequently fell into ruin, Gregory III rebuilt the church from its foundations, making it larger and painting all of it. This church is a titular cardinalate church. There is a station on the Thursday after the second Sunday of Lent. On the octave of the Assumption of our Lady there is a plenary remission from sins. On the first day of the year, there is an indulgence of twenty-five thousand years and a plenary remission from sins. There are the bodies of SS. Calixtus I, Innocent and Julius, all popes and martyrs, and St. Quirino Bishop. *It is a collegiate church.*

San Crisogono. This church too is located in Trastevere. It is a titular cardinalate church *with a monastery of Carmelite friars.* There is a station on the Monday after the fifth Sunday of Lent. The following relics are conserved: an arm of St. James the Greater; a shoulder of St. Andrew; the head and hand of St. Crisogono; some wood from the cross; some of Christ's hair; a rib of St. Stephen; some relics of St. Sebastian, SS. Cosmas and Damian, St. Julian Martyr, St. Peter, St. Paul, *St. Andrew,* St. Matthew the Apostle, St. Urban Pope, St. Lawrence, St. Primo, St. Felician, St. George, St. Cecilia, St. Prisca, St. Ninfa, St. Dionisio, the tomb of Christ, Mont Zion and of the holy earth of Jerusalem. *There are still the seven privileged altars as in the church of San Paolo outside of Rome. This church was rebuilt from its foundations by the Very Reverend Cardinal Giovanni da Crema in 1129 because it had earlier fallen into ruin. The columns which are in this church used to form part of the Taberna Meritoria. It is decorated with the most beautiful marbles and porphyry.*[16]

San Francesco *has a monastery for Franciscan friars.* On his feast day and for the whole octave, there is a plenary remission from sins. In this church there is a chapel where the body of the Blessed Ludovica Romana is buried and makes miracles. *St. Francis lived here when he was in Rome.*

San Cosimato is situated where the Naumachia of Caesar used to be.[17] It has a convent for venerable Roman women who are attached to the Order of the Observant Franciscans. There are many indulgences and pardons for sins.

San Pietro in Montorio *has a monastery for Franciscan friars.* This church is on the Janiculum and was restored by Ferdinand the king of Spain. As a cardinal, Clement VII commissioned the high altarpiece and the tabernacle *from Raphael of Urbino who can never be too highly praised.*[18] To the right hand side, on entering from the principal door, there is a picture of Christ at the Column painted by Brother Sebastiano of Venice, a very excellent painter.[19] That round chapel which is outside the church occupies the site where St. Peter the Apostle was placed on the cross.[20] Paul III conceded many indulgences for this which appear in a marble tablet over the door leading to that chapel. Now there is a very beautiful tomb made through the sanctity of Pope Julius III for his uncle Cardinal del Monte.[21]

San Pancrazio *has a monastery for Ambrosian friars.* This church is situated outside the Porta Aurelia, along the Via Aurelia, and was built by Honorius I. It is decorated with very beautiful porphyry. It is a titular cardinalate church and there is a station on the Sunday of the Apostles [*on the Sunday after Easter*]. There are the bodies of St. Pancratius Bishop and Martyr; St. Pancratius Cavalier and Martyr; SS. Vettore, Malco, Madiano, and Gotteria. In the cemetery of St. Calipodio, Priest and Martyr, which is underneath this church, there are an infinite number of martyrs' bodies. One may look at them and touch them, but not carry them away without permission from the pope, under punishment of excommunication.

Sant'Onofrio *has a monastery for the Friars of St. Jerome.* This church is located between the Porta Settimiana and Porta Santo Spirito on a pleasant hill. There are many relics and pardons for sins. *It is a titular cardinalate church. There are very kind fathers who lead an exemplary life.*

In the Borgo

Santo Spirito in Sassia. This hospital was built by Innocent III and endowed with fine revenues. Sixtus IV restored it and added to its income. It is called "in Sassia" because Saxons lived there at one time. Many alms are collected there. Many sick people and orphans are housed on a continuous basis. *Every year a large number of orphan girls are married off.* Recently, the Reverend P. N. Lando, commendator of this hospital, [*Lately, Lando, commendator*] has built a very beautiful church from its foundations.[22] There is a pardon on the Sunday closest to the Feast of St. Anthony and on Pentecost *for the whole octave.* There is an arm of St. Andrew, a finger of St. Catherine and many other relics of saints.

Sant'Angelo. This church was built by the very blessed Pope Gregory.[23] As he marched in procession and sang litanies with the clergy and Roman people, the angel Michael appeared on top of the fortress on the castle and put back a bloody sword in his sheath. Many relics are there. There is a plenary indulgence for the remission of sins which lasts for the whole octave of his feast. There is a company of noble Romans who marry off poor spinsters each year.

Santa Maria in Camposanto. At this spot there is a cemetery of holy earth, brought from Jerusalem, where pilgrims and poor people from every nation are buried. According to general belief, these corpses disintegrate in three days. There are many indulgences and relics *and very long lists of the dead.*

Santo Stefano degli Indiani. The home of Indian people is located behind the church of San Pietro in Vaticano.[24] They officiate at the divine services in their own tongue. There are many indulgences conceded by the holy popes.

Sant'Egidio Abbate. This church is located outside the Porta San Pietro in the Vatican. It is held in great devotion by the Roman people so that on the first of September they go there to be protected from the fever. There is a plenary indulgence.

Santi Lazzaro, Marta e Maddalena is outside the Porta San Pietro and at the foot of Monte Mario.[25] On 22 July there are many indulgences and pardons from sins. This church is located outside of Rome because there is a hospital attached for poor people who are contagious *with the disease of St. Lazzaro*. They are well cared for here.

Santa Caterina. This church is on the Piazza San Pietro.[26] On the Feast of St. Catherine, there is a plenary remission from sins. There is some of the milk which poured from the neck of St. Catherine, instead of blood, when she was decapitated as well as some of the oil which comes out of her grave.

San Giacomo Scossacavallo. This church is located on the Piazza of the Very Reverend Cardinal Salviati [*the piazza in the middle of the Borgo*]. There is the stone on which our Saviour was presented in the temple on the day of his circumcision and the one on which Abraham wanted to sacrifice his son. St. Helena brought these to Rome to place them in San Pietro. When the stones reached the site of the present church, the horses which had carried them fell dead. They were never able to be moved elsewhere and thus this church was constructed for their installation. *A company is located here.*

Santa Maria in Traspontina.[27] In this church are the two columns against which the very blessed Peter and Paul were flagellated. *There is a crucifix which spoke to these Apostles and many other relics as well. There is a monastery for Carmelite friars.*

From the Flaminian Gate,
Now the Popolo, As Far As the Foot of the Capitoline.

Sant 'Andrea is outside the Porta del Popolo on the Via Flaminia. It is a round chapel of great art and beauty built by the Lord of our Lords, Pope Julius III, who conceded plenary indulgence for all the living and dead on the Feast of St. Andrew at the end of November.[28] On that day there is a solemn procession of all the Roman companies and fraternities from San Lorenzo in Damaso to San Pietro in Vaticano *where the head of St. Andrew is displayed.*

Santa Maria del Popolo. The bones of the emperor Nero were buried on the site of the high altar in this church, under a nut tree. They were guarded by demons who used to plague anyone passing by that spot. Due to a vision of the most blessed Virgin, Pope Paschal excavated the bones, threw them in the Tiber and established an altar. Sixtus IV renovated it from the foundations. There are one thousand years and as many quarantines of indulgence for each day from the middle of Lent until the whole octave of Easter. There is a plenary remission from sins on the Feasts of the Nativity, Purification, Annunciation, Visitation, Assumption, and Conception of the Virgin Mary, their octaves and every Saturday of Lent. There are many relics and one of the pictures of our Lady painted by St. Luke. *Augustinian friars live there.*

Santa Maria dei Miracoli is next to the walls of the Porta del Popolo.[29] This church is heavily frequented. It has been blessed with many miracles. There is a plenary indulgence and remission from all sins.

Santa Trinità. This church is situated on the Pincian Hill. It was built as a result of the prayers of St. Francis of Paola, and Ludovico XI, King of France.[30] *It has a monastery for its own friars.*

San Giacomo in Augusta. There is a hospital on this spot in which they raise many alms. They care for those ill with incurable disease. There is a plenary remission from sins on the Feast of the Annunciation of the Virgin Mary, the first day of May and the Day of the Dead. There is a remission of the third part of sins on all Saturdays during the year *and many other privileges, as one can read on the marble tablets.*

Sant'Ambrogio is at the bottom of the hill of the Trinità [*is in the street that leads from the Popolo*]. This church was built by the people of Milan with a hospital for their poor.[31] Pope Clement VII conceded great indulgences and privileges to it.

San Rocco on the Ripetta is where the mausoleum of the emperor Augustus used to be. The church with a beautiful hospital for the people of Lombardy was built recently by the Company of St. Martin.[32] Every day there is a plenary indulgence conceded by many holy popes, *especially by Pius IV. There is a company.*

San Girolamo degli Schiavoni is also on the Ripetta. This is a church of great devotion. There is a hospital for the Slavic people where they are given lodging and food. *There are many relics.*

San Lorenzo in Lucina. In ancient times, this church was the Temple of Juno Lucina. Celestine III dedicated it to St. Lawrence Martyr. It is a titular cardinalate church. There is a station on the Friday after the third Sunday of Lent. There are the bodies of SS. Alexander, Eventio, Teodolo, Severino, Pontiano, Eusebio, Vicentio, Peregrino, and Gordiano as well as two phials with the flesh and blood of St. Lawrence, a vase full of his burned flesh, a portion of the grating on which he was burned and a cloth with which the angel cleaned his very holy corpse in addition to many other relics. *This is a collegiate church.*

San Silvestro. This church was built by Simaco I. It is a titular cardinalate church. There is a station on the Thursday after the fourth Sunday of Lent. There is a plenary remission from sins on the Feast of St. Clare and St. Silvester. There are the heads of St. John the Baptist, St. Stephen Pope, the Blessed Margarita of the Colonna family who was a nun in this establishment; a piece of the mantle of St. Francis; some relics of St. Francis and of many others [*the mantle of St. Francis and of many others*]. *It has a monastery for Franciscan monks.*

Le Convertite. This is a convent dedicated to St. Mary Magdalene for penitent prostitutes.[33] There are many plenary indulgences conceded by Pope Clement VII and Pope Paul III, *and many others. They follow the Augustinian order.*

Santi Apostoli. This church was built by Constantine the Great in honor of the twelve Apostles. Because it was ruined by the heretics, the holy popes Pelagius and John restored it. It is a titular cardinalate church. There are stations every Friday of the four periods, the Thursday between the octave of Easter and the fourth Sunday of Advent. There is a plenary remission from sins on the first day of May. There are the bodies of St. Philip, the Apostle James, St. John, Pelagius Pope and Martyr, SS. Theodore, Cirillo, Honorato, Colosio, Buono, Fausto, Proto Giacinto, Giovino, Mauro, Nazario, Superantio, Basilio, Primitivo, Eugenio,[34] Claudia, Sabino, a large part of SS. Grisante and Daria, a rib of St. Lawrence, a knee of St. Andrew, a shoulder and arm of St. Biagio, some wood from the cross, a sleeveless vestment belonging to St. Thomas the Apostle, and the scapular of St. Francis. *There are Franciscan friars.*

San Marcello. This church was built by a noble Roman woman in honor of St. Marcellus Pope, who was confined to that place (which was a stable) on the orders of Maxentius. He died here from the great stench which emanated. It is a titular cardinalate church. There is a station on the Wednesday after the third Sunday of Lent. There is a plenary indulgence on the Feast of St. Marcellus. There are the bodies of SS. Degna, Merita, Marcellus, Feda, John the Priest, Biagio, Diogene, Longino, and Felicita, with seven sons; the heads of SS. Cosmas and Damian, a jaw-bone of St. Lawrence, an arm of St. Matthew the Apostle and Evangelist and many other relics. *Likewise there is the famous Company of the Holy Crucifix which now produces them in a remote oratory.*[35] *The Servite friars are there.*

Santa Maria in Via Lata. This is a titular cardinalate church. There is a plenary remission from sin on the Feast of the Purification and Nativity of the Virgin Mary. There is the oratory of St. Paul the Apostle and of St. Luke, where he wrote the Acts of the Apostles. He painted the picture of the Virgin Mary which is in this church in the manner in which St. Luke had the first account of her. Thus he painted her with a ring on her finger which, until our own times, one sees in this oratory on the figure of the glorious Virgin which worked many miracles. Many Christians came to give thanks to her and returned joyful and exuberant. It was first called the oratory of SS. Paul and Luke. *It is a collegiate church.*

San Marco. This church was built by the blessed Mark Pope. As it had fallen into ruin, Paul II restored it. It is a titular cardinalate church. There is a station on the Monday after the third Sunday of Lent. There is a plenary remission from sins on the first day of the year, the Feast of St. Mark Evangelist, the octave of the body of Christ, on the Epiphany, on the Feast of SS. Abdon and Sennem, and from the Holy Monday until the Tuesday of Easter. There are many relics which are placed on the high altar on festival days of this church. *It is a collegiate church.*

Santa Maria di Loreto. This church is situated in the forum by the Antonine column [*by Trajan's Column*].[36] The church is held in high devotion and it was built with a very beautiful design *by the bakers of Italy*. There is a plenary indulgence for the living and the dead on the eighth of September.

Santa Marta in the Region of the Pine is a convent for holy women who are destitute. There are many privileges and a plenary indulgence for whoever visits this church. Nearby there is another convent named the Malmaritate.[37]

Santa Maria della Strada, *now called the Company of Jesus*, is also in the region of the Pine—on the Piazza Altieri.[38] Here every day a very great indulgence is conceded to the church fathers of the Company of Jesus, called reformed priests. They perform many devoted works through prayers, confessions, communions. They have founded colleges where one learns the humanistic letters such as Hebrew, Greek and Latin in every faculty— all offered free of charge for the use of the Roman people *and the poor.*

Santa Maria sopra Minerva. This church occupies the former site of the Temple of Minerva Calcidica. There is a company which every year arranges marriages for many spinsters. [*There are three famous Companies—the Holy Sacrament, the Rosary, and the Annunciation—which every year on the Feast of the Annunciation arrange marriages for many spinsters*]. On the Feast of St. Dominic there is a plenary remission from sins. Whoever celebrates, or has celebrated for him a mass on the high altar of this church liberates a soul from the punishment of Purgatory. There are some of the clothing and hair of the Virgin Mary, *the body of St. Catherine of Siena* and many other relics. *It has a monastery for Dominican friars. It is a titular cardinalate church.*[39]

Santa Maria Rotonda. In antiquity this church was the Temple of the Pantheon. Boniface IV obtained it from the Emperor Phocas.[40] On 12 May he consecrated it to the Virgin Mary and all the saints. There are stations on the Friday between the octave of Easter and the Feast of the Invention of the Cross; the Feasts of the Assumption, the Nativity and the Conception of the Virgin Mary. There is a plenary remission from sins on All Saints Day and its whole octave. There are the bodies of SS. Rasio, Anastasio, and many others. *It is a collegiate church.*

Santa Maria Maddalena. In this church there is plenary remission from sins on the Feast of the Magdalene. *It belongs to the Company of the Gonfalone.*

Santa Maria in Campo Marzio. In this church there are nuns who have come from Greece for the last three [*four*] hundred years. There is a picture of Christ of great devotion which is called the Pieta. There is the head of St. Quirino Martyr and the body of St. Gregory Nazarene. Two other monasteries are situated near this convent which follow the Franciscan rule and are called of "Montecitorio."

Santa Elisabeta [*Santa Maria in Aquiro, otherwise Santa Elisabeta*] is on the Piazza Capranica.[41] *This is a cardinalate church.* It has many relics and pardons conceded by the holy popes, above all by Pope Paul III for the poor young boys and girls who are maintained in this place by alms and instructed in letters and virtue *in the love of God.*

San Macuto. In this church there are many relics of saints and privileges conceded in the name of SS. Bartholomew and Alexander for the company and territory of Bergamo on 25 August. *On the same piazza there is the large college of the Company of Jesus, recently constructed for public use of whoever wants to study letters and good customs. Everyone is taught for free.*

Sant'Eustachio. This church was built by Celestine III. It is a titular cardinalate church. There is some of the blood, draperies, crown of thorns and cross of Christ; part of the cross of St. Andrew; some of the charcoal over which St. Lawrence was burned; some relics of St. Eustachius, Teopista his wife, and Teopisto and Agapito his sons, and many others. *It is a collegiate church.*

San Luigi is in the region of Sant'Eustachio. This church was constructed by the French nation with a beautiful design. Mass is well-celebrated and there are many privileges and a plenary indulgence every day in the Chapel of the Saviour *which is at the side.* In this church there are some relics of St. Apollonia and many other saints. *The Company of the Holy Medici in Rome is there.*

Sant'Agostino. This church was redone from its foundations by the Reverend Cardinal Guglielmo of Rouen. On the Feast of St. Nicholas of Tolentino there is a plenary remission from sins. There is the body of St. Monica and a picture of the Virgin Mary which was painted by St. Luke. This brought about many good graces [*many miracles*] at the time of Innocent VIII. *It has an Augustinian monastery.* In the church of San Trifone which adjoins this church there is a station on the first Saturday of Lent.[42] It has the head of St. Ruffina.

San Trifone. This church is contiguous to the church of Sant'Agostino.

There are many relics. *There is a station on the first Saturday of Lent. It has the head of St. Ruffina. It belongs to the Company of the Shoemakers.*

Sant'Antonio dei Portoghesi is near what is called the "Scrofa." This church was dedicated by Pope Gelasius to SS. Anthony and Vincent. He endowed it with many indulgences and privileges for the Portuguese nation. At this spot they have a hospital which provided housing and board for the poor foreigners from that land who came to Rome.

Sant'Apollinare. This church was once the Temple of Apollo. Hadrian I dedicated it to St. Apollinare. It is a titular cardinalate church. There is a station on the Thursday after the fifth Sunday of Lent. There are the bodies of SS. Eustrasio, Nardario, Eugenio, Oreste and Ausentio. *It is a collegiate church.*

San Giacomo degli Spagnoli. This church was built by Alfonso Paradina, a Spaniard and Bishop of Civita. There is a plenary remission of sins on 25 July. There is a hospital for the Spanish nation.

Santa Maria dell'Anima. In this spot there is a hospital which provides lodging for any German for three nights.

Santa Maria della Pace. This church was built by Sixtus IV. There is a plenary remission from sins on the Feasts of the Purification, Annunciation, Visitation, Snow, Assumption, Nativity, Presentation and Conception of Mary, and all Saturdays of Lent. There are one thousand years and as many quarantines of indulgence for half of Lent until the whole octave of Easter. There are many relics which are placed on the high altar during solemn occasions. *It has a monastery for regular canons.*

San Tommaso in Parione. This is a titular cardinalate church. It was consecrated by Innocent II on the twenty-first of December 1139. On the high altar he placed an arm of SS. Damasus, Calixtus, Cornelius, Urban, Stephen, Silvester and Gregory, Popes; some vestments belonging to the Virgin Mary; some loaves of barley; some of the rocks with which St. Stephen was stoned; some blood of St. Lucy; some relics of *St. Lucy* . . . SS. Nicholas, Valentine, Sebastian, Tranquilino, Foca of the Four Crowned Martyrs, John, Paul, Crisante, Daria, Cosmas and Damian, Ninfa, Sofia, Balbina, Martha, and Petronilla. Their relics were concealed until the year 1546, the twelfth year of the reign of Paul III. *The Company of the Writers of the Roman Court is in this church.* The rector of the church was then the very Reverend Monsignor Giuliano Gallo and they were discovered by the Reverend Monsignor Ambrogio Maggio, doctor of one and another law, vice-rector of this church.

San Salvatore in Lauro is in the Region of the Ponte. This church was built by Cardinal Latino Orsini and embellished by a very beautiful building and privileges. It has a monastery for friars of the Order of San Giorgio in Alga. *The Company of the Chamberlains is here.*

San Giovanni dei Fiorentini on the Via Giulia was initiated in a great hurry in order to construct a beautiful church.[43] There is a plenary indulgence on 24 June.

San Biagio della Pagnotta. This church was built at the time of Alexander II. There is some wood from the cross as well as clothing of the Virgin Mary, relics of SS. Andrew, Biagio, Crisante, Daria and Sofia. It is on the Via Giulia where Pope Julius II wanted to build the Palace of Justice [*of Religion*] of Rome. *It belongs to the Chapter of San Pietro.*[44]

Santa Lucia, known as the Chiavica, is in the Region of the Ponte. In this church every day there is a plenary indulgence conceded by many holy popes for the venerable Company of the Gonfalone which maintains its very well endowed oratory near this church.

San Giovanni in Agina is near the Savella Court. In this church there is a company with many people known as of the "Oration," alternately known as "of Death."[45] With good works and *living* a holy life, they have a plenary indulgence every second Sunday of the month *and many other days of the year.*

San Girolamo is near the Farnese Palace. In this church, every day there is a plenary indulgence for the remission of sins. Many alms are collected here for the poor and needy people of Rome by the Company of Charity which gathers in this church. *The church belongs to them.*

La Casa Santa. The church has a convent for nuns who lead a holy life. With much erudition, they teach and demonstrate virtue to young girls. On 8 December there is a pardon.

San Lorenzo in Damaso. This church was built and endowed by the blessed pope Damaso. He donated a silver patent weighing twenty pounds, a vase weighing ten pounds, five chalices and five crowns. As it was half ruined, the reverend cardinal of San Giorgio reconstructed it from the foundations and instituted a choir of singers.[46] It is a titular cardinalate church. There is a station on the Tuesday after the fourth Sunday of Lent. There are the bodies of SS. Buono, Mauro, Faustino, Giovino, Eutirio and his brothers; the head of St. Barbara; the flesh of St. Lawrence; a foot of St. Damaso and many other relics. There are still two companies: one is of the Holy Sacrament which collects many alms and is the first of its kind in Italy and the other is of the Conception of our Lady which every year marries off many spinsters on the Feast of the Conception. *Another is of St. Sebastian. It is a collegiate church.*

Santa Barbara. This church is located between the Piazza Giudea and the Campo dei Fiori. There is some of the hair of St. Mary Magdalene as well as some clothes of the Virgin Mary, the veil and cape of St. Barbara, some relics of SS. Bartholomew, Philip and James Apostles, of SS. Margaret, Felice, Ioricio, Christopher, Sebastian, Alessio, Mario, Marta, Lawrence, Petronilla, and many others.

San Martinello is in the Region of the Regola.[47] This church was built by one Walter, a monk of San Salvatore, at the time of Pope Honorius III. There are a part of the tunic and the vestment which the blessed Virgin Mary made for her son Jesus Christ, which went to the grave with him.

San Salvatore in Campo is in the Region of the Regola. In this church every day there is a great pardon. The Company of the Holy Trinity is here which helps those poor pilgrims to live who come to Rome [*which accepts with charity those poor pilgrims who come to Rome*]. Those sick, poor people who come out of the hospitals not completely cured may recover here. *Now it is called the Madonna of the Trinity. It works infinite miracles.*[48]

Santa Maria in Monticelli. This church is in the region of the Regola. There are the bodies of St. Ninfa Virgin and St. Manciliano Bishop and other relics.

Santi Vincenzo e Anastasio is on the river. This church belongs to the Company of the Cooks.[49]

San Tommaso is beside the Farnese Palace.[50]

Santa Caterina is at the Savella Court. This is a parish church. It belongs to the Chapter of San Pietro. The Company of the Hoosiers is there.[51]

San Tommaso is at the same spot. Here is the hospital for the English nation.[52]

Sant'Andrea at the same spot is a parish church. The Company of the Tailors, called the Holy Gentleman is there.[53]

Santa Brigida is on the Piazza Farnesina.

Santa Caterina da Siena. This church is located on the Via Giulia and it belongs to the Sienese people.

Santa Maria di Monserrato is at the Savella Court. In this church there are quite a few relics and infinite indulgences. It was renovated recently. It is very well tended by Spanish priests. It belongs to the Aragonese Crown.

Sant'Eligio. This is a very beautiful temple on the river, near the Via Giulia. It belongs to the Company of Goldsmiths.

Santo Stefano alla Chiavica of Santa Lucia is a parish church. It is located near the Hospital of the Poles.[54]

Santi Celso e Giuliano is at the Banchi. In this church there is a foot of the Magdalene and many other relics. There is a Company of the Blessed Sacrament with many indulgences. It is a collegiate church.[55]

San Biagio. This church is also located in the Regola. There is the ring of St. Biagio and many other relics.

Santa Maria del Pianto. This church was once called the Holy Saviour. On account of the miracles which the glorious image has worked recently and which she continues to work, there is a plenary indulgence every day [*On account of the miracles which were worked here at one time by the glorious Virgin, and which continue, it is called St. Mary. Every day there is an indulgence*]. There is a company.

Santa Caterina dei Funari. In this church there is a convent for miserable spinsters who, with a holy life and good habits, are nourished until
the time that they are capable of being married. Then they either wed
or become nuns. In this place every day there is a general pardon. On
the Feast of St. Andrew there is a plenary jubilee conceded by the holiness of our Father Pope Julius III *as well as many other indulgences. Cardinal
de Cesis just lately has built a small temple here which is as charming and beautiful
as any seen in Rome.*[56]

Sant'Angelo. This church is in Pescheria. It was formerly the Temple of
Juno. It is a titular cardinalate church *to which the Roman Senate offers a chalice
every year on the Feast of St. Angelo in May. There are many relics, such as that found
in 1560 when the high altar of the place was moved and underneath that altar a wooden
box was found which was full of relics with a lead plaque inscribed with letters in
the vernacular which read: "Here lie the bodies of the holy martyrs Sinforiana, her husband Zotico and her children — all were transferred here by Pope Stephen." These relics
are shown twice a year with plenary indulgence on the Feasts of St. Sinforiana on July
8 [18?] and of St. Angelo on 29 September.* There are the bodies of St. Sinforiana and her companions, as well as many other relics. Each year the
Senate offers a chalice.

San Nicola in Carcere. This church is located on the site of the ancient
prisons. At the time of the Consuls C. Quinto and M. Attilio, the Temple of the Pietà was constructed here for this reason: A man had been
condemned to die by starvation in prison and one of his daughters, on
the pretext of paying him a visit, used to give him milk every day. When
the guards realized this, they consulted the Senate. For such an act of
mercy, the Senate pardoned the father and provided both of them with
food for the duration of their lives. This church is a titular cardinalate
church. There is a station on the Saturday after the fourth Sunday of
Lent. On the Feast of St. Nicholas there is a plenary remission from sins.
There are the bodies of SS. Mark, Marcellinus, Faustina, and Beatrice. There is
a rib of St. Matthew the Apostle, a hand of St. Nicholas, and an arm
of St. Alessio *as well as many other relics.*

Santa Maria in Aracoeli. This church is on the Capitoline Hill. It is decorated with beautiful columns and different marbles. It was built over the
ruins of the Temple of Jupiter Feretrius and the Palace of Augustus. On
the Feast of St. Anthony of Padua; St. Bernardino; the Assumption, the

Nativity, and the Conception of the Virgin Mary; St. Louis Bishop; and the Nativity of our Saviour there is a plenary remission of sins. There are the bodies of SS. Artemio, Abondio, and Abondantio. In front of the choir there is a round stone, covered with iron grating, in which remain the traces of footsteps belonging to the angel at the time of the consecration by Pope Gregory. There is an image of the Virgin Mary, painted by St. Luke, shown in the way she appeared at the Crucifixion. At the approach to this church, there is a very wide [*a very long*] marble stairway of one hundred and twenty-eight steps which were fashioned from the decoration of the Temple of Quirino which was on the Monte Cavallo. *In our day the choir has been enlarged and altered. There is a monastery for Franciscan friars. There are other privileges and infinite indulgences with the maximum on the first of the year.*

From the Capitoline to the Left to the Hills.

San Pietro nel Carcere Tulliano. This church is at the foot of the Capitoline. St. Silvester consecrated it. SS. Peter and Paul were imprisoned there. When they wanted to baptize Processo and Martiniano, the guards at this prison, a fountain arose miraculously. Each day there are one thousand two hundred years of indulgence and remission from a third part of all sins. On feast days, these are doubled. There are the bodies of SS. Processo and Martiniano. *Above is the Church of San Giuseppe belonging to the Company of the Carpenters.*

Sant'Adriano. This church as well is in the Roman forum. In ancient times, it was the treasury. Honorius I consecrated it to St. Adrian. It is a titular cardinalate church. There are the bodies of SS. Mario and Marta, the relics of St. Adrian and many others.

San Lorenzo in the Boarium or the Roman Forum is in the portico of Antoninus and Faustina.[57] *The Company of the Spicemakers is there.*

Santi Cosma e Damiano. This church is in the Roman Forum. In ancient times it was the Temple of Romulus. Felice IV dedicated it to SS. Cosmas and Damian. When it fell into ruin, the blessed Gregory restored it. It is a titular cardinalate church. There is a station on the Thursday after the third Sunday of Lent. Every day there are a thousand years of indulgence. There are the bodies of SS. Cosmas and Damian and many other relics. Those copper doors are ancient. *The Franciscan friars live there.*

Santa Maria Nuova. This church is near the Arch of Titus. It was built by Leo IV. When it fell into ruin, Nicholas V restored it. It is a titular cardinalate church. There are the bodies of SS. Nemesio, Giustino, Sinforiana, Olimpio, Essemperio, and Lucilla. The body of St. Francis of Rome, who was canonized by Alexander VI, is in front of the high altar in that tomb covered with iron grating. There is one of the pictures painted by St. Luke in a marble tabernacle which used to be in Greece in the city of Troy. It was brought to Rome by the illustrious cavalier Angelo Frangipane. When the church burned at the time of Honorius III, this picture did not suffer any damage whatsoever. *The Benedictine monks from Monte Oliveto live there.*

San Clemente. This church is located between the Colosseum and San Giovanni in Laterano. It is a titular cardinalate church. There is a station on the Monday after the second Sunday of Lent and a plenary remission from sins. Every day there are forty years and as many quarantines of indulgence. During Lent they are doubled. There are the bodies of St. Clement and St. Ignatius. In the chapel outside the church there is the body of St. Servolo. There are also many relics which are shown on the high altar on the day of the station. That woman who was made pope gave birth on the site of that little chapel of the Saviour outside the church facing the Colosseum. Thus the pope does not pass along this street when he goes to San Giovanni in Laterano, but travels on the one in the direction of the Seven Rooms.

In that [*In this*] little chapel called Santa Maria Imperatrice facing San Giovanni in Laterano there is a picture of the Virgin Mary which spoke to St. Gregory. He conceded to whomever said the Pater Noster and the Ave Maria three times on this spot fifteen years of indulgence for each time.

Santi Quattro Incoronati. This church is on the Caelian Hill. It was built by Honorius I. When it fell into ruin, Leo IV reconstructed it and Paschal II restored it. It is a titular cardinalate church. There is a station on the Monday after the fourth Sunday of Lent. There are the bodies of SS. Claudio, Nicostrato, Semproniano, Castorio, Severo, Severiano, Carposoro, Vittorino, Mario, Fellicissimo, Agapito, Hippolito, Aquila, Prisco, Aquinio, Narciso, Marcello, Marcellino, Felice, Apolline, Benedetto,

Venantio, Diogene, Liberale, and Festo; the head of St. Proto; of SS. Cecilia, Alexander [*and*] Sisto [.], Sebastian, and Prassede. *During our day, Pope Pius IV has enlarged and decorated the place with a new building at very great expense. Male and female orphans have been placed there. A direct road from the entrance of the church to the Arch of San Giovanni in Laterano has been made.*

Santi Pietro e Marcellino. This church is also located between the Colosseum and San Giovanni in Laterano. It was built by Constantine the Great who gave it a gold patent weighing thirty-five pounds, four golden candelabra measuring twelve feet each, three gold chalices decorated with precious stones, a silver altar weighing two hundred pounds and a gold vase weighing twenty pounds. When it fell into ruin, Alexander IV restored it on the tenth of April 1260. It is a titular cardinalate church. There is a station on the Saturday after the second Sunday of Lent. There are the so-called relics of SS. Peter and Marcellino in addition to many others as appear inscribed on that marble tablet along the exterior wall of this church. *It belongs to the Chapter of San Giovanni in Laterano.*

San Matteo in Merulana. This church is located in the street which goes from San Giovanni in Laterano to Santa Maria Maggiore. On the Feast of St. Matthew, there is a plenary remission from sins. Every day there are one thousand years and as many quarantines of indulgence, as well as the remission from a seventh part of all sins. *It is a titular cardinalate church. Augustinian friars live here.*

San Pietro in Vincoli. This church was built by Eudoxia, the wife of the emperor Arcadio, over the ruins of the old curia. Sixtus III consecrated it. When it fell into ruin, Pelagius restored it. It is a titular cardinalate church. There is a station on the first Monday of Lent. On the first day of August there is a plenary remission from sins. There are the bodies of the Maccabean SS., the chains with which St. Peter was tied in prison in Jerusalem, a part of the cross of St. Andrew and many other relics. There is also a marble Moses below the tomb of Julius II which is sculpted with marvelous artifice by the most divine Michelangelo *Florentine*.[58] *Regular canons live here.*

San Lorenzo in Panisperna. This church is located on the Viminal Hill on the spot where St. Lawrence was martyred. It was built by Pius I on the ruins of the emperor Decius' palace. It is a titular cardinalate church. There is a station on the Thursday after the first Sunday of Lent. There are the body of St. Bridget, an arm of St. Lawrence, pieces of the grating and the coal with which he was burned, and many other relics. *The nuns of St. Francis live there.*

Sant'Agata. This church was the maternal house of St. Gregory. He consecrated it to St. Agatha. It is decorated with different marbles. *It is a titular cardinalate church.*

San Lorenzo in Fonte. This church is located between Santa Potenziana and San Pietro in Vincoli. It was the prison where St. Lawrence was held. When he decided to baptize St. Hippolito and St. Lucilla, a fountain arose which can be seen still today.

Santa Potenziana. This church was once the paternal house of this saint. The Novitian baths were there. Pius I consecrated it. When it fell into ruin, Simplicio restored it. It is a titular cardinalate church. There is a station on the Tuesday after the third Sunday of Lent. Every day there are three thousand years, as many quarantines of indulgence and a remission from a third part of all sins. The cemetery of Priscilla is here in which lie the bones of three thousand martyrs. In the chapel near the high altar, St. Peter the Apostle celebrated his first mass. For whoever celebrates mass or has it celebrated for him in this chapel, a soul is liberated from the punishment of Purgatory. In the Chapel of San Pastore there is a well with the blood of three thousand martyrs which was collected and installed in that spot by St. Potenziana. While a priest was celebrating mass in that chapel, he doubted whether the consecrated host was the real body of Christ. Because of this doubt, the host went from his hand and fell to the ground where it left a stain of blood. This stain can be seen still today and it is covered by a small iron grating.

San Vito in Macello. This church is close to the Arch of Gallieno. It is a titular cardinalate church. On the Feast of St. Vitus there are six thousand years and as many quarantines of indulgence [*six thousand years of indulgence*] and every day there are six thousand years of indulgence. There are the relics of St. Vitus which are used to make an oil for treating the bites of mad dogs. Over that marble stone covered with iron grating, an infinite number of martyrs have been killed.

San Giuliano. This church is also located near the aforementioned Trophies [*near the Trophies*].[59] There are the relics of SS. Julian and Albert which are used to make a water for treating all types of fever and other sicknesses. *Carmelite friars live there.*

San Eusebio. This church is also a short distance from the Trophies. It is a titular cardinalate church. There is a station on the Friday after the fourth Sunday of Lent. Every day there are seven thousand eight hundred years and as many quarantines of indulgence. [*Every day there is a great quantity of indulgences*]. There are the bodies of SS. Eusebio, Vincenzo, Romano, Orosio, Gregory Nazarene, Paul the Confessor; some of the bridle of Constantine's horse made from a nail which fastened our Saviour to the cross; some of the column at which he was beaten; part of his tomb; some relics of SS. Stephen Pope, Bartholomew, Matthew, Helena, Andrew, and of many others. *The Light Blue friars live here.*[60]

San Luca at Santa Maria Maggiore. This church belongs to the Company of Painters.[61]

Santa Bibiana. This church is located beyond the Trophies of Marius in the Via Labicana. It was built by Pope Simplicius. When it fell into ruin, Honorius III restored it. On All SS. Day, there are six hundred thousand years of indulgence and every day there are nine thousand years of indulgence. There is the cemetery between the two laurel trees in which are the bones of five thousand martyrs. There is an herb planted by St. Bibiana which cures epilepsy.

San Martino. This church is on the Esquiline Hill. It was dedicated by Sergius I. Simaco installed a silver tabernacle weighing one hundred and twenty pounds on the high altar. It is a titular cardinalate church. There are the bodies of SS. Silvester, Martin, Fabian, Stephen, and Soter Popes; of Asterio, Ciriaco and many others, as appear inscribed in a stone tablet along the right hand side of the choir in this church. *In our day, it has been beautifully decorated by the good gentleman Diomede Carafa, the cardinal of Ariano. Carmelite friars live there. There is a station on the Thursday after the fourth Sunday of Lent, which was re-instituted in our day by Paul IV.*

Santa Prassede. This church is located near Santa Maria Maggiore. It was consecrated by Paschal I. It is titular cardinalate church. There is a station on Holy Monday. Every day there are twelve thousand years and as many quarantines of indulgence as well as remission from a third part of all sins. The body of St. Prassede is under the high altar. In the chapel known as the Garden of Paradise where women never enter, there are the bodies of SS. Valentine and Zeno, and above, the column at which our Saviour was flagellated. This was brought to Rome by Cardinal Colonna, named Giovanni. In the middle of this chapel, under the round stone, forty martyrs are buried, among whom number eleven popes. Whoever celebrates a mass, or has one celebrated in this chapel will liberate a soul from the punishment of Purgatory. In the middle of the church, on the site of that round stone protected by iron (which was covered by Leo X after he saw this same blood) there is a well holding the blood of infinite martyrs. St. Prassede went around Rome with a sponge collecting it and carried it to this well. There are also many relics which are shown on Easter Day after vespers. *Friars of the Vallambrosan order live here.*

Sant'Antonio. This church is near Santa Maria Maggiore and Santa Prassede. It has a hospital which maintains many sick people. On the Feast of St. Anthony, there is a plenary indulgence. There are many relics.[62]

San Quirico. This church is close to the Tower of the Conti. It is a titular cardinalate church. There is a station on Tuesday after the fifth Sunday of Lent. There are many relics.

Santa Susanna. This church is on Monte Cavallo. It is a titular cardinalate church. There is a station on the Saturday after the third Sunday of Lent. There are the bodies of SS. Susanna, Sabino her father, Felice her sister; some of her clothing; wood from the cross and tomb of Christ; some clothing and hair of the Virgin Mary; relics of SS. Luke, Thomas, Lawrence, Marcellus, Simon, Silvester, Boniface, Clement, Anthony Abbot, Lione, Biagio, Saturnino, Agapito, Lino, Luciano, Grisante, Daria, Proto, Giacinto, Vitale, Stephen Pope, Gregory Nazarene, Catherine, Dalmatio, Martin, Tecla, Prassede, Copio Martina and many others. *Augustinian friars live there.*

San Vitale. This church is situated in the valley of Monte Cavallo. As it had fallen into ruin, it was restored by Sixtus IV. It is a titular cardinalate church. There is a station on the Friday after the second Sunday of Lent. *It is a collegiate church.*

Santa Costanza. This church is outside the Porta Sant'Agnese *now called the Porta Pia* and it is round in form. In ancient times, it was the Temple of Bacchus. Alexander IV dedicated it to St. Costanza, the virgin daughter of Constantine the Great, who is buried in this church in a very beautiful tomb of porphyry.

Also in this location is the church of Sant'Agnese built by the same St. Costanza in honor of St. Agnes because she had cured her of leprosy. It has copper doors. It is decorated with diverse stones. There is a ring sent down from heaven to [*by*] St. Agnes. *The friars of San Pietro in Vincoli maintain it. Sheep are kept here in order to make wool for the cloaks of the archbishops.*

Santa Maria degli Angeli. On 5 August 1561 Pius IV dedicated the stupendous building of the Baths of the emperor Diocletian situated on the Quirinal Hill, today called Monte Cavallo, to the Madonna of the Angels.[63] *With the universal consent of the Roman people, he gave it to the Carthusian monks who earlier had lived at Santa Croce in Jerusalem. He conceded the same privileges, stations and indulgences to this church that are enjoyed by Santa Croce. Moreover, he gave a plenary indulgence to everyone who visited it on the Feasts of the Nativity; the Resurrection of Our Lord; the Pentecost; the Nativity, Purification and Assumption of the Madonna; and the dedication day of this church.*

From the Capitoline to the Right *Toward the Hills.*

Santa Maria Liberatrice. This church is also in the Roman Forum.[64] St. Silvester consecrated it after having bound the mouth of a dragon who had lived there in a very deep grotto while he poisoned the air of Rome with his breath. After his mouth was sealed with the sign of the very Holy Cross, he never did any more harm. Every day eleven thousand years of indulgence are conceded here.

Santa Maria della Consolazione. In this church there is a picture of the Virgin Mary which works many blessings. On the second Sunday of June, between the first and second vespers, there is a plenary remission from sins, conceded by Sixtus IV. In the Chapel of Santa Maria delle Grazie there is one of the pictures painted by St. Luke. There is a hospital in which many alms are collected and which receives continually all the sick who go there.

San Giovanni Decollato. This is a very beautiful church, built by the Florentine na-tion, which has a company dedicated to the Misericordia. This company buries all the condemned dead. On the Feast of the Beheading of St. John there is a plenary indulgence and on that day one person with a life sentence is freed from prison. In the same place, they have a very beautiful oratory for this nation.[65]

Sant'Alo. The Company of the Blacksmiths is here.[66]

Sant'Anastasia. This church is a titular cardinalate church. It used to be the titular church of St. Jerome. There are stations on the Tuesday after the first Sunday of Lent, on the Feast of the Nativity of our Lord at dawn, and the Tuesday of the octave of Pentecost. There is a chalice of St. Jerome as well as many other relics.

Santa Maria in Portico. This church is a titular cardinalate church. It was once the house of Galla, the daughter of Symmachus, a Roman patri-cian. She was a woman of holy life to whom during the pontificate of John I, while she was dining, a sapphire of wonderful splendor was car-ried by angels to her credence table. It had an impression of the Virgin Mary with the Saviour in her arms. Gregory VII, moved by this mira-cle, consecrated this church. He placed the same image in a tabernacle covered with iron grating over the high altar. This may be seen still to-day. That round temple at the Ponte Santa Maria was called the Temple of Pudicitia in antiquity.

San Gregorio. This church was the paternal house of St. Gregory Pope who consecrated it to St. Andrew the Apostle during the second year of his pontificate. He prayed to the omnipotent God that whoever should elect to be buried in this place, as a faithful Christian, should be conced-ed eternal life. As he finished the oration, an angel appeared and said to him: "Oh Gregory, your prayer has been granted." On the day of the commemoration of the dead and for the whole octave, there is a plenary remission from sins. Whoever celebrates a mass, or has one celebrated in that chapel which is next to the sacristy will free a soul from the punish-ment of Purgatory. An arm of St. Gregory and a leg of St. Pantaleone are there. *The monks of St. Gregory live there.*

Santi Giovanni e Paolo. This church is on the Caelian Hill. It is a titular cardinalate church. There is a station on the first Friday of Lent. There are the bodies of SS. John and Paul; St. Saturnino; Prestina, Donata and Seconda; some relics of SS. Stephen, Silvester, Nicholas, Grisante, Daria, Cesas, Saturnino, Sebastian, Mamiliano, Alexander, Prassede, Lucy, Matthew, Constantine, Secondo, and Peregrino; some of the drapery, cross, and tomb of Christ, and the stone on which SS. John and Paul were decapitated. It is the one that is on the altar in the middle of the church. Their bodies are in the wall opposite the same altar.[67] *The Gesuati monks live there.*

Santa Maria [*in Domnica, otherwise known as*] della Navicella.[68] This church is a titular cardinalate church. There is a station on the second Sunday of Lent. It is called the "Navicella" because of the stone which is in front of this church. It also is located on the Caelian Hill.

Santo Stefano Rotondo. This church is on the Caelian Hill. It was once the Temple of Fauno. Simplicio I dedicated it to St. Stephen Protomartyr. As it had fallen into ruin, Nicholas V restored it. It is a titular cardinalate church. There are stations on the Friday after the fifth Sunday of Lent and on the Feast of St. Stephen. There are the bodies of Sts. Peter and Feliciano; the relics of SS. Domicilla, Augustine, and Ladislao; and of many other. *The white monks of Hungary live there.*

San Giorgio. In this church there is a station on the second day of Lent. It is a titular cardinalate church. The head of St. George, iron from his lance and part of his standard are there as well as many other relics.[69]

San Sisto. This church is near that of San Gregorio. It was endowed by Innocent IV. It is a titular cardinalate church. There is a station on the Wednesday after the third Sunday of Lent. There are the bodies of SS. Sisto, Zeferino, Lucio I, Lucio II, Luciano, Felice, Antero, Massimo, Giulio, Sotero I, Sotero II, Partenio and Calocerio del Latte; some of the Virgin Mary's hair; some of St. Dominic's clothing; the veil and breast of St. Agatha; some relics of SS. Martin, Agabito, Andrew, Peter, Lawrence and Stephen, and many others; and a picture of the Virgin Mary painted by St. Luke; and one of those pictures of the Virgin Mary that St. Luke painted [*sic*]. *Dominican friars live there.*

Santa Sabina. In antiquity, this church was the Temple of Diana. It is on the Aventine Hill. It is a titular cardinalate church. There is a station on the first day of Lent. As it had fallen into ruin, it was rebuilt by a Slavic bishop during the pontificate of Sixtus III. It used to be the house of St. Sabina. During the time of Honorius III, it was the papal palace. He gave it to St. Dominic and confirmed his order in the year 1216. *His friars are here.* There are *still* the bodies of SS. Sabina, Serafina, Peregrina, Eventio, Teodolo and St. Alexander Pope; a thorn from the crown of our Saviour; a piece of the reed with which his head was beaten;[70] some of St. Dominic's clothing; part of the tomb of the Virgin Mary; some of the holy earth from Jerusalem; a piece of St. Andrew's cross; a rib of one of the Innocents; some relics of SS. Peter, Paul, Bartholomew, Matthias, Philip, James, John Chrysostom, Cosmas, Damian, Apollinare, Stephen Protomartyr, Lawrence, Orsola, Margaret, Christopher, Jerome, Julian, Gregory Pope, Martin, Sebastian, Cecilia, and St. Mary of Egypt. In addition, there is a silver crucifix full of relics in the middle of which there is a little cross made from the wood of the cross. That black stone, which is attached to the high altar, was thrown at St. Dominic in order to kill him while he made an oration on that spot. However, it split apart miraculously and he was not harmed at all.[71]

Sant'Alessio. This church is on the Aventine Hill. It used to be the house of St. Alessio. One can still see a certain wooden staircase to the right of the high altar where he did penance after his return from a pilgrimage until the end of his life (this lasted for seventeen years). It was never known by his father or by any other member of the household. In this church there is a plenary remission from sins on the Feast of St. Alessio. Every day there is an indulgence of one hundred years and as many quarantines. The bodies of St. Alessio, St. Boniface, St. Hermete the Martyr and many other relics are under the high altar. That picture of the most blessed Virgin which is in the high tabernacle used to be in a church in the city of Edessa. The very blessed Alessio, when he was in that city, often made orations in front of this. Going to this church one day to pray, he found the doors locked. Twice did this picture tell the caretaker to let Alessio, a man of God, enter because he was worthy of heaven.[72] *The friars of St. Girolamo live there.*[73]

Santa Prisca. This church is also on the Aventine Hill. It used to be the Temple of Hercules constructed by Evander. St. Peter the Apostle lived there. As it had fallen into ruin, Calixtus III rebuilt it. It is a titular cardinalate church. There is a station on Holy Tuesday. There are the

bodies of St. Prisca, St. Quila, her mother and St. Aquilo priest and martyr; St. Peter's stole; a marble vase in which he used to baptize and other
relics. *It is a collegiate church.*

Santa Saba Abbate. This church is also located on the same hill. There
is a fountain with the mantle of St. Saba inside. This water has a wonderful quality in that it cures many infirmities, especially the flow of blood.
The bodies of the emperors Vespasian and Titus are in a marble tomb
near the choir. *The friars of St. Bernard live here.*

Santa Balbina. This church is on the same hill. It was consecrated by
St. Gregory. It is a titular cardinalate church. There is a station on the
Tuesday after the second Sunday of Lent. Every day there are seven years
of indulgence. There are the bodies of St. Balbina, St. Quirino and five
other saints, whose names are written in the book of life.

San Giovanni before La Porta Latina. This church is at the Porta Latina. It is a titular cardinalate church. There is a station on the Saturday
after the fifth Sunday of Lent. On the sixth of May there is a plenary
remission from sins. That little chapel [*That round chapel*] which is outside
this church is on the site where St. John the Apostle was put in boiling
oil at the command of the emperor Domitian. He came out of it without
any wound.

Sant'Anastasio. This church is outside Rome along the Via Ostiense.[74]
It was consecrated by Honorius I in the year 1201 with twenty-one cardinals present. There is a column over which St. Paul the Apostle was decapitated. After his head was severed from his bust, it bounced three times
and three fountains miraculously arose which can be seen still today. On
the Feast of St. Anastasius there is a plenary indulgence. Every day there
are six thousand years. *The heads of SS. Vincent and Anastasius Martyrs are
there as well as a good number of relics.*

*Santa Celi. This church is near Sant'Anastasio on the Via Ostiense.[75] Every day there
are many indulgences. On 27 January a soul is liberated by whomever celebrates mass,
or has it celebrated, under the altar where the bones of ten thousand martyrs are located.
These may be seen, but not touched. There is the knife with which these martyrs were
killed. Every day there are ten thousand years of indulgence.*

Santa Maria Annunciata. This church is located on the same street. It was consecrated in the year 1220 on the ninth of August. On the Feast of the Annunciation, there is a plenary remission from sins. Every day there are ten thousand years of indulgence. In the midst of the road between this church *of SantʼAnastasio* and that of San Sebastiano, on the site of that cross, there are the bodies of ten thousand martyred soldiers.

Santa Maria in Via. In this church there are infinite indulgences. There is an image of the Madonna which is very much venerated due to a great number of miracles. It is a titular cardinalate church. The Servite friars live here.

THE END

Part III

Appendix: La guida romana

Introduction

La guida romana per tutti i forastieri che vengono per vedere le antichità di Roma offered a short tour of Roman antiquities in the form of three itineraries spread over two and a half days. The author of the guide, an Englishman named Schakerlay, shows a nearly obsessive thoroughness as he doggedly records the location of every notable antiquity. As a result of his stilted prose and pedantic style, *La guida romana* has limitations as a literary work. Nevertheless it offers a fresh perspective on the state of Roman ruins during the sixteenth century, and the author emerges as an authority by way of his first-hand contact with Roman monuments and customs. In this respect the book is a novelty, even a landmark, in the history of descriptive accounts of antiquity. The guidebook was a product of personal experience and direct observation, and the author's obvious fascination with the ancient city must have prompted the tourist to share in his enthusiasm.

Palladio's *Descritione de le Chiese* first acquired *La guida romana* as a companion text, or appendix, in the small octavo edition of 1557 (see List of Editions Consulted). The final sections of the book consisted of *I nomi de i sommi Pontefici*, an historical table of the popes, emperors and monarchs, updated to the year of the guidebook's publication. When these three sections were combined as *Le cose maravigliose di Roma*, Palladio's text not only was linked permanently with Schakerlay's, but the names of both authors were lost to posterity.[1] Palladio was credited only in the heading of the Stations and Indulgences: "Le Stationi, Indulgentie . . . etc. novamente poste in luce da M. Andrea Palladio," which may have resulted from an oversight on the part of the printer who otherwise removed all traces of Palladio's authorship. Schakerlay's preface to *La guida romana*, where he reveals his name and nationality, was dropped from all editions after 1562. Yet his description of antiquities continued to serve as a counterpart to the account of sacred Rome for generations to come.

The Roman publishing firm of the Dorico Brothers first recognized the demand for a practical guide to the city's treasures, and they may even have commissioned *La guida romana* from the author who clearly composed the work in a hurry. The text appears to have been written after September 1557; it reached print before the end of the same year.[2] The Dorico Brothers issued a reprint the following year and already by 1561, when it must have been evident that they had a best-seller on their hands, they had the guide translated into Spanish by Hernando de Salazar.[3] Then, in 1562, the press of Antonio Blado issued *La guida romana* using a new typography and a list of popes updated to include Pius IV.[4] Although it survives only in a fragmentary state, enough of the text remains to show that it was consistent with the original edition of 1557 (Fig. 17).

The first edition of *La guida romana*, produced from 1557–1563, included a preface with a statement of the author's purpose. Schakerlay, who calls himself an Englishman, writes that he composed the guide to Roman antiquities on behalf of all foreigners—not only his own countrymen but the French, Flemish and people of other nations as well. His intention was to make a succinct presentation of the material for the sake of impatient tourists who otherwise would have time to visit only a fraction of the city's treasures. The emphasis on haste permeates the narrative as the author appears alternately apologetic and ill-tempered about having assumed the awesome task of compressing the tour of ancient Rome into two and a half days.

The three separate itineraries of *La guida romana* show the tourist a sequence of antique monuments or "curiosities," which are identifiable on a contemporary map designed by Pirro Ligorio as an archaeological reconstruction (Fig. 14). It is striking how accurately Shakerlay's descriptive narrative matches the visual evidence, real and imagined, of the ancient city. The starting point of the Ponte Sant'Angelo introduces the first day's tour of the Vatican Borgo which continues through Trastevere and then takes the visitor across the island to the Forum Boarium. From here the route meanders along the city bank of the Tiber as far as the Gate of San Paolo, back along the Via Ostiense to the site of the Piscina Publica, returning by the Via Appia to the inner circuit of the walls as far as the Lateran and the amphitheater at Santa Croce in Gerusalemme. After a visit to the area around Santa Maria Maggiore and the Trophies of Mars (near the Capitoline), the tourist is admonished not to attempt more sightseeing. On the second day, the tour resumes at the Mausoleum of Augustus and then turns north as far as the Gate of the Popolo, then back to the center of the ancient city. The itinerary leads to sites at the Quirinal including the Baths of Diocletian and the Esquiline Hill. The visitor must still see the Roman Forum and the Capitoline and finally walk back to the Campo dei Fiori, by way of the Theatre of Marcellus. By the third day, the rigors of the program have diminished considerably as the tourist is instructed to visit attractions in the area of the Campo Marzio and Capitoline Hill, ending his trek at the Piazza Navona. At the Tiber he is advised to take a boat to San Pietro in order to visit the Belvedere. Several noteworthy sites — a private palace and monuments outside the walls — are added at the end as afterthoughts. Nevertheless the concept of establishing itineraries imparts a sense of order to the tour of the city's ancient monuments, but the haphazard quality of the author's observations and the progressive reduction of demands made on the tourist lend credibility to his claim at the end that "I, for certain, can no longer walk" (Trans., *La guida romana*, p. 138).

It is this spontaneity of expression, at once a virtue and a defect of literary expression, which gives *La guida romana* a special character. The author does not seem learned, but he is knowledgeable. While the writing lacks scholarly accuracy and a pleasing style, it offers unexpected insights into a contemporary appreciation of sixteenth-century Rome. A sense of excitement pervades the author's description of the Baths of Diocletian and his thwarted exploration of the subterranean grottoes (Trans., *La guida romana*, p. 131). Yet, he makes crucial errors and omissions in his itinerary, as in the brief description of the Roman Forum (Trans., *La guida romana*, p. 134).

The buildings of contemporary Rome hold little attraction for the author of *La guida romana* who uses current place names as landmarks for ancient topography, but exhibits no interest in medieval or Renaissance monuments. In general, *La guida romana* leaves the reader with the impression that objects of antiquarian interest were readily accessible.

Ancient buildings and sculptures dot the urban landscape, but famous "curiosities" also await the tourist in cardinals' *vigne* and collectors' palaces. In his haste, the author of *La guida romana* notes the location of these private collections, but never describes an interior. His concern is focused on the construction of an itinerary which permits a survey of major monuments in the open air. The guidebook was neither for the specialist nor for the scholar but for the one-time visitor to Rome. The tourist most likely was a pilgrim who, having visited the stations and relics of the churches described in the first section of *Le cose maravigliose*, desired a rapid look at the rest of the city.

La guida romana met with immediate and enduring success. The two and a half day itinerary through Rome became a permanent fixture of all future editions of *Le cose maravigliose* beginning in 1563 when a conscientious editor corrected and updated the text.[5] Many revisions pertained to the palaces of contemporary collectors as five palaces were deleted from the original text. Families like the Farnese or the Capodiferro replaced earlier patrons whose importance had declined (Trans., *La guida romana*, p. 135). The pope of the intervening years, Pius IV (1559–1565) had changed the urban layout of Rome and his major projects, such as the Strada Pia and Santa Maria degli Angeli, appear for the first time. The updated version of *La guida romana* also incorporated changes in the itinerary—logical modifications of the original route where it had shown inconsistencies. Thus the tourist proceeds to the Belvedere of the Vatican when making the rounds of the Borgo, and not as an afterthought (Trans., *La guida romana*, p. 126). Finally the editor corrected outright mistakes, inserted qualifying remarks and generally improved the style of writing. Subsequent editions retained the structure of *La guida romana*, while periodic revisions reflected the current state of knowledge about Roman antiquities.[6]

Shortly after its inception, Onofrio Panvinio identified *La guida romana* as an important guide to Roman antiquities. He cited descriptions of the ancient city compiled during the 1550s in the introduction to his own projected corpus of writings, recalling the works of Fauno, Mauro, Aldrovandi, Palladio, and Gamuccio and adds: "Publicatus est etiam incerto auctore libellus lingua italica, cui *guida romana* nomen est, adiectus libro de mirabilibus rebus urbis in nostrum idoma verso."[7] The publication of the *Antiquitatum Romanarum libri centum* was interrupted by Panvinio's death in 1568. He must have composed the preface in the 1560s because he referred to the latest edition of *La guida romana*, one which appeared after 1563 without the author's name. Panvinio singles out Palladio's guide to antiquities, but ignores *Le Chiese*, probably because the bibliographic discussion concerned texts on ancient Rome. Panvinio therefore recognized Schakerlay's work as distinct from *Le cose maravigliose*, but few other scholars have acknowledged the significance of the text. Early in this century, the sixteen folios of *La guida romana* of 1562 came to light in the binding of a sixteenth-century book. The date in the colophon and the reference to Palladio on the last page of his list of the stations established the text as the appendix to the 1562 edition *Le cose maravigliose*.[8] The fragment included the original preface signed by Schakerlay, the Englishman.

Schakerlay remains an elusive personality. While the author reveals himself as a foreigner of English origin, his unsophisticated opinions indicate that he was neither a cultivated aristocrat nor a scholar. Nor was he a wealthy tourist for his extensive and practical knowledge of Rome suggests that he was a resident of the city.[9] He has been identified as the Peter Shakerley who produced an English edition of Ecclesiastes in 1551 and called himself "poor Shakerley."[10] More credible is the assertion that the author was the "English organist Thomas Shakerley, resident of Rome."[11] In the earliest version of the guide, Schakerlay mentions a collection of musical instruments and an Academy of Music at the house of the Monsignor of Piacenza which may betray his own professional interests (Trans., *La guida romana*, p. 138). Regardless of his qualifications as an authority on the city, it is credible that the author of *La guida romana* was a foreigner who, proficient in the Italian language and familiar with local customs, still continued to marvel at the city's "curiosities" with the enthusiasm of an outsider.

The conspicuous English presence in Rome in the mid-sixteenth century explains the selection of the author and also suggests why an appreciative audience would have enjoyed his account of historical sites. English visitors gravitated to the Hospice of St. Thomas on Via Monserrato where Cardinal Reginald Pole served as guardian after 1538.[12] Reconstituted as the English College in 1579 under the auspices of the Society of Jesus, the institution continued to attract travellers, especially pilgrims.[13] With the spread of Protestantism, English Catholics who moved to Rome identified Cardinal Pole as a willing protector. Catholic travellers, however, found the road to Rome an arduous one, and they often considered the viewing of monuments of minor importance.[14] But Rome satisfied the scholarly curiosity of Protestant visitors, even after the Inquisition, with the vogue for Italian culture peaking at mid-century. The scholar William Thomas (c. 1507–1554) spent about three years in Italy, stayed in Rome in 1547 and subsequently authored a History and Italian Grammar.[15] Anthony Munday's lively account of *The English Romayne Lyfe 1582*, printed after his return to England, depicts the customs of English students who interrupted their religious devotions with visits to the *vigne* every third or fourth day for playful pursuits.[16] Munday did little to hide his cynical opinion of Catholic practices, but the devotion to relics particularly aroused his disdain.[17]

The Protestant Englishman found that his fortunes in Rome fluctuated with the contemporary political climate. The reign of Sixtus V (1585–1590) brought about a resurgence of Protestant persecutions, and Fynes Moryson who toured the city in 1594 went to such extremes to conceal his whereabouts that his behavior begins to smack of paranoia. He paid the requisite visit to Cardinal Allan and then changed his lodgings in secret to "a vitling house, in the Market-place, close under the Pope's Palace, where I thought they, or any one else would least seeke mee."[18] The spirit of Counter-Reformation Rome also pervades the account of Gregory Martin, a devout Catholic who recorded the sacred traditions of the city. In 1576–1578, Martin taught at the English College and maintained close relations with the Jesuits. When he composed *Roma sancta* about two years later in Reims, he surely had consulted secondary sources because his narrative fuses first-hand observations with theological accounts. His description of the churches of Rome, their relics and stations derives in large part from *Le cose maravigliose*. He also assumes a defensive position in a section on "Certaine scrupulous doubtes about Relikes resolved."[19] The English Catholic surely consulted *Le cose maravigliose* with the expectations of any devout pilgrim.[20] Only after visiting the churches would the same traveller turn to *La guida romana* for a handy overview of the city's antiquities.

In its practical orientation, Schakerlay's guide was not unlike the lists of *Stations and Indulgences* which had been produced for foreign visitors to Rome since the thirteenth century. In 1452–1453, the Augustinian friar John Capgrave composed a guide for British pilgrims which consisted of the *Mirabilia*, a list of churches and stations and an account of indulgences and relics.[21] By the sixteenth century, British travellers circulated journals based on their Italian trips and, increasingly, guides written by Italian authors appeared in England. As the English fascination with antiquity accelerated, important descriptions of Rome emerged in the writings of Thomas Hoby (1548–1550) and Richard Smith (1563).[22] *La guida romana* was not a comparable literary work, although it would have provided such authors with a useful itinerary through ancient Rome. Because the guide was published in Italian rather than Latin, it was available to all tourists—foreign and indigenous, scholarly and unlettered alike. Schakerlay realized his stated objective of constructing a quick tour of ancient monuments, thus divulging the secrets of Rome's past to the general public.

Many descriptions written by Roman visitors reflect the influence of *La guida romana*. With inevitable variations, tourists followed the established itinerary and remarked on the standard set of monuments. Typical was a certain Englishman who started in the Vatican Borgo, followed the route through Trastevere and into the heart of old Rome. Many anecdotal details of his account conform with the information in *La guida romana* such as his reference to the Church of Santa Maria in Cosmedin as the present site of "La Bocca della Verità," formerly the school of Sant'Agostino.[23] Similar observations about the area of the Forum Boarium emerge in Fynes Moryson's description which moreover alludes to the "foot of Mount Aventine (where the Jews use to fish)."[24] But no intelligent tourist, then as now, relied on a single authority, and travel diaries reflect disparate literary sources, among which *La guida romana* held a primary place of importance.

The guidebook owed its inception and continuing popularity to the rise of tourism. Sojourners in Rome found no shortage of professional guides for hire, although the qualifications of these *ciceroni* left a lot to be desired. Montaigne had a low opinion of hired guides; he had initially engaged a French guide to take him around the city, but dismissed him and turned to his own resources: "he piqued himself that by his own study he was able to master that science with the help of various maps and books which he had read to him in the evening . . . so that in a few days he could have easily reguided his guide."[25] Fynes Moryson was equally critical of hired guides: "All the rest . . . inquiring after my lodging, promised to be my guides in Rome . . . I went from them. I well knew that such guides would be very troublesome to me for they (according to the manner) disputing of Religion . . . besides that to gratifie them for their courtesie, I must needes have runne into extraordinary expences."[26] The discriminating tourist inevitably found that the study of current literature and maps was essential to a proper understanding of the city. To judge from the number of guidebooks issued during the sixteenth century, a lively commerce existed in publications for tourists. The success of printing enterprises like that of Antoine Lafréry meant that city plans were available to tourists after mid-century. Even floor plans of contemporary churches were sold to the public on street corners.[27] Such material allowed the traveller to do advance research for a tour of Rome in the most expedient manner possible.

A knowledgeable traveller such as Fynes Moryson managed to visit seven churches in one day by hiring a mule. He then embarked on a four-day tour of antiquities.[28] Another English tourist recommended boat, coach, or foot depending on the departure point within the city.[29] Most itineraries were planned with reference to those neighborhoods in the city center where travellers found reliable lodgings. Because foreigners tended to stay in the area of Campo Marzio, it became a common point of departure and conclusion. The route outlined in *La guida romana* began near the well-known Albergo del Orso, and on the second day returned to this area after mention of a Hosteria near Santa Maria Maggiore.[30] Pilgrims found accommodations at charitable institutions, like the hospice at SS. Trinità dei Pellegrini founded by Filippo Neri in 1548, in the heavily populated *rioni* of *Ponte* and *Regola*.

The compactness of *La guida romana* allowed even the most frenzied visitor to extract a list of the city's outdoor monuments — statuary and architectural marvels — as well as the private collection of antiquities open to the public. Great family palaces filled with antique treasures awaited the tourist who could expect to gain entry. It was customary for collectors to allow the public access to prized antiquities which, in a sense, never left the public domain.[31] Thus our Elizabethan Englishman provides a thorough description of the interiors of the Villa Medici and the Farnese Palace. His advice on entry to the latter: "Go in on the right-hand under the vault, and there dwells the overseer that hath the key; he will show you every thing in order: — Bestow something upon him to drink."[32] In this fashion, the tourist obtained an intimate view of cherished objects while surveying the splendor of antiquity recreated in the grand rooms and courtyards of private palaces in sixteenth-century Rome.

The *vigne* (for which no satisfactory equivalent in English exists) figured prominently among these attractions, as the sixteenth-century traveller sought out antiquities displayed in the parcels of natural landscape which, though private property, were open to the public. Antique fragments and statuary mingled in the picturesque settings evocative of Rome's past grandeur, areas with strong appeal to admirers of ancient Rome. Montaigne delighted in the untamed glory of these sites which, in his opinion, set off the intrinsic beauty of the works of art. He listed the outstanding *vigne*, calling these sites "beauties open to anyone . . . for any purpose . . . to sleep . . . if the masters are not at home, and they do not often go there."³³ The rural character of large areas of Rome, particularly to the east and south of the city center, is apparent on many a sixteenth-century map, and the landscape is dotted with *vigne* which belonged to a cross-section of Roman society.³⁴ With urban development, city dwellers came to use their plots of land as farms, vineyards or country retreats. The more affluent owners turned these areas into estates complete with park-like structures and overnight accommodations. The elaborate gardens, also called *orti* or *giardini* by the mid-sixteenth century, were famous throughout Europe. The *vigne* mentioned by Schakerlay were among the most important of their day: the lands owned by the cardinal of Ferrara, the cardinal of Carpi, the cardinal of Sant'Angelo and Pope Julius III (Trans., *La guida romana*, pp. 130–38).

La guida romana made the marvels of ancient Rome accessible to the general public. The first practical walking tour of the city was composed by an author well-versed in practical matters and unencumbered by scholarly tradition. By approaching his subject in a straightforward manner, Schakerlay provided a comprehensive overview of the city's treasures. This itinerary became the basis for first-hand experience which in turn was to generate the more literate and imaginative responses produced by later travellers to Rome.

The Guide to Rome
For All Foreigners Who Come to See the Antiquities of Rome, One By One, In a Very Fine Way and with the Utmost Brevity.

༈

From the author to the very dear readers,

Do not think, Gentlemen, that I seek praise or any reward in this small work. Rather I only expect to show you that which I know is dear to you because it is very evident that from day to day we English and the French, the Flemish and people from many other nations come to Rome, very anxious to see her things and to know very well that of which many times, not even a third is seen. However as I am motivated to make you happy, I have taken the bold step of being the guide to your wishes. Beseeching you to be kind to me and not to ask me too many things along the way, but to leave it to me and I will show you the truth about everything and, with as much brevity as possible, I will make sure that you remain fully satisfied.

Your,

Englishman Schakerlay[1]

Of the Borgo *on the first day.*

Whoever wants to see the ancient and marvelous things of Rome needs to start off in an orderly fashion. Don't behave as many do—that is by looking at this and that and then finally leaving without having seen even a half. In order to see everything and be completely satisfied, I want you to begin at the Ponte Sant'Angelo as it is now named[2] which used to be called Ponte Elio by the ancients. When you are on it, look down in the Tiber and you will see in the water the remains of the Ponte Triumphalis over which all the triumphs used to pass on route to the Capitoline in antiquity.[3]

Next, then, turn directly to your right and you will see the Castle which was really the tomb of the emperor Hadrian which was not very distant from where there was a gilt-bronze pine cone of wondrous size which today can be seen in the bronze doors of San Pietro in its real form, and there still is one of those pine cones in front of the church.[4] [*on the top of which (as Pope Clement VII used to say) was a gilt-bronze pine cone of wondrous size which today can be seen in the middle of the open courtyard of San Pietro. But before you depart from San Pietro you will go into the Belvedere where there are many beautiful statues in the secret garden, and especially the famous Laocoön and Cleopatra*].[5]

Then, after passing the Porta San Pietro which goes to the cemetery, as you are in the street to the right-hand side, look[6] and you will see the obelisk, which is now called the "Guglia" of San Pietro, of a wondrous height. On the summit are the ashes from the bones [*body*] of Julius Caesar. Just set a little bit apart from this was the miraculously beautiful circus of Nero which occupied the Borgo toward the Tiber.

Of Trastevere

Once you have seen this, come back up until you reach the Porta Santo Spirito through which the duke of Bourbon entered during the Sack of Rome.[7] As you will be outside, look up to the right and you will see a certain little church called Sant'Onofrio. Beginning there, all the way to San Pietro in Montorio, the whole of that hill the ancients used to call the Janiculum, one of the seven hills of Rome. Where you pause in front of San Pietro in Vaticano is also one of the seven hills.

Now, as I tell you, looking from Sant'Onofrio all the way to San Pietro in Montorio, at the base was the Circus of Julius Caesar of the [*of great*] width and length which you will be able to see if you go on the hill, in front of the Porta San Pietro in Montorio.

Thus, going straight along the road which goes toward the Ripa, as far as Santa Maria in Trastevere, is where now you will see the church which formerly was called the Meritoria of the pious and ancient Romans. When the poor soldiers, who were miserable, mutilated or [*and*] wasted by war, came there, they were able to maintain themselves and find refuge for as long as they lived. In front of this church is the spot where a fountain spewed forth oil in a very great quantity for a whole day when Christ *our Saviour* was born.

Then, continue walking in the direction of the Ripa where one sees the wine [*where wine is sold*]. Look at all those gardens, churches and houses which you will find [*will see*] here. The arsenals of the Romans used to be in these, which were the banks of the Ripa, and you will be able to judge what size they were [*here where the arsenal of the Romans used to be which, from above the banks of the Ripa, you will be able to judge what great size it was*] because one can still see the remains.

Of the Island in the Tiber.

Then going along toward the Ripa, you will find an island on the left which the ancients used to call Tyberina and where the Church of San Bartolomeo and San Giovanni, a convent for women, are now located. Two temples were on this island—one was of Jupiter Licanius and the other of Aesculapius. If you will observe closely, this island is shaped like a ship. Also on this island, there are two bridges for access which were called by the ancients "Fabricius," one, and the other "Cestius"—both have no other names today [*which today have no name other than the Bridge of the Four Heads*].

Of the Ponte Santa Maria, the Palace of Pilate and other things.

Once you have seen this, cross to the other side of this island, and proceed always next to [*always toward*] the Tiber along a road which you will find at the foot of this forenamed island's bridge. Continue walking straight until you come to a new bridge which today is called the Ponte Santa Maria, and the Ponte Senatorio by the Ancients.[8] At its foot you will find a palace in ruins which is said by some to be the Palace of Pilate. And opposite this you will see a certain ancient temple which was of the Moon and, on the other side, that of the Sun—very ancient.

After passing these, you will see across the way a white marble which is large and round. The interior is shaped like a face, which is commonly called the Mouth of Truth. It is propped up against the Church of Santa Maria which is still[9] called the Schola Greca, and this is where St. Augustine used to read. After this, you will reach the foot of the Aventine Hill and near where you will see Jews fishing was the site of the Ponte Sublicio where Horatius Coclius fought against all of Tuscany.[10]

And walking beneath this hill near the Tiber and toward San Paolo, you will find *vigne* to the right, alongside the Tiber, within which the Romans had one hundred and forty granaries which were *very* large, as their remains in the *vigna* of Signor Giuliano Cesarino demonstrate.[11]

Of Monte Testaccio and many other things.

Then, having passed by this, continue going toward San Paolo and you will find a very beautiful field, where the Romans held their Olympic games. In this field you will see Monte Testaccio which is made up entirely of broken vases because *they say that* the sealer-artisans [*the vase makers*] lived nearby and they used to throw away their broken and shattered vases there.

And look at the Porta San Paolo and you will see a very ancient pyramid which is [*walled up*] in the [*middle of the*] wall. It is said to be the tomb of Cestius.

Then take the street which goes near the Hosteria at the Gate [*the street*] of San Paolo which will lead you to San Gregorio where you will pass along the ridge of the Aventine Hill. Look and you will find [*You will see*] great ruins of buildings. This street will take you to the site of an aqueduct [*a river*] and you will find women who are always washing [*where women always wash*] below San Gregorio. Look carefully from there because you are in the Circus Maximus where Roman youth used to fight on water as they performed [*where they used to race with carriages and stage naval battles*]. You will also see certain [*three orders of*] tall columns, one on top of the other, which is called the Settezoni [*the Septizonium of Severus*].[12]

Of the Antonine Baths and other things.

Once you have seen this, a little higher up you will see the Antonine Baths, marvelous and stupendous things to see,[13] and on the other side near Santa Balbina, the cemetery of Presidia and Basil, but they are all ruined.

Then walk as far as San Sisto, a convent for women, along the straight road which goes to San *Se*bastiano and take a certain path on the left which will take you to Santo Stefano Rotondo, which in antiquity was the Temple of Fauno. Close by you will see the high [*certain*] walls which *they say* were aqueducts that went to the Capitoline. And the Caelian Hill is located on this spot.

Of San Giovanni in Laterano, *Santa Croce* and other things.

And you will pass by those until San Giovanni in Laterano where you will see the basilica [*the baptistery*] in which Constantine the Emperor was baptized as well as the four bronze columns in the church, stupendous things to look at. Next take the street of Santa Croce in Gerusalemme and in front of the door of the church you will find the former site of the Temple of Venus in which the ancient[14] courtesans of *that time* used to celebrate *her holiday* every year on the twentieth of August. The Theatre of Statilius Taurus made of bricks used to be in the actual Church of Santa Croce and it was very beautiful and large as one can well imagine.[15] Once you have seen this, turn toward the new [*the old*] Rome because at the moment you are actually in old Rome[16] and take the street from Porta Maggiore which goes to Santa Maria Maggiore. Always walking straight ahead, you will find the Triumphs [*the Trophies*] of Mars, a very beautiful thing.[17]

And *then* coming toward Rome, you will pass the Arch of Gallieno, now called the Arch of San Vito, still in one piece, where you will see the keys of Tivoli attached above [*below*] at the Hosteria of Santa Maria Maggiore.[18] Now that you have seen all these things, turn home and don't search anymore, because this is enough for you to see in one day [*for the first day*]. In fact, when I came to Rome for the first time, I did not see as much in a month with all the guidance at my disposal.[19]

SECOND DAY

Of the tomb of Augustus and other things.[20]

The next morning you will begin at San Rocco where behind the church you will see a large part of the tomb of the emperor Augustus, which with its surrounding forest occupied the area as far as the Church of

Santa Maria del Popolo. That large pyramid which you will see broken in the street below the street[21] of San Rocco, was from his tomb, with many other beautiful ornaments which have already been excavated.

From the Gate of the Popolo.

Then the gate which is now called the Porta[22] del Popolo, and which was called the Flaminia *or Flumentana* by the ancients, is that which you will see[23] attached to the Church of the Madonna [*del Popolo. In our times, this has been enlarged and so well decorated by N. S. PP Pius IV who likewise straightened and repaired this beautiful road called the Flaminia. But you will be able to appreciate it better when we return to the great vigna of Pope Julius III*]. But don't let it happen that you proceed to the Gate for you have to turn upward toward the Trinità where the street goes from [*Now we will turn around toward the Trinità*] below which you will walk along. You must have known it was the large Circus of Augustus, like that of Maximus which I told you about earlier. Where today[24] the Church of the Trinità is seen and extending as far as Monte Cavallo *they say* the very pleasant gardens of Salustius used to be in antiquity.

Then going toward the Quirinal *Hill* which today is called Monte Cavallo, below the *vigna* of the very reverend cardinal of Ferrara, you will see certain ancient grottoes. In a nearby piazza, the Romans used to conduct the so-called Games of Flora with total dishonesty. All the dishonest women used to live in those grottoes. Above this place, still, the altar of Apollo was situated, I mean the place which may be seen in the *vigna* of the above-named Ferrara.

Of the Marble Horses which are on Monte Cavallo and of the Baths of Diocletian.

Then you must take a small street which goes up Monte Cavallo, and when you have arrived, you will see two marble horses sent from Egypt to Nero whose palace you will see nearby.[25] But (the view is) better from the other side at the site of the nearby church, which, it is said, was the Temple of the Sun. That is not true because one sees today that a secret road came from his palace. There were beautiful columns as far as the place called the Oratory of Nero. One sees a large part of the church still standing. These are not far from the horses.

After you have seen this, take the straight road which goes toward the Baths of Diocletian. On the left, right in the *vigne [which belonged to Leonardo Boccaccio]* where you will see Giovanni Boccaccio written in different places, exactly there began the Baths of the Emperor Constantine and they extended as far as Santa Susanna.[26] On the other side of these baths was the Senate of the Matrons, poor widows and little orphans and before the Romans went inside, they used to visit the altar of Apollo which was opposite this place.

Then walking, as I have told you, you will reach the Baths of Diocletian. But I would not want you to leave there until you have looked carefully. You will ask how it is possible to make another building like this and I will answer to you that neither the emperor, nor the king of France nor all the Christian kings could make another one similar to that. I have been told by a venerable monk that there are grottoes and secret underground roads — one which goes to the Capitoline, another to San *Se*bastiano and the third under the Tiber which goes to the Vatican. But I have never been there. However, I would like very much to go. He pointed out to me clearly the spot in the *vigna behind the culvert* behind certain grottoes where one evening I wanted to enter with others. We went, according to our estimate, about a half mile, but not straight.[27] *But pardon me if I must turn back a bit, for it would be such a shame to pass by so many beautiful things in silence.*

Of the Strada Pia.

This street, which you will see here is so spacious, so long and so straight, has recently been redone in such a beautiful aspect by the Holiness of N. S. Pope Pius IV. From his name he has deservedly called it Pia.

Of the vigna of the Cardinal of Ferrara.

Here you may contemplate the very agreeable and wonderful vigna of the very illustrious monsignor and very reverend cardinal of Ferrara which, in my opinion, has no equal in modern times, nor do I believe that it even suffers much in comparison to the ancients.[28] Here you will be able to enter and see it at your pleasure because it belongs to a gentleman who is very correct and truly very splendid.

Of the vigna of the Cardinal of Carpi and other things.

From this one you deservedly will be able to see the place near that of the very illustrious and very reverend Cardinal of Carpi which is full of antique and modern things, all excellent. In the same street you will see infinite other things, all beautiful, and if they were not placed in comparison to those two mentioned above, they would all be held to be most beautiful.[29]

Of the Porta Pia.

At the top of this very beautiful street is a gate suitable for it, also built and called Pia on account of the name of his holiness.

Of Sant'Agnese and other curiosities.

Now you can also move along as far as Sant'Agnese on the Via Nomentana which has been very well repaired by our Holiness as well. Here you will see an ancient and very beautiful temple which they say was dedicated to Bacchus, and likewise you will see there a porphyry tomb so large and so beautiful like no other I have ever seen.[30] *But should going on right now tire you, let us return along the same street to the stupendous Baths of Diocletian which have been consecrated by the same Pope Pius IV in honor of the glorious and ever virgin, Maria degli Angeli.*[31] *I hope you don't regret that I have brought you here two times; you can see yourselves that the work merits the double effort, yes or no. But I forgot to tell you before that below these Baths there are* many doors and other streets to be found as well, like those under the Antonine where I have been still even further. Now having seen this well,[32] take the narrow[33] road which goes to Santa Maria Maggiore. Below this church, in the valley, you will find a church called Santa Potenziana where the Novitian Baths were located in antiquity.

Above on the hill on the present site of the monastery of San Lorenzo in Panisperna were the baths of the Olympians—very large buildings. So that they can go from one side to the other, as people who go underneath Santa Maria Maggiore can see clearly [*better*] poor gypsies often come here to live.

Of the Temple of Isis and other things.

And where the present church of Santa Maria Maggiore is located, the Temple of Isis used to be in ancient times which was greatly esteemed by the Romans. Where the Chapel of San Luca is located at the Church of Santa Maria (Maggiore) and all the way below, there was the forest dedicated to Juno, greatest goddess of the Romans. Above this, in the *vigna* of Sant'Antonio, was the very rich and marvelous Temple of Diana where the Romans made their sacrifices with very great riches. Then on the other side, where the Church of San Martino is now, was the Temple of the God[34] Mars whom all the captains and soldiers worshipped.

Of the Seven Rooms, the Colosseum and other things.

Then having passed the aforementioned church, you will find a road which will lead you right to San Pietro in Vincoli. But leave this street and take the first alley that you find on the left which will take you to the Seven Rooms, as they are called, inside which you will see a marvelous thing which the emperor Diocletian [*Titus*] made for his pope in those times.

Once you have seen this, turn around from there and pass below along the first street in the *vigne* which will take you to San Clemente, the monastery for friars. Thus you will keep going straight toward Rome until you find a stone erected [*a little chapel*] in the street, set a little apart from the theater [*colosseum*]. On that very spot Pope Joan the Englishwoman gave birth. Everyone thought her to be a man when, going in procession, she gave birth. *However, the popes do not pass along there.*

Then arriving at the stupendous *and ancient* theater *of Vespasian* called the Colosseum, you will certainly never see another one made like this [*you will see a creation certainly unlike any other you will see*] in the whole world, although that of Verona is beautiful. This one as well is of marvelous construction because the ancient Romans who went there to watch when a show was presented numbered one hundred and ninety thousand people and everybody saw well [*because one hundred and ninety thousand people were there and each one saw well, when the ancient Romans staged a spectacle*].

Then when you have passed to the other side, nearby you will see the Arch of Constantine, still very beautiful to look at. Nearby in the garden belonging to the monks of Santa Maria Nuova, you will see remains from the Temple of the God Serapis. Going a little further, you will pass the Arch of Vespasian[35] which was built for him when he returned *triumphantly* from Jerusalem.

Of the Temple of Peace, *and the Palatine Hill
now called* the Palazzo Maggiore,
and[36] other things.

And further along in front of this you will see the Temple of Peace,[37]
nearly ruined and, opposite that, *the Palatine Hill now called* the Palazzo
Maggiore *where* now *there is* a beautiful *vigna* up high[38] which belongs to
the cardinal of Sant'Angelo.[39]

Near this spot was the Temple of Romulus which today is the Church
of Santi Cosma e Damiano. Nearby was the Temple of [*Marcus Aurelius
and of*] Faustina, the wife of Marcus Aurelius [*his wife*] and the daughter
of the Divine Antoninus Pius whose palace is behind that temple. Opposite that was a beautiful temple dedicated to the goddess Venus which
is now called Santa Maria Liberatrice from the Punishment of the Inferno.

And those three columns which you see standing in the piazza alone
used to be a secret road [*in the middle of the Campo Vaccino, they say that there
was a bridge*] which passed along the Capitoline from [*to*] the Great Palace
for the Senate who travelled it thus.[40] [*There they say was the Lake of Curtius.*]

Then that church which you will see with the door of bronze near the
Arch of Septimius *they say* was the Temple of Victory [*of Saturn, treasury
of the Roman People*]. The arch which I mentioned to you before was of
Lucius Septimius *Severus* and it was [*is*] very beautiful.[41] That statue
which you will see against *a corner of* the street is the so-called Marforio.[42]
Where you will see eight [*three*] columns on the other side of the arch
was the Temple of Concord.[43]

Of the Capitoline and other things.

Now you have come to the Capitoline, which was called the Tarpeian
Hill in antiquity, at the foot of which the Temple of Jupiter used to be.
When it burned, it was never again rebuilt, but only the aforementioned
place remained. Near there was also the Temple of Ceres. Today you
will see a man on a *bronze* horse on this spot which is said to be of *Emperor*
Marcus Aurelius. From this spot you will see *almost* the greater part of
Rome in the most beautiful view, and many of the things which you have
seen already. But from here it is necessary to turn around, to where a
little down the road *at the base* of the back of the Capitoline you will find
certain deep cisterns made by the Romans *perhaps* to store salt or grain,
called "horrei" in antiquity.

And from here you will pass by Santa Maria della Consolazione. A little beyond there you will see the Arch of the Boarium, but I would like you to see things of greater importance; that is the Theater of Marcellus, where the cardinal Savella lives now.[44] Inside this theater was the Temple of the Pietà, something very much cherished by the Romans.

Of the Portico of Octavia and of Septimius and of the Theater of Pompei.

At a little distance from this for the approach to the fish-market were the porticoes of Octavia, the sister of Augustus. However, one sees little remaining of these now. Then further along within the entrance to Sant'Angelo in Pescaria are the porticoes of L. [*Lucio*] Septimius *Severus*.

Then walking as far as the Campo dei Fiori, you will find the Palace of the Orsini which was the Theater of Pompei in antiquity.[45] Behind was its portico. [*Here nearby you will see the beautiful palace of the Capodiferro,*[46] *and further on you will find that of the Signori Farnese built with wonderful architecture and full of very beautiful curiosities.*][47] Now, on this day, I don't want you to tour any more, but when you have reached home, note well what you have seen. Don't be like the others who, by going to look and then forgetting, remain idiots. They don't know how to keep anything in their heads.[48]

THIRD DAY

Of the two Columns — one of Antoninus Pius and the other of Trajan — and other things.

On the third day, you will begin from the Campo Marzio or, better said, from the Piazza Colonna where you will see the Column of Antoninus Pius of one hundred and seventy-six feet in height, with the spiral staircase inside of one hundred and forty steps with fifty-six windows.[49]

Having seen this, go afterwards along a street to the Piazza Sciarra. Turn to the right, as you are at the Grocer's which is a little below the street; go up to the Vestal Virgin, a church which was very esteemed by the Romans and now is full of little orphans, a very pious institution. When you have seen this, take [*turn down*] the same street, along which you came and proceed always straight ahead toward San Marco, until you have reached the *place called the* slaughterhouse of the crows, as it is called.[50] Ask where the Column of Trajan is, which anyone will show you. It is one hundred and twenty-three feet high; the spiral staircase inside has one hundred and fifty-five steps and it has forty-five windows.[51] From now on, head back to the Church of the Minerva which was called by the same name in antiquity, but then was destroyed along with other very beautiful buildings, as you will see as you go along.[52] *But I have omitted telling you that if you want to see rare things in sculpture or in painting, ask at Montecitorio for the home of Monsignor Girolamo Garimberto, bishop of Galese. There you will be shown, courteously, an infinite number of things, all of which are rare.*[53]

Of the Rotonda or the Pantheon.

A bit further on the other side you will see the Pantheon, now called the Rotonda, which is a very old church [*built by Marcus Agrippa, a very beautiful work and very much appreciated*] where, going on top, you will be able to clearly read who made it.

Of the Baths of Agrippa and Nero.

Nearby this in [*from the side at*] the rear where now one sees wooden panels, there were once the Baths of Agrippa who constructed the Rotonda.[54] And behind Sant'Eustachio there were the Baths of Nero *of* which *a part* are in the Palazzo Madama. All around you will see *very* substantial remains.

Of the Piazza Navona and *Master* Pasquino.

Then having passed the Piazza di Madama, you will enter the Piazza Navona where every Wednesday the market is held. But the Romans built it for making appearances and[55] showing games *and spectacles*, as the spot is very beautiful.[56] And at the foot of this piazza *in Parione* under a *large* Palace of the House of the Orsina (*sic*),[57] you will find attached the very ancient M. Pasquino Romano [*the statue of Maestro Pasquino*][58] and I will leave you with him until you have dined because no other old curiosities are to be found more than those which I have told you about [*that I know about*].

But in the house of certain cardinals and of other particular people there are many beautiful things to see which because they move from place to place, I will not attempt to tell about them so that when you go there and do not find them, you will not be able to blame me. But I will mention only a very beautiful place which you will find outside the Porta del Popolo.

I have shown you all the things which are within Rome. Now nothing remains but the vigna which Pope Julius built where there is a very beautiful fountain with many beautiful statues and you will see many things.[59] *Yet, despite all the things you have seen and all the things you will be able to see, still there will always remain something else to see. With the reminder that I am tired by now, I leave you with this.*

But in the house of certain cardinals there are many beautiful things to see which I shall show you once you have dined.[60]

Then, after the meal.

Of the old Curiosities of Monsignor d'Aquino and of the Palace of San Giorgio and that of Montepulciano.

Now we go to the house of Monsignor the Bishop of Aquino. We will see a very beautiful type of ancient curiosity, held in the highest esteem.[61]

And then the Palace of San Giorgio which is one of the most beautiful things to see which is found in all Europe, where you will see many beautiful ancient curiosities[62] and also the Palace of the cardinal of Montepulciano, very beautiful to see, with many ancient curiosities inside of a very noble quality.[63]

Of the Belvedere.

Then you will be able to proceed by boat along the Tiber behind the aforementioned palace. Go to San Pietro to see the Belvedere which is very sumptuous and full of various things which are lovely to see and very magnificently made.

So that you have seen all these things, it seems to me that you will be quite well-satisfied and quite happy with these things.

Of Roman Women.

However, if with all these things you want to see beautiful and very honorable Roman women as they go out and in what garments, go to the Pace or to the Minerva, Santi Apostoli or San Girolamo. You will see their behavior and very noble comportment.[64]

Of the Monsignor of Piacenza, the Tomb of Bacchus and the *vigna* of Pope Julius.

And if you take pleasure in passing the time and heat of the day in a virtuous way, go to the house of the Monsignor of Piacenza who lives near Sant'Agostino. You will find every type of musical instrument, where the Academy of Honorable and Excellent Noblemen is held for singing and playing in a heavenly way. Of the rest, I don't know how to tell you more. I have shown you all the things which are within Rome. Now you are missing nothing except the Tomb of Bacchus which is outside the walls at Sant'Agnese.[65] Outside the Porta del Popolo is the *vigna* which Pope Julius built where you will see still many beautiful things. Yet, despite all the things you have seen and all the things you will be able to see, there still will always remain something else to see. In order that I acquit myself as by now I am tired, I will leave you with that which you have seen and I, for certain, can no longer walk.

THE END

Notes

Notes to Introduction

1. Hereafter the two guidebooks will be referred to as *Le Chiese* and *L'Antichità di Roma*.

2. A recent census cites about ninety editions. Ferrari (1976), 475–550. This estimate does not necessarily include examples appended to other texts, such as the Venetian edition of 1711 where *L'Antichità di Roma* was joined to the *Quattro Libri*. Trettenero (1938), 15.

3. For the facsimile reprint, see Murray (1972). The guidebook is included in Lionello Puppi, *Andrea Palladio; scritti sull'architettura (1554-1579)*, Vicenza: Neri Pozza, 1988, published while this study was in press. The extant copies are discussed in chapter three below.

4. The full title is: *Le cose maravigliose dell'alma città di Roma, dove si tratta delle chiese, stationi, indulgenze & reliquie de i corpi santi, che sono in essa. Con un breve Trattato delle Antichità, chiamato La Guida Romana. Et i nomi de i Sommi Pontefici, de gl'Imperadori, de i Re di Francia, Re di Napoli, de i Dogi di Venetia & Duchi di Milano.* Hereafter referred to as *Le cose maravigliose*.

5. Schudt (1930), 26–31, 198–217.

6. A recent exception is Olivieri (1981, pp. 99–104) who treats the guidebook as a statement of Palladio's utopian and spiritual ideals. Puppi (1975, p. 441) reviewed the circumstances of its publication, recognizing that the guidebook "should be given greater attention than it has so far received," although with some mistaken information about the date of subsequent editions. Other useful accounts are Burns (1975), 95; Puppi (1980), 57.

7. Hereafter referred to as the *Quattro Libri*. Puppi (1975), 441–42.

8. "E perchè fin dalla mia giovanezza mi son grandemente dilettato delle cose di Architettura . . . mi son trasferito ancora spesse volte in Roma, & altri luoghi d'Italia, e fuori; dove con gli occhi proprii ho veduto, & con le proprie mani misurato

i frammenti di molti edifici antichi." Palladio (1570), 7. The standard English translation reads slightly differently: "Guided by a natural inclination, I gave myself up in my most early years to the study of architecture . . . and set myself to search into the reliques of all the ancient edifices. . . . I began very minutely with the utmost diligence to measure every one of their parts . . . I have very frequently not only travelled in different parts of Italy, but also out of it" Palladio (1738), n.p.

9. Tiepolo (1980), 71.

10. As he indicates in his introduction to the work. Puppi (1975), 442; Puppi (1980), 57–58.

11. Palladio had studied the treatise under the tutelage of Giangiorgio Trissino as early as 1533–38. Isermeyer (1979), 253–71. For an intriguing discussion of Palladio's approach to the *Commentari*, see G. Barbieri (1982), 43–44.

12. Puppi (1975), 442; Puppi (1980), 60–61. See the introduction in Burlington (1730).

13. Gualdo (1958–59), 94: "Fece parimente alcune nobilissime fatiche sopra Polibio dedicandole a Francesco Gran Duca di Toscana, che mostrò averle sommamente care." See Hale (1977), 240–55.

14. Interestingly, this is in direct contrast to the attitude he assumes in the preface to *L'Antichità di Roma* where he cites the authors, ancient and modern, whom he consulted.

Notes to Chapter 1

1. Gualdo (1958–59), 93. An English translation of Gualdo's text appears in Lewis (1981), 3–4. The mention of the *Mirabilia Romae* should not be mistaken for a reference to Palladio's own *Le Chiese*. Gualdo had probably seen a copy of *L'Antichità di Roma* bound together with an older Latin edition of the *Mirabilia*, a practice which was not uncommon. The continuing popularity of the Latin version of the *Mirabilia* suggests that, despite Palladio's intentions of superceding the medieval text, *Le Chiese* did not actually replace it. Other biographers followed Gualdo's lead by omitting any mention of *Le Chiese* in an account of Palladio's writings: Temanza (1762), viii; Magrini (1845), ix–xii; Zanella (1880), 14–15. More recent authors have done the same: Trettenero (1938); Pane (1942).

2. Zorzi (1962), 14–51. For a comprehensive account of Palladio's career see Puppi (1975); Lewis (1982).

3. The early relations between the architect and his mentor are discussed by F. Barbieri (1980), 191–96. For his contribution to the design of the Villa at Cricoli, see Lewis (1981), 16–18.

4. Wittkower (1971), 57–58.

5. "Scorgendo esso Trissino il Palladio esser giovane molto spiritoso ed inclinato molto alle scienze matematiche, per coltivar questo ingegno s'indusse egli stesso ad esplicarli Vitruvio, et a condurlo anco seco a Roma tre volte, dove misurò e tolse in dissegno molti di quei più belli e stupendi edifici, reliquie della veneranda antichità Romana" Gualdo (1958–59), 93.

6. The evidence for Palladio's early travels is offered by Puppi (1975), 10-11. The source for Trissino's stays in Rome is Morsolin (1894), 241-45. He established that Trissino made only two trips in the company of Palladio because the young architect absented himself on the second occasion to go briefly to Venice. He then returned to Rome to resume residence, thereby accounting for the three trips noted by Gualdo. See Zorzi (1959), 17.

7. Puppi (1975), 10; Lotz (1962), 61-66. Forssman (1965, 32) posits that this first trip was devoted to the study of modern buildings.

8. Bruschi (1978), 13, 18-19. For Palladio's trips to Verona and Padua, see Zorzi (1959), 15-16; Lewis (1981), 30-33. For the sites covered on his trips to and from Rome in 1541, see Zorzi (1959), 17-18; Lewis (1981), 28-29.

9. While Serlio's *Fourth Book* had been published in 1537 in Venice, his *Third Book* on the antiquities of Rome was published only in March 1540, before he moved permanently to France. See Lewis (1982), 351-53. The drawing of "Raphael's House," often attributed to Palladio is refuted by Lewis (1981), 50-56.

10. The biographical information on Trissino comes from Morsolin (1894), 69-241.

11. The date of XIII Kal Aug. Ann MDXLI Roma appears on fols. 1a-1b, while the epigram is on fol. 2 of Biblioteca Vaticana, Vat. Lat. 3744. The poem is mentioned by Morsolin (1894), 241-45. Trissino later wrote a letter to Paul III dated 19 September 1543, when he was in Vicenza, concerning a Paduan scholar who taught Greek. Dorez (1932), 1:43.

12. Trissino wrote to his son in 1546 of his welcome at the papal court: "Sono tanto ben veduto e accarezzato in questa terra, quanto dir si possa, e specialmente dalla Santità di Nostro Signore, il quale sempre mi vede volentieri ed usa meco parole onorevoli ed amorevoli e buonissime" (Morsolin [1894], 278). See also Berger (1978), 239. Speculation that Palladio's drawing of the Villa Madama resulted from a papal introduction, arranged by Trissino in 1541, is in Lewis (1981), 55.

13. Michelangelo's *Last Judgment* was completed on 31 October 1541. See Dorez (1932), 1:29, 145.

14. For the probability that Palladio saw early projects and a wooden model of San Pietro, see Frommel (1977), 108. For the chronology of building at the Farnese Palace, see Chastel (1981), 1:145-52.

15. Palladio presented a drawing for the Loggia of the Basilica in Vicenza on 5 March 1546. Zorzi (1922), 15,16. For evidence concerning the dating of the trip, see Puppi (1975), 13, n. 17.

16. Morsolin (1894), 270-80, 339; Zorzi (1959), 17.

17. For Trissino's house, see Puppi (1975), 13, n. 71. Trissino lived in a common house with Thiene until January 1546 when he moved to a place near the Pantheon. Morsolin (1894), 273-74. Marco Thiene and Trissino remained intimate friends until the latter's death on 13 December 1550. Mantese (1969-70), 82.

18. Zorzi (1922), 24.

19. Mantese (1969-70), 90.

20. Morsolin (1894), 279.

21. He reported on a project for a memorial statue at the time of Thiene's death in 1556. In Vicenza, Maganza's home was close to those of Palladio's sons and the Thiene family. Mantese (1969-79), 83-84.

22. Now in the collection of Count Angelo di Valmarana, Vicenza. The newly-discovered portrait is discussed by Puppi (1980), 104–113. For Maganza's career as a painter see Noe (1976), 98–105; Sgarbi (1980), 101–6. Maganza's literary works provide information about Palladio and his circle. He recited poems — his own and those of other authors — at Palladio's funeral, according to Gualdo (1958–59), 94.

23. "Giov. Battista Maganza, pittore insigne . . . ha riconosciuto l'essere e l'educazione di questa mia casa, essendo stato condotto in Roma anch'egli in compagnia del Palladio dove apparò le più vive maniere del colorire e l'eccellenza della sua professione" MS. A.T. in Morsolin (1894), 279, n. 2.

24. Wittkower (1971), 57–64; F. Barbieri (1980), 191–99.

25. Ligorio was connected with the "Accademia dei Virtuosi" from 1543. Burns (1973), 187, n. 12; Vignola, from 1550. Chastel (1981), 2:472. The use of the term "Accademia" by Francesco Sansovino — a contemporary of Palladio — is of interest. It connoted a group of humanists who studied the ancient authors, theology, the liberal arts, Latin, Greek and the vernacular. See Sansovino's letter of 5 October 1540 in Grendler (1981), 318–19. Palladio was of course no stranger to such endeavors, beginning with his training at Cricoli and culminating, in 1556, with his participation in the Constitution of the Accademia Olimpica.

26. Morsolin (1894), 279; Zorzi (1959), 17–18.

27. Palladio repeatedly emphasizes his first-hand familiarity with antique monuments in the *Quattro Libri*. See Zorzi (1959), 16–17. For example, he mentions witnessing the excavations on the Quirinal Hill. Palladio (1738), 92. However, he may have stressed specific sites on purpose. He was not able to sketch every building *in situ*, and relied instead on his drawing collection. Lotz (1962), 65.

28. Zorzi (1959), 19; Lotz (1962).

29. Note the metopes and triglyphs in the drawing associated with this stage of the design (RIBA, XIII/9) which is thoroughly analyzed by Lewis (1981), 108–9.

30. "La breve trasferta vicentina dell'acerba primavera del '46 per portare i famosi disegni non richiesti — e maturati nell'ambito delle conversazioni romane con l'ormai settantenne mecenate — e, più ancora, il ritorno definitivo dell'artista nel luglio del '47, sono poi avvenimenti dal significato preciso" F. Barbieri (1980), 200. For deliberations about the Basilica, see Lewis (1982), 355–56.

31. Morsolin (1894), 279–80; F. Barbieri (1980), 200–201.

32. For an account of the competition for the Basilica facade, see Kubelik (1980), 49–52.

33. Gualdo (1958–59), 93. For the exact dates of Palladio's stay, see Zorzi (1959), 19–20.

34. Morsolin (1894), 339.

35. For conjecture on this encounter, see Puppi (1975), 14; Frommel (1977), 108.

36. For Michelangelo's influence on Palladio, see Zorzi (1959), 20. The Last Judgment of the Sistine Chapel was to become a source for the important fresco cycle at Palladio's Villa Foscari at Malcontenta by the artist, Battista Franco. Lewis (1981), 148–50.

37. "Vi andò anco la quinta volta con alcuni Gentiluomini Veneziani amici suoi, dove pure si diede a rivedere misurare e considerare la bellezza e la grandezza di quei meravigliosi edifici e stampo anco a quel tempo un libretto di esse Antichità,

che comunemente si vende con quel libro intitolato Mirabilia Romae" Gualdo (1958–59), 93.

38. The notary act, placing Palladio in Vicenza, seems never to have been connected to Palladio's Roman journey. Zorzi (1922), 147. The trip is assigned to February–November, 1554 by Zorzi (1959), 21. Its duration is shortened to February–June 1554 by Puppi (1975), 14, 231, while the inclusive dates of February–July are cited in Burns (1975), 91. In January of 1554, Palladio had been defeated for the important post of "Proto" in the Venetian Ufficio del Sale. Zorzi (1965), 8.

39. For Barbaro's Paduan experiences see Boucher (1979), 278, n. 3. For Maganza's relation to Barbaro, see Noe (1976), 98–99. For the connections between Trissino, Barbaro, and Palladio, see Lewis (1982), 350–51.

40. Forssman (1966), 68.

41. Zorzi (1959), 20; Forssman (1965), 72.

42. Lewis (1981), 40, 44. For Palladio's practice of employing other architects' drawings, see Lotz (1962), 61–68. For Palladio's connection to Ligorio, see Burns (1973), 173, n. 12.

43. Mandowsky/Mitchell (1963), 2–3.

44. Cardinal d'Este was away from Rome from 1552 to 1554. Coffin (1979), 203. This visit to Tivoli and the impact on Palladio's designs for the Nymphaeum and Villa Barbaro at Maser are discussed by Forssman (1966), 75.

45. Mandowsky/Mitchell (1963), 40–41.

46. That Palladio travelled to Rome in 1554 to consult Michelangelo and Vignola is only speculation. Puppi (1975), 14.

47. Gualdo (1958–59), 93.

48. "Il disegno del Ciborio dell'Altar Maggiore: la Cappella in mezzo l'hospedale è architettura di Andrea Palladio." It is clear, however, that Palladio's projects do not date from his final visit of 1554, as Zocca states in Celio (1967), 82, 93, n. 275.

49. The illustrations come from a treatise on the history of the Order of Santo Spirito and reproduce the altars of both the hospital and church. The former is frequently overlooked as it is missing from at least one copy of Pietro Saulnier, *De capite sacri ordinis S. Spiritus dissertatio* (Lyon), 1649. For a summary and bibliography on the works at Santo Spirito, see Puppi (1975), 265–66, who reproduces only the illustration of the ciborium in the church. For the literary descriptions, see below n. 57.

50. For example, his drawing of the Temple of Vesta, Rome (Olin Library, Cornell University, Ithaca, New York). A drawing of a small temple front (RIBA XVII, 18r) was identified as a project for the hospital tabernacle by Zorzi (1967), 24. This association, however, has been convincingly refuted by Lewis (1981), 122–23. The similarities to the *Tempietto* and San Pietro are distinguished by Puppi (1975, 265–66), who also discusses the relationship of the cupola design to Palladio's own project for the Cathedral of Vicenza.

51. See Berger (1978), 235–36, 238. Since the mid-nineteenth century, skepticism has surrounded the attribution of the altar in the Corsia Sistina. Magrini (1845, pp. 247–48) notes that contemporary documents are missing: "Vecchie memorie dell'Archivio dell'ospitale di S. Spirito da me consultate confermano un altare eretto dal Palladio nell'ospitale e nella chiesa, oltre il ciborio indicato dal Temanza. Mancano però documenti contemporanei."

52. For documentation and a description of the alterations to the hospital, see Howe (1978), 65–66, 124–30. For the original plan of the Corsia Sistina, see Heinz (1977), 170–75.

53. For Guidiccione's relations to Paul III, see Dorez (1932), 29.

54. For payments to Antonio da Sangallo, see Bertolotti (1878), 209.

55. A small ciborium over the altar appears in a drawing from the Sangallo workshop, published in Frommel (1964), 29. An unpublished drawing by Sangallo is cited, but not reproduced, by Berger (1978), 238, n. 678. It should be noted that Palladio seems to have had first-hand knowledge of the Vatican Chapel designed for Paul III. See its inclusion in Palladio's *L'Antichità di Roma* (1554), n. pag.

56. This is the thesis put forward by Berger (1978, pp. 237–39) who, however, limited Palladio's intervention to the ciborium in the church.

57. Well-known is Titi's description published in 1674. Of the hospital: "ha un vago Altare con la sua Tribuna sostenuta da quattro colonne e Tabernacolo simile operato il tutto da Andrea Palladio Architetto." And of the church: "il ciborio dell'altar maggiore fu architettato da Andrea Palladio." Titi (1674), 29–34. See also Pane (1961), 114–15. Although more informative, Titi's account of the altars is by no means the earliest as has always been assumed (see n. 48, above). The first reference to an altar in the middle of the Corsia dates from 1536. Already in 1581, Francesco del Sodo described "un simile altare dove usì conserva li santi sagramenti" in the hospital. A central chapel with a tribune, white marble columns and a gold tabernacle was the site of a daily mass by 1601. The four marble columns were noted by Alveri in the mid-seventeenth century. Authors like Alveri and Titi relied on earlier literary accounts for their information, explaining why they did not record the renovated form of the altar. For these descriptions, see Howe (1978), 128–30.

58. The altar and the lost ciborium are attributed to Palladio by Lavagnino, n.d., pp. 27–42. Lavagnino (1962), 52–58; Pane (1961), 114. The possibility of an emblematic reference in the decoration is not discussed by Berger (1978), 234–39.

59. Bassi (1978), 126–27, n. 24. The contract of 8 October 1575 reads: "et justa le sagome che da esso misier Andrea li saranno date, ecetuando però le quattro colonne che vano nel mezo di esso altare, le quali con li suoi capi (telli) et base siano fatte far per detto Hospitale, et la corn (ice) sotto il volto che va in mezo della Pala, la qual non vi (è) et intendendo che quelle colonne grandi che sono dissegnate si intendano pilastri canellati, con cinque scalini battudi da ben, li quali habbiano d'haver il suo basamento justa la sagoma ordinaria del sopra dito misier Andrea Palladio." It was a common Venetian practice, noted by Burns (1973, 179), for the architect to give a "sagome" to the stonecutter for execution. See also Ellero (1982).

60. "Il Palazzo di Fiorenza in Campomarzo la parte interiore è del Palladio, aniome con il Principato verso Borghese" Mola (1663), fol. 31.

61. "Queste cose dimostrano chiaramente che tra la schiera di tanti eccellenti Professori, che allora fiorivano in Roma, faceva anch'agli onorata comparsa. Vuolsi pure ch'ei architettasse la facciata sopra Campo Marzio del Palazzo del gran Duca di Toscana" Temanza (1762), vii.

62. Nova (1988), 213. See also Magrini (1845), 347. The palace is illustrated in the engravings of Letarouilly who applies the title of the "Loggia del Primaticcio"

to the ground floor level. Reproduced and described by Loukomski (1927), pl. xxii–xxix.

63. For an account of the building activity at the di Firenze, see Nova (1988), 213–220; Montini (1958).

64. He is documented in Rome in 1571 and in 1572, immediately after Cardinal Ferdinando de' Medici had moved into the palace and determined to build it "ex novo" Fossi (1976), 37.

65. Hager (1974), 225–42.

66. The attribution is rejected by Berger (1978), 235.

67. No exception should be made for the watercolor drawing of a later Renaissance building (RIBA, XIV, 7r) which lacks notations and measurements. It represents the elevation of a three-story palace on Piazza Montevecchio. Once exhibited as a study by Palladio, it bears little relation to his style. De Angelis d'Ossat (1959), 57–59.

68. The famous drawing of Palazzo Caprini (RIBA X 18) — the so-called House of Raphael — is attributed to a follower of Bramante by Lewis (1981), 52–53. Further discussion of Palladio's drawings of sixteenth-century Rome is provided by Burns (1973); and Lewis (1981), 50–51, 54–55.

69. Frommel (1977), 107–24; Bruschi (1973), 69–71. For the altered opinion of Michelangelo, see Bruschi (1977), 180–81.

70. "Since Bramante was the first who brought good, and beautiful architecture to light, which from the time of the ancients had been hid; for several reasons it seemed to me fit, that his works should have a place among the ancients" Palladio (1738), 97. Palladio's praise evokes the well-known statement by Sebastiano Serlio that Bramante was the inventor and light of all good architecture. Bruschi (1977), 9.

71. For his observations on the Portico of Pompei, see Palladio (1738), 35.

72. Vasari's account is related by Bruschi (1977), 73.

73. Palladio also praises Vignola in the *Quattro Libri*. Palladio (1738), 97.

74. Coffin (1979), 167.

75. W. Lotz, "Palladio e l'Architettura del suo tempo," in Cevese, ed. (1973), 29–30.

Notes to Chapter 2

1. "Per essermi venuto (non so come) alle mani un certo libretto intitolato: Le cose maravigliose di Roma, tutto pieno di strane bugie & conoscendo quanto sia appresso ciascuno grande il desiderio d'intendere veramente l'antiquità & altre cose degne di cosi famosa città, mi sono ingegnato di raccore il presente libro" Palladio, *L'Antichità di Roma*, n. pag. A later biographer perhaps unwittingly recognized Palladio's motive in composing *Le Chiese* and *L'Antichità di Roma* by relating the following account of a visit to Rome: "In una di queste sue visite alla città dei Cesari venutagli per le mani una piccola guida, intitolata *Le cose maravigliose di Roma*, tutta piena di bugie, se ne indispetti a modo da porsi a comporne una, che in poche pagine presentasse una esposizione chiara, precisa e bene ordinata delle antichità di Roma" Barichella (1880), 20.

2. For the critical antiquarian method adopted by Ligorio and Biondo, see Mandowsky/Mitchell (1963), 3, n. 3.

3. Castelli (1753), 112.

4. Castelli (1753), 74; De Beer (1942), 58–60.

5. The map is at the end of volume 2. Trissino tried to arrange a contract with the Roman publisher Tramezzino, but turned to the Dorico brothers after his efforts failed. Morsolin (1894), 279–80. *Italia liberata* was later printed in Venice as well. Palladio's participation in these negotiations must have provided him with valuable experience for his own projects. For a discussion of *Italia liberata*, see Burns (1975), 81–82.

6. "Da molti fidelissimi autori, antichi e moderni, che di cio hanno diffusamente scritto, come da Dionisio Alicarnaso, Titto Livio, Plinio, Plutarco, Appiano Alessandrino, Valerio Massimo, Eutropio dal Biondo, dal Fulvio, dal Fauno, dal Marliano & da molti altri." See the preface to Palladio, *L'Antichità di Roma*, n. pag.; Zorzi (1959), 19.

7. This conclusion is based on the inventory of books in Trissino's house at the time of his death in 1550. The "libro del Giubileo" appears together with works of classical and contemporary authors. Morsolin (1894), 444. Clearly, *Le cose maravigliose* of 1550 was a best-seller. It reappears in an inventory of the library of Claudio Thiene, dated 1685: "De Jubileo de Indulgentiis, in 8°, stampato in Roma, 1550." Mantese (1968), 38.

8. The quality and number of illustrations vary with each edition: 1556, 1567 (Italian and Latin). Palladio executed only the most important images. Forssman (1966), 68. It is clear that Palladio also carried out his own scholarly projects while working with Barbaro. In his commentary on Vitruvius, Barbaro mentions that the architect was about to publish a book on private houses, probably Book 1 of the *Quattro Libri*. Forssman (1965), 49.

9. Forssman (1966), 30; Paschini (1962), 97–102. For Barbaro's written works in general, see Burns (1975), 94–96. For the villa at Maser, see Huse (1974).

10. Alberigo (1964), 92–93.

11. "Perchè essendo in mezzo a gente che la vera credenza aveva disprezzata, si riducesse in stato di non trarre dalla conversazione con quelle pregiudizio veruno nel fatto di Religione." Paschini (1962), 30. See also Alberigo (1964), 91. But Barbaro composed fifteen letters on religious subjects for his aunt, a nun at the convent of Santa Chiara in Murano.

12. For the passage from Barbaro's commentary on Vitruvius, see Boucher (1979), 279, n. 12. Barbaro's opinion recalls the view related by Pirro Ligorio about the propriety of certain forms for sacred and secular architecture. Of Michelangelo, Ligorio wrote: "Quello (che) si dave da' gentili alli Dii della morte, l'ha dati et introducti nelli templi d'Iddio aeterno et immortale acui si dedicano sempre le cose integre." See Zander (1974), 346–47 for the impact of the Council of Trent on Ligorio.

13. Boucher (1979), 277–82.

14. For discussion of the Venetian press and the Counter-Reformation in general, see Grendler (1981), 26–36. Antiquarian works included topographical studies of ancient Rome. Zander (1974), 333–44.

15. The index was initiated in 1549. For references to Barbaro's conciliatory position, see Zaccaria (1777), 143, 148. For a discussion of censorship and the Roman Inquisition, see Grendler (1981), 48–53.

16. For the official position, see Schroeder (1941), 215–17, 483–85. Lea (1896), 3:380–442.

17. At the twenty-fifth session on 3-4 December 1563, the Council issued a decree "On the Invocation, veneration and relics of Saints, and on sacred images." The reforms included a decree on indulgences:

Since the power of granting indulgences was conferred by Christ on the Church, and she has even in the earliest times made use of that power divinely given to her, the holy council teaches and commands that the use of indulgences, most salutary to the Christian people and approved by the authority of the holy councils, is to be retained in the church, and it condemns with anathema those who assert that they are useless or deny that there is in the Church the power of granting them . . . and thus the gift of holy indulgences may be dispensed to all the faithful piously, holily, and without corruption. Schroeder (1941), 214-17, 253-54.

18. Resulting in a sentence two years later from the Rota Romana. Paschini (1962), 86-87. It is tempting to conclude that Barbaro's trip to Rome was not motivated solely by his study of Vitruvius.

19. See the bull of convocation of 22 May 1542. Schroeder (1941), 2-3. As early as 1524, Clement VII alerted his nunzio in Venice about the sale of Lutheran books. In 1547, a letter from the Venetian Council refers to heretics occupying the "piazze" of Vicenza: "contro l'honore de Dio, contro la fede et religione cristiana. . . ." Other reasons why Barbaro himself was not immune from suspicions of heresy are provided by Puppi (1973), 30-32, 41-43.

20. In his introduction to the *Quattro Libri* Palladio singled out the aristocrats of Vicenza who studied architecture — dilettantes to be sure. For their ties to Protestant ideas, see Puppi (1973), 12, 36-40; Burns (1975), 9-12, 83-84; F. Barbieri (1980), 204.

21. Giangiorgio Trissino's will reveals that he had disinherited his older son on account of his Lutheran sympathies. Giulio received a sentence from the Roman Inquisition on 7 May 1556. Tiepolo (1980), 13.

22. Alessandro was imprisoned on 14 March 1563, but escaped to Switzerland. He eventually settled in Geneva where he became a leader in the community of Italian exiles. For further discussion of his beliefs, with mention of Giulio Trissino, see Olivieri (1967), 54-76; Burns (1975), 77-78; Olivieri (1980).

23. For Marco Thiene and Maganza, see Burns (1975), 82-84. For Maganza's fresco commission, see Noe (1976), 98-99. Burns (1975, pp. 74-75) speculates that Palladio introduced Maganza to many of his patrons. For Maganza's association with the humanist reformer, Luigi Groto, see Mantese/Nardello (1974), 19-27.

24. Palladio called his Vicentine patrons "nobilissimi intelletti" in the preface to the *Quattro Libri*. Palladio (1570), 7. Palladio's reputation among his contemporaries emerges in the poems composed at his death by Luigi Groto. Mantese/Nardello (1974), 32-33, n. 46.

25. Rigon (1980), 46.

26. The relevant passages appear in Palladio (1570), in the preface, 8: "s'egli sarà piaciuto a Dio, ch'io non m'habbia affaticato in darno."

Book 2, chapter 2, 3: "Ma si come Iddio Benedetto ha ordinati questi membri nostri, che i più belli siano in Iuoghi piu esposti ad esser veduti."

At the end of Book 2, 66: "E con questa inventione sia a laude di Dio posto fine a questi due libri."

In the preface to Book 3, 5: "Perlaqual cosa in questo libro, nel quale io do principio alle mie antichità, & ne gli altri, che piacendo Iddio seguiranno."

In the preface to Book 4, 3: "cio senza alcun dubbio si deve fare ne i Tempi, ne quali esso Fattori, e Datore di tutte le cose DIO. O.M. deve essere da noi adorato."

Book 4, chapter 2, 6, 7: "e attissima a dimostrare la Unità, la infinita Essenza, la Uniformità & la Guistitia di Dio. . . .la purità del colore, e della vita sia sommamente grata a Dio."

27. Gualdo (1958–59), 93. Moreover, Palladio was in Venice in January of 1554. See above chapter one, n. 38.

28. Schudt (1930), no. 639, 640; Ferrari (1976) 483–85. The publication of *L'Antichità di Roma* by two presses already had been noted by Temanza (1762), viii. No privilege for publication rights to *L'Antichità di Roma* is recorded in the permissions granted by the Senato Terra from 1542 to 1560. Pagan is mentioned only in connection with a world map: "1561 18 agosto—Mattheo Pagano libraro & stampator in questa città per il disegno et intaglio da lui trovato d'un mappamondo di fogli dodici grandi zeali per anni quindici sotto l'istesse pene." Archivio di Stato, Venezia, Senato Terra, Registro 43, fol. 96v. On 20 agosto 1558 a fine was to be paid for unknown reasons to M. Pagan. ASV, "Stampatori Ricerca Duca di Rivoli," no. 64, Schede 64.

29. Puppi (1975), 441. The pervasive assumption that the Venice edition preceded Lucrino's Roman printing is convincingly dismissed by Ferrari (1976), 483–85. There is no reason to assume that Palladio made a special trip to Venice in order to give the text to Pagan as he was already travelling with Venetians who could have delivered it for him.

30. This reference, however, is suspect as the same author makes a misleading observation about the 1570 edition of Palladio's *Quattro Libri*. Moreover, he does not reveal where he consulted this copy. Bernoni (1890), 253, 353–54. Searches in the major collections—including the Biblioteca Vittorio Emmanuele, Rome—have produced no traces of an edition by Blado. The edition by Blado is not included in Fumagalli and Belli (1891).

31. For Arrighi, see Johnson (1926), 6–8; Barberi (1965), 13.

32. Ascarelli (1953), 68.

33. De Frede (1969), 21–30. The first list of prohibited books was printed by the Venetian press of Giolito in 1554. Johnson (1926), 19. For the works of the Blado Press, see Schudt (1930), no. 52, 1663; Fumagalli and Belli (1891), 1, no. 207; Barberi (1965), 15.

34. For their production, see Barberi (1965), 221–61. For Antonio Labacco, see Bellini (1975), 20.

35. Masetti-Zannini (1980), 167–68. Lucrino's name appears variously as: "Vincenzo Luchino, Vincentio Lucrino, or Vincent Lucchino." Ascarelli (1972), 319, 339. He was originally from Brescia, not Bologna as stated by Ascarelli (1953), 70.

36. Such practices were not uncommon. For these important observations, see Barberi (1965), 229–31, n. 17, 20, 21.

37. The most celebrated example of a printmaker who worked in different professional capacities was Antoine Lafréry. Bellini (1975), 20.

38. The three prints here connected to Lucrino are in the Novacco Collection of the Newberry Library. The view of Monte Testaccio, designed by I. T. F. (1530–50?), appears in its first state of 1557. The engraving of San Pietro is inscribed: "1564 Forma partis Templi Divi Petri in Vaticano. Pio IIII P. M. dicatum. Micael Angelus Bonarotus. Inventor. Romae Vicentius Luchinus excu. Cum privilegio MDLXIIII." Finally, the important map of Italy reads: "Italia Nuova. Romae cum privilegio 1558. Vincentii Luchini aereis formis ad Peregrinum."

39. For Lucrino's permission, see Ascarelli (1953), 70. An official dispenser of paper was not established in Rome until 1574. See Barberi (1942), 42, n. 2.

40. For documentation of the preceding activities, see Masetti-Zannini (1980), 21, 102, 125, 182.

41. See the *Short Title Catalogue of the British Museum*. A longer span of time, (1527–1599), is indicated by the list in Ascarelli (1972), 343.

42. For more on Lucrino's emblem, see Barberi (1965), 229–31.

43. See Bellini (1975), 33. The Dorico brothers conducted their business at the Campo dei Fiori until 1555; the "chiavica di S. Lucia" (near Via dei Banchi Vecchi); Via dei Pellegrini by 1557; Via dei Coronari (under Lucrezia) in 1569. Barberi (1965), 225. Via dei Pellegrini was also the location of the Roman branch of the Tramezzino Press. The brothers Francesco and Michele maintained a shop there from c. 1539–1577. See Ascarelli (1953), 68; Masetti-Zannini (1980), 135.

44. The later edition includes an image of a saint holding a cup with a serpent (St. John the Evangelist), as in the copy at the Hertziana. The woodcut, however, is pasted on the verso of the title page; its likely provenance is a Blado edition of *Le cose maravigliose* of 1548.

45. Polanco mentions organizing a press for the Jesuits at the Collegio Romano in a letter of 1556. Rinaldi (1914), 56; Castellani (1933), 11–16.

46. The privilege, dated 17 November 1560, has escaped notice until now. It refers to "Vincenzo Luchino Libraro in Roma," ASV, Senato Terra, Registro 43, fol. 23. No other record of Lucrino's press appears in the documents of the fondo from 1542 to 1560.

47. Ascarelli (1953), 70, 197, 203. Valgrisi became a controversial figure when in 1559 he protested the *Index of Prohibited Books* under Paul IV. He was tried and sentenced to acts of penitence. See de Frede (1964), 29–30; Ferrari (1976), 479.

Notes to Chapter 3

1. See, for example Ascarelli (1972), 343; Barberi (1965), 236.

2. Classified as no. 57 by Schudt (1930), 198.

3. The London copy is owned by the Royal Institute of British Architects. Another copy survives at the Österreichischen Nationalbibliothek, Vienna. See Trenkler (1976), 12. The fifth example of *Le Chiese* is a recent addition to the University Library at Madison, Wisconsin. I thank John Tedeschi for bringing this to my attention. A sixth copy at the Bibliotheca Hertziana is bound at the back of a 1550 edition of the *Mirabilia urbis Romae* which apparently was unknown to Schudt. Three copies of *Le Chiese* are mentioned in Burns (1975), 92; Ferrari (1976), 477.

4. For example, Hertziana A (Schudt [1930], no. 57) has the following marginal corrections: fol. 21v: "Favola"—text underlined in reference to the foundation of Santa Maria del Popolo; fol. 23v: "Traiana"—text underlined in reference to the so-called Antonine Column; fol. 24: "Hoggi si chiama la Chiesa del Giova nobiliss in tutte le cose"—text underlined at Santa Maria de la strada; fol. 24: "edificato da Pompeo Magno"—in reference to the Temple of Minerva Calcidica. D. Moreau s Dauteil, whose name and coat of arms appear on the title page, may have added these notes in 1579, the date which is inscribed on the copy of *L'Antichità di Roma*, bound with this volume. Ferrari (1970, p. 477) identifies it as "un ex-libris di lettore francese." The Vatican copy (Schudt [1930], no. 57) is also inscribed with the name of the owner, Julio d'amadeo, who presumably added the notations to the list of indulgences at the end of the guide. Of those copies examined, only *Le Chiese* of the RIBA shows little sign of use.

5. As suggested by the mutilated remnant of *Le cose maravigliose* in the British Library. Schudt (1930), no. 60.

6. Puppi (1980), 56–57.

7. Valentini & Zucchetti (1953), 4:459. It was noted by Murray (1972) that Albertini, like Palladio, introduced a guidebook about the old and new cities.

8. For the various editions, see Schudt (1930), 95–98, 311–12; Murray (1972); Valentini & Zucchetti (1953), 4:459–60.

9. "Io. Tortellium e Blondum e Pomponiumque." He also acknowledged Poggio in the discussion of the walls of Rome. See the *Opusculum* in Valentini & Zucchetti (1953), 4:463–64.

10. "Reverendus Galeottus, dixit: 'Francisce, bonum opus operatus es. Quare et mirabilia Romae, imperfecta fabularumque nugis plena, non corrigis?'" Albertini, *Opusculum* in Valentini & Zucchetti (1953), 4:462.

11. Albertini refers to the book as: "Cum enim opusculum de stationibus et reliquiis Urbis ad Imperatorem" Valentini & Zucchetti (1953), 4:462. In his dedicatory letter to Baccio di Montelupo he writes, "ma quello compuosi allo Imperatore Maximiliano (*le stationi di Roma*) lo farò anchora in vulgare ad istantia di alcune persone devote senza littere" Schmarsow (1886), xi, n. 1.

12. For example, in the description of the Lateran, he writes: "in stationum opusculo satis dictum est" Valentini & Zucchetti (1953), 4:500. See also Olschki (1924, 483) who notes the case of the Lateran. But Albertini also mentions his work on the stations in the description of Santa Maria Maggiore and, finally, of San Lorenzo. For the *Epigrammata*, see Olschki (1924), 487–88.

13. Schmarsow (1886, p. xi) notes that we do not know if Onofrio Panvinio and Pomponio Ugonio had access to this guide. Valentini & Zucchetti (1953, 4:462, n. 4) assert that Albertini's guidebook treated the history of the construction of the Vatican as well as some Roman churches. It is more likely that *De stationibus* belonged to the tradition of the *Libri indulgentiarum*.

14. The author of *De varietate fortunae* of the early 1430s, Bracciolini omitted any reference to Christian Rome. Schudt (1930), 139–40.

15. Now dated to c. 1433. Valentini & Zucchetti (1953), 4:209–22.

16. For a list of the various editions up to Palladio's day, see Schudt (1930), 362–64. Biondo also wrote *De Roma triumphante* and *Italia illustrata*, the earliest guidebook to the peninsula, printed in 1471. Trenkler (1976), 25–27.

17. For Fulvio, see Trenkler (1976), 28–29; Schudt (1930), 140–43, nos. 597–601.

18. Schudt (1930), 135–36. For the medieval origins, see Valentini & Zucchetti (1953), 3:3–10; De Beer (1952), 39–40. For a census of the manuscript redactions and incunabula see Valentini & Zucchetti (1953), 3:10–16; Nichols (1889), ix; Borroni (1962), 2:13–62.

19. The *Indulgentiae* originated in the mid-fourteenth century. De Beer (1952, 39) points out that the title, although inconsistent, arises from conventional usage to distinguish these guides from the *Mirabilia*. See also Huelsen (1927), xxi–xxiv, 137–56. For examples of variant editions, see J. R. Hulbert (1922–23).

20. Capgrave (1911); Valentini & Zucchetti (1953), 4:325–39; Parks (1954), 596–600.

21. Brewyn (1933), iv, n. 1. Not mentioned by Schudt (1930).

22. Trenkler (1976), 9–10. Schudt (1930, 19–26) asserts that this "pure" type originated around 1350. See also the expanded Latin version of 1489 by the German printer Stephan Planck (Schudt, 1930, 185).

23. Schudt (1930, no. 53) records the earliest edition of *Le cose maravigliose* as 1541. See also Pescarzoli (1957), 1:265–66. However, the New York Public Library owns an edition of 1532 (Rome, Dorico) and a copy in the Biblioteca Nazionale, Florence dates from c. 1540 (Rome, Da Borgo). A translation into French had occurred before 1540. For the Latin editions, see Schudt (1930), no. 1–48; Pescarzoli (1957), 1:255–63. There is little consistency in the earlier editions. The *Indulgentiae* published in Rome between 1494 and 1504 include lists of indulgences, relics and stations. Another edition, of 1504, omits the separate list of indulgences and introduces a discourse on the Holy House at Loreto. See the copy at the Biblioteca Vittorio Emanuele, Rome.

24. Comparison of *Le cose maravigliose* (Dorico, 1550); the *Mirabilia* (Blado, 1550); and *Le cose maravigliose* (Fontaneto, 1544) shows only slight variations in the text.

25. For example, Stephanus Pighius relied on Leandro Alberti in a similar manner for his guidebook of 1587: "Where Alberti's matter is suitable, Pighius simply translates it; this was not crude plagiarism but in accordance with the best literary practice of the time." De Beer (1942), 60.

26. Palladio's probable contact with Ligorio has been discussed above in chapter one, "Daniele Barbaro and the Trip of 1554." While the map of 1552 may have aided Palladio in his research, it had more bearing on *L'Antichità di Roma* than on *Le Chiese*. The use of archaeological views as stimulus for literary descriptions had at least one precedent. In composing *Roma Instaurata* (1444–46), Flavio Biondo seems to have referred to a map of Rome. Scaglia (1964), 154.

27. Huelsen (1933), 12–14.

28. The city view (Fig. 15) is inscribed: "LA CITTA DI ROMA DELINEATA NEL PONTIFICATO DI PIO IV L'ANNO MDLXII 1562." The sketch is conserved among the Palladio drawings at the RIBA and at one time was connected to his hand. Lanciani (1895), 645–50. Now attributed to Giovanni Antonio Dosio, it is a drawing in pen presumably prepared for the engraver. Frutaz (1962), 2:177. For a discussion of Dosio's connection to the *Forma urbis* and other Roman views, see Dosio (1976), 12–13.

29. For a partial list of the plans issued for the Holy Years, see Huelsen (1933), 10–11, n. 1. For early itineraries and city plans, see Lanciani (1895), 645–46.

30. A reference to an edition of 1555 published by the Roman press of Antonio

Blado appears in Bernoni (1890), 253, 355. No trace of this book has been found. There is also a reference to an edition of 1556 published by Accolti in Puppi (1980), 57. However, this may be a misprint because Puppi, in his informative essay in Cevese (1973, 176), comments on the Accolti edition of 1566.

31. The general organization, presented in this edition of *Le cose maravigliose*, lingered until the 1750s. See Ferrari (1976), 495; Schudt (1971), 26–31.

32. In the Dorico edition of 1558 at the Hertziana, the first page has been damaged. A small woodcut representing St. John the Evangelist (symbol of the Lateran) has been pasted on the verso of the title page. It is difficult to sustain De Beer's observation that "These figures are probably very much more than ornaments; the figures of the Saints evoke the essence of this church," De Beer (1952), 40. See also Barberi (1965), 258. A testimony to the pervasiveness of guidebooks appears in the 1575 deposition of Ottavio di Domenico, a bookseller: "Io, signore, so libraio, cioe che ligo delli Sette Salmi et Mirabilia Rome et altri libricciuoli che servo mastro Marco Amatore a Monte Giordano" Masetti-Zannini (1980), 49.

33. To my knowledge the Vatican Library copy of the 1561 Dorico edition of *Le cose maravigliose* is unique. It is listed erroneously in the card catalogue under *Mirabilia Romana*. This edition resembles that of 1563 in the following passages:

Santa Celi: description inserted between Sant'Anastasio and Santa Maria Annunciata.
Santa Cecilia:account of the oratory is included;
San Crisogono: comes before Santa Maria in Trastevere, account of seven privileged altars is included;
Santa Maria in Traspontina: sentence about crucifix, but not monastery of Carmelites, is included;
Santa Elisabeta: alternate name of Santa Maria in Aquiro is included;
San Trifone: station and head of Santa Ruffina is included (but not Company of Shoemakers);
San Nicola in Carcere: continues after arm of Sant' Alessio, with many other relics;
Sant'Agata: information about titular Cardinalate church is included;
Sant'Antonio: description inserted between San Prassede and San Quirico;
San Giovanni Decollato: description inserted between Santa Maria della Consolazione and Sant'Anastasia (Sant'Alo is not included);
Santa Maria della Navicella: name changed to Santa Maria in Domnica;
San Giorgio: description inserted between Santo Stefano and San Sisto;
Sant'Anastasio: last sentence about heads of martyrs and relics included;

The 1561 edition also brings the list of the popes up to date in ending with Pius IV (1559–65). Schudt mentions a Spanish translation of *Le cose maravigliose* printed in 1561, but he describes the editions published from 1558 to 1562 as identical. Schudt (1930), 30–31, n. 1.

34. Listed in the British Library as a "Fragment of 'Le cose maravigliose dell'alma città di Roma,' consisting of sixteen leaves of the appendix of 'La Guida Romana' with a preface headed: 'L'Autore alli Lettori carissimi' and signed: 'Schakerlay Inglese.'" See "A Sixteenth Century Guidebook" (1902), 204. The typeset, however, differs

from the Dorico editions, and the colophon reads: "Stampata in Roma per Antonio Blado Stampator Cam. l'anno MDLXII."

35. Schudt (1930), no. 62. I have not examined this edition.

36. Despite Schudt's calculation of 132 churches. Schudt (1930), 31.

37. The sets of woodcut illustrations are different. It also should be noted that the Amador edition of 1565 was issued with a copy of *L'Antichità di Roma.* See Borroni (1962), 7904[17]. The Varisco edition of 1565 is erroneously attributed to Franzini in the catalogue of the British Library.

38. For Panvinio, see Huelsen (1927), xxvi–xxvii.

39. He appears in the documents as Francino, Francini, or Franzini. Later he is called "Libraro in Roma al segno della Fonte," but his origins were Venetian. Schudt (1930), 32. See also Barberi (1965), 221. A facsimile reprint of the 1588 edition has been published by Vivarelli e Gulla (Rome, 1973): *Le cose maravigliose dell'alma città di Roma dove si veggono il movimento delle guglie & gli acquedotti per condurre l'Acqua Felice. E si tratta delle chiese rappresentate in disegno da Gieronimo Francino.*

40. The value of these woodcuts was recognized by Armellini who used them as illustrations for his compendium on Roman churches. Armellini (1942), 2 vols. See also Schudt (1930), 32–33.

41. Ashby (1923); Ashby (1925a, 1925b); Waetzoldt (1969), 4–5.

42. For the surge in illustrations between 1587 and 1687, see the account compiled by Waetzoldt (1969), 5–13. Even much later, guidebooks reused the same Francini woodcuts. See for example, *Les Merveilles de la Ville de Rome* (Rome: Ansillion, 1750).

43. Named "Santi Solinori da Monte Sansovino, frate Agostiniano" in a papal bull issued by Sixtus V in 1587. Ashby (1923), 346; Huelsen (1927), xxxiv–xxxv. For Fra Santi and the Guida Angelica, see Schudt (1930), 117.

44. Concerning the woodcut of the obelisk intended for the piazza of Santa Croce in Gerusalemme, see Ashby (1925), 201; Ashby (1923), 345–46.

45. Other additions to the text are noteworthy for insights into recent architectural and artistic projects. See, in particular, the sections on *Santi Faustino e Giovita, Santa Faustina e Iovita, Sant'Antonio.* Some of this new information is mentioned by Schudt (1930), 33.

46. "Et in questa chiesa hora vi si fa un bellissimo solaro." *Le cose maravigliose* (Rome: Giovanni Martinelli, 1589, n.p.). See *Le cose maravigliose*: List of Editions Consulted.

47. For example, the 1594 Zannetti edition reused the frontispiece of the 1589 Martinelli edition, and the 1591 Accolti edition. The woodcuts illustrating the basilicas were identical in the 1591 Accolti, the 1597 Muti and the 1600 Zannetti editions. See *Le cose maravigliose* List of Editions Consulted. For the complex relationships between Roman typographers, see Nardelli (1984).

48. An intriguing example of continued use appears in a copy of the 1589 Martinelli edition (Biblioteca Vaticana). Eleven pages of handwritten notes are dated with the year 1699 and signed by the owner: "Essendo io andato a Roma, a Loreto, et ad Assisi in quest'anno 1699 di molte cose considerate in Roma si ho notato le seguenti.

Io. Gio. Battista di Carlo, di Vicenzo Lando da

Genova Bolognesi Rome 1699/Bologna 1700"

He follows this introduction with a list of sites including a description "Della Cathedra di S. Pietro," ascribed to Bernini. He evidently copied the measurements of certain monuments from a "manuscript" in Rome. Also interesting are the notations in the 1595 Faccioto/Franzini edition belonging to the Newberry Library: This copy fell into the possession of Frederick Ballrillo who notes that he found it in 1864 in a hotel in San Moritz. Next to the description of San Giovanni in Laterano, he remarks: "In 1809 from this balcony the pope Pius IX let fly 2 plenary indulgences papal. I was in the church below and one paper came straight towards me and I *caught it.*"

49. He described *San Giovanni in Laterano, San Pietro* and *San Paolo fuori le Mura.* Significant as well are the sections on *Santa Cecilia, Santa Maria dei Monti, Il Gesù, San Salvatore in Lauro, Santo Salvatore e Santo Stanislai, Sant'Andrea* (in Piazza Siena or delle Valle) and *Santa Maria e San Gregorio in Vallicella.* See the comments by Schudt (1930), 34.

50. Andrea Palladio, *Les Antiquitez et Merveilles di La Ville di Rome,* trans. Pompee de Launay (Arras: Maudhuy, 1612).

51. For Felini, see Waetzoldt (1969), 1–14; Huelsen (1923), xxxviii. Inexplicably, Schudt (1930, pp. 34–37, 233–35) tends to separate the text from the evolution of *Le cose maravigliose.*

52. He also referred to the "libro della vita"—a necrology—in his description of *Santa Balbina* (Trans., p. 110).

Notes to the Translation

1. Palladio thus informs the reader that *L'Antichità di Roma* was already complete. It was published twice in 1554, by Matteo Pagan in Venice and Vincenzo Lucrino in Rome.

2. Much of the information on the history of Rome comes directly from *Le cose maravigliose (Mirabilia Urbis Romae nova recognita* in Latin) or *Le Indulgentie e Reliquie de le chiese de Roma* which Palladio could have consulted in any number of editions published between 1540 and 1550. The source cited for the story of Constantine is Jacobus de Voragine's *Legenda aurea.*

3. The Italian *quarantene* derives from the Latin *quadragenae,* here meaning a period of forty consecutive days.

4. Although Palladio uses the Italian word for copper, he clearly means to identify the metal as bronze. He refers to these columns in the *Quattro Libri*: "This metal [copper] mix'd with tin, lead and brass (which last is only copper coloured with *lapis calaminaris*) makes bronze, or bell-metal, which is often used by architects in making bases, columns, statues and such-like ornaments. There are to be seen in the church of *San Giovanni Laterano* in Rome four brass columns (one of which only has its capital) made by the order of Augustus of the metal that was found in the prows of those ships he had taken in Egypt from Mark Anthony" Palladio (1738), 5.

5. The legend that the pope had to submit to this examination of his masculinity seems to originate in the "Visions of the Dominican Robert D'Usez" (d. 1290). Brewyn (1933), 33.

6. The date of the original foundation of the SS. Sanctorum is unknown but it was renovated in 1278–80. Krautheimer (1980), 211.

7. The Chapel of the Holy Cross was founded by Hilarius III (461–68) and destroyed in 1558. Krautheimer (1980), 50–51.

8. Descriptions from the sixteenth century often mention the bronze tiles of the interior roof. Ciampini (*De sacris aedificiis*) noted their presence in the central nave and transepts. Du Pérac identified their origins as the Temple of Jupiter Capitolinus, the Rotonda or some other ancient monument and recalled their restoration by Benedict II (684–85). Ashby (1916), 31.

9. Two of the bronze peacocks remain with the Pinecone in the semicircular niche of the upper Belvedere, the so-called Garden of the Pine, where the famous monument was moved by Paul V (1605–21). Other statues were reportedly melted down in order to create the Virgin erected on the Column of Santa Maria Maggiore in 1613. Ashby (1916), 39. Debate about the origins of the bronze pine cone persisted during the sixteenth century. Palladio followed the opinion of the medieval chroniclers, most notably in the *Mirabilia*, when he attributed the first location to the cupola of the Pantheon. Legend held that when the Devil hurled the pine cone at San Pietro, it landed in the courtyard. Brewyn (1933), 34. The 1563 edition of *Le Chiese* substituted the more current theory of the pine cone's origins as the Tomb of Hadrian, an idea which, however, found its critics. For example, Du Pérac suggested that it came from the Circus of Nero. Antonio Labacco endorsed this version of the story by citing the authority of Clement VII (1523–34). Ashby (1916), 35–36; Labacco (1552), pl. vi. In actuality, the pine cone had belonged to a fountain near the Serapeum in Campus Martius. It subsequently was installed under a canopy in front of the the the early Christian church of San Pietro where it attracted the attention of travellers during the Renaissance. For an example of a contemporary rendering of the monument, see the sketch executed by Giovanni Antonio Dosio (c. 1565). Dosio (1976), 136–37.

10. Du Pérac also noted that "to the left, on entering the courtyard, is a marble tomb with Emperors Otto II, Honorius and Valentinian II, Augusti" Ashby (1916), 35.

11. The wooden, gilt ceiling is also mentioned by Panvinio (1575).

12. Now attached to the Hospital of the Fatebenefratelli. The order of nuns occupied the convent until 23 November 1573 when, due to serious flooding on the island, they were transferred by Gregory XIII. Ashby (1916, 68) cited the 1568 edition of *Le cose maravigliose*, mistaking it for the first, to confirm the presence of the nuns. Du Pérac mentioned that the Benedictine nuns moved to the Convent of Santa Anna (Santa Maria in Iulia, Santa Anna dei Falegnami or dei Funari) in 1581. He erred in calling this a Jesuit church. Pope Gregory XIII granted it to the Brothers of San Giovanni di Dio (the Fatebenefratelli). Ashby (1925a), 207–9.

13. The mistaken attribution of the foundation to Gelasius II (1118–19) was repeated often, as in the accounts of Andrea Fulvio and Etienne Du Pérac. The confusion may result from a misreading of the inscription over the door which honors Pope Paschal II (1113). Ashby (1916), 68.

14. The severe flood of 1557 caused the destruction of the facade and its mosaics. Restoration took place in 1583 and the facade was rebuilt by Martino Longhi the Younger in 1625. Armellini, 2:621.

15. One of the more "modern" churches mentioned by Palladio, it was founded in 1488–89 (and not in 1419 as indicated by Armellini). The company was organized

in 1492-95. Huelsen (1927), 537. The present day church was rebuilt around 1566 by Guidetto Guidetti. Dosio (1976), 260-61.

16. In the 1563 edition of *Le cose maravigliose*, the description of San Crisogono precedes that of Santa Maria in Trastevere.

17. Also known as Santi Cosmate e Damiani "trans Tiberim" or "in Mica Aurea."

18. It is curious that Palladio neglected to mention the name of Raphael whose *Transfiguration* was installed on the high altar in 1523.

19. In 1518, Sebastiano Luciani (del Piombo), a protege of Michelangelo, painted the *Flagellation* for the chapel of Pier Francesco Borgherini.

20. It is indicative of Palladio's circumscribed objectives that he did not even mention Bramante's name when referring to the *Tempietto*.

21. An early reference to the Chapel of San Paolo inside the church. Giorgio Vasari designed the architecture, completed in 1552, and painted the altarpiece. The tombs of Cardinal Antonio del Monte (d. 1533) and Vincenzo del Monte (d. 1504) were sculpted by Bartolommeo Ammannati. The sculptural program was completed in 1553-55, but Palladio's account confirms that the Tomb of the Cardinal was finished by 1554. For discussion of the commission, see Pietrangeli, *Trastevere* 1:170.

22. Known as Santa Maria in Saxia, or Sassia, during the Middle Ages. Here Palladio refers to the rebuilding of the church by Antonio da Sangallo from 1538-44.

23. A reference to any of the following institutions: Sant'Angelo de Castro S. Angeli (founded in the seventh century, but not mentioned again in sources after the fourteenth century), S. Angeli prope Castellum S. Angeli (thus named in the Catalogue of 1555 and perhaps the same as Sant'Angelo in Burgo—its name in 1492—or Sant'Angelo in Corridoio), Sant'Angelo propre S. Petrum in civitate Leonina (destroyed in the late eighteenth century—otherwise first mentioned in 1555—situated outside the Gate of the Cavalleggieri). Huelsen (1927), 196, 527. The story of its foundation by Gregory the Great and the apparition of the archangel Michael appears in the *Mirabilia Urbis Romae*.

24. Probably founded under Eugenius IV c. 1439. Now called Santo Stefano degli Abissini or dei Mori. Huelsen (1927), 447-78.

25. The earliest known reference to the name of San Lazzaro (degli leprosi) which later appears in the List of Pius V 1566. Located on Via Trionfale, the same church was formerly called Santa Maria Magdalena. Huelsen (1927), 379-80.

26. Situated at the entrance to San Pietro, it was demolished under Alexander VII in 1659. Huelsen (1927), 235-36.

27. Represented in Dosio's view of 1564. Egger, 1:22. The demolition of the church took place in the same year due to the fortifications for Castel Sant'Angelo commissioned by Pius IV. It was reconstructed in the Borgo Nuovo and completed in 1566. Huelsen (1927), 370-71.

28. The earliest known reference to Sant'Andrea Rotundi, a centralized church designed by Vignola for Julius III. Huelsen (1927), 527; Schudt (1930), 28.

29. Founded by the Confraternity of San Giacomo degli Incurabili in 1525. Andrea Fulvio referred to a chapel situated by the interior of the Aurelian walls which had earlier housed a miraculous Madonna. Huelsen (1927), 537-38.

30. Actually founded by Charles VIII, king of France. Existence first documented in 1492. Huelsen (1927), 543.

31. Sant'Ambrogio dei Lombardi, founded by Sixtus IV in 1471. Replaced the former San Nicolai de Tofo. The church was rebuilt as San Carlo a Corso from 1612–19. Huelsen (1927), 407.

32. The earliest record of the existence of the church. See Schudt (1930), 28.

33. Also known as Santa Lucia delle Convertite during the sixteenth century. Demolished during the eighteenth century. Huelsen (1927), 302.

34. In the 1563 edition of *Le cose maravigliose*, the four preceding names are omitted.

35. The Oratory of the Crucifix, attached to San Marcello, was built c. 1568 after the designs of Vignola. Dosio (1976), 262–63.

36. Thus Palladio's erroneous identification of the column stands corrected in the edition of 1563.

37. The present church of Santa Marta at the Collegio Romano was not founded until 1561. The catalogue of Pius V (1566) lists the Convent of the Malmaritate as closed. Huelsen (1927), 540.

38. The name of Santa Maria Alteriorum was still in use in 1551 as indicated on Bufalini's map. The catalogue of Pius V (1566) lists the church as the property of the Jesuits. Huelsen (1927), 313–14. Rebuilding of the church began in 1568.

39. Designated a cardinalate church in 1557 by Paul IV. Pietrangeli, *Pigna* 2:54.

40. Called Santa Maria ad Martiri before AD 1000. It was dedicated by Boniface IV in 609. Krautheimer (1980), 72.

41. Santa Maria in Aquiro was the name of the old church. Huelsen (1927), 310.

42. San Trifone often is mentioned in connection with Sant'Agostino after 1470. Enlargement of the convent of Sant'Agostino brought about the demolition of the church in the eighteenth century. Huelsen (1927), 495, 528.

43. In 1519, Leo X entrusted the church to the Company of the Pietà dei Fiorentini who began the reconstruction. Huelsen (1927), 410–11. When Palladio mentions that it was built in a hurry, he must be referring to the early stage of the rebuilding, in 1520–21. Work then came to a halt until Giacomo della Porta took over in 1583–1602. Pietrangeli, *Ponte* 4:16.

44. A reference to the Palazzo dei Tribunali, designed by Bramante but never completed. The later name of the Palace of Religion recalls the building's function as the seat of the Curia. Note that Palladio does not refer to Bramante's plan for the church of San Biagio della Pagnotta (beg. 1508), although he sketched the project, but rather to an earlier foundation. For the drawing, see Lewis (1981), 54. In 1575, construction began on SS. Faustino e Giovita dei Bresciani which would replace Bramante's unfinished church. Dosio (1976), 147.

45. An early reference to "la chiesa della morte," as it was called in 1566. Armellini (1942), 1:512.

46. Cardinal Raffaelle Riario began the reconstruction of the palace as well as of the church in 1486. Armellini (1940), 1:458.

47. Also known as San Martino ai Pelamantelli, formerly located near the Ponte Sisto. Demolished during the eighteenth century. Huelsen (1927), 383.

48. The original church was destroyed in 1639. Huelsen (1927), 434.

49. Located near the Ponte Sisto. Destroyed c. 1888. Huelsen (1927), 173. Conceded by Paul III to the Confraternity of the Cooks and Pasticcieri in 1537. Armellini (1940), 2:1236.

50. San Tommaso della Catena, or degli Spagnoli, was close to the Palazzo Farnese. Now called San Petronio dei Bolognesi. Huelsen (1927), 492.

51. Santa Caterina alli Cenci. The earliest mention of this lost church which also appears in the 1566 catalogue of Pius V. Huelsen (1927), 530.

52. San Tommaso degli Inglesi or, after 1575, also called San Tommaso di Canterbury. Huelsen (1927), 493–94.

53. Sant'Andrea a Corte Savella was demolished in 1573. Huelsen (1927), 178–79.

54. Destroyed c. 1870. Huelsen (1927), 482.

55. A church of a cruciform plan designed by Bramante. It was begun c. 1509, but left incomplete. Later demolished.

56. Commissioned by Cardinal Federico Cesi in 1544. Armellini (1940), 2:696. The present church was built by Guidetto Guidetti in 1560–64. See the drawing of the facade by Dosio (1976), 258–59.

57. Mentioned in the *Mirabilia urbis Romae*, San Lorenzo in Miranda was built into the ruins of the Temple of Antoninus and Faustina. In 1430, Martin V gave it to the College of the Apothecaries or Pharmacists. Huelsen (1927), 288.

58. One of the few contemporary works noted by Palladio, the *Moses* appears in all later editions of *Le cose maravigliose*.

59. Formerly near the "Trofei di Mario," at the present site of Piazza Vittorio Emanuele. Destroyed 1874. Huelsen (1927), 279.

60. Given to the Celestines during the fifteenth century. Transferred to the Jesuit Order in 1820. Pietrangeli, *Esquilino*, 28.

61. Given to the Guild of Painters, or Company of San Luca, by Sixtus IV. Joined to Santa Martina when the original structure was demolished during the renovation of the Piazza of Santa Maria Maggiore under Sixtus V. Huelsen (1927), 299–300.

62. The Church of Sant'Antonio Abate, founded in 1308 according to Armellini (1940), 2:1006–7. The contiguous hospital was reconstructed by Pius V (1559–65), probably accounting for the inclusion of the church in later editions of *Le cose maravigliose*. It already had been mentioned in the edition of 1561. For the history of the church, see Pietrangeli, *Esquilino*, 80–92.

63. A complete and unusual account of the foundation of Santa Maria degli Angeli. Michelangelo's sketches for the project date from 1560–63. Ashby (1916), figs. 72, 73. Construction began in 1561, and ended in 1564 with the death of Michelangelo. This is one of the earliest records of the existence of the church which otherwise made its way into travel literature with the Catalogue of the Anonimo Spagnuolo of c. 1570. Huelsen (1927), 535.

64. Destroyed in 1900 due to the excavation of Santa Maria Antiqua.

65. The same description of San Giovanni Decollato appears in the 1561 edition of *Le cose maravigliose*.

66. Formerly, San Iacobo d'Altopascio. Rebuilt as Sant'Eligio in 1562. Huelsen (1927), 264.

67. *Le cose maravigliose* of 1575, published by Degli Angeli, mentions a new tabernacle of 1573 and the visit of Gregory XIII.

68. The designation of "Navicella" arises during the sixteenth century.

69. This description appears also in *Le cose maravigliose* of 1561.

70. All of the aforementioned relics, as well as the papal palace, were noted by

Du Pérac in 1581 who adds that the palace was let to the Ruffini family by Paul III. Ashby (1916), 3.

71. Du Pérac repeats the story of the Devil throwing the stone at San Domenico. He also describes the stone at the high altar as "of Lucullan marble . . . an ancient weight of the Romans" Ashby (1916), 3.

72. The legend holds that Alessio married the emperor's daughter, fled to Palestine on his wedding day and returned as a beggar in disguise to live under the stairs until his death. Related by Du Pérac. Ashby (1916), 3. The painting of the miraculous Madonna is still there.

73. The Gerolomitani, or Hermits of San Girolamo, were installed by Martin V in 1426.

74. Santi Vincenzo e Anastasio near the Tre Fontane.

75. Santa Maria Scala Coeli near the Tre Fontane. The description also appeared in *Le cose maravigliose* of 1561.

Notes to *La guida romana*, Introduction

1. For the assimilation of Palladio's *Le Chiese* and *La guida romana* into *Le cose maravigliose*, see Ferrari (1976), 481–82; Schudt (1930), 26–31.

2. The text may be dated on internal evidence because of the reference to damage, presumably the flood of 15 September, in the area of Santa Maria sopra Minerva (Trans., *La guida romana*, 136). The list of popes also provides a terminus postquem by the inclusion of Paul IV, elected in 1555. There is no evidence of an earlier edition of *La guida romana*. The reference to a 1555 edition of *Le cose maravigliose* published by Blado is possibly a mistake. Bernoni (1890), 253, 355. The first known edition, the Dorico of 1557, belongs to the Bibliotheca Hertziana. Listed as "Besitz der Firma Leo S. Olschki," by Schudt (1930), 198. See also Peddie (1948), 694; Borroni (1962), 38–39. The itineraries in *La guida romana* are described by Dickinson (1960), 41–65.

3. Schudt (1930), 30–31, nos. 59, 161; Peddie (1948), 694; Borroni (1962), 50–51. Blado (Rome) published a Spanish translation of the *Mirabilia urbis Romae* in 1561.

4. Blado's name and the date appear in the colophon. See "A Sixteenth Century Guidebook" (1902), 204. Also Schudt (1930), 28–31, no. 60; Borroni (1962), 39. The *British Museum Short Title Catalogue* lists this edition erroneously as G. Franzini.

5. Ashby (1925a, 204–5) refers to the revisions in the 1566 edition, but later acknowledges the edition of 1563 (1925b, 38–39).

6. It was not updated again until the Francini (Venice) edition of 1588. That text remained the standard one until 1600 when three Roman publishers (Zannetti, Fei-Facchetti and Giovanni Francini) all issued a new version. An illustrated *La guida romana* appears in the *Descrizione di Roma antica e moderna* (Rome: G. Fei, 1650). The latest edition of *La guida romana* that I have located is in a French translation in *Les Marveilles de la Ville de Rome* (Rome: Ansillion, 1750) with eight woodcut illustrations.

7. Panvinio includes a curious reference to the work of the German author "Hermundus" whom he praises but who must remain anonymous because his book was on the list of "Librorum prohibitorum incidis." "Onuphrii Panvinii" (1842), 657.

8. Published by Blado (Rome) and catalogued in the British Museum as Shaker-

ley, "A Fragment of Le cose maravigliose" (1562), 8 o, Voyn. 36. See also "A Sixteenth
Century Guidebook" (1902), 204; Ashby (1925a), 201–6.

9. The anonymous notice in the copy of *La guida romana* at the British Library
calls Schakerlay a "wealthy tourist."

10. The assumption of the author of "A Sixteenth Century Guidebook" (1902),
204. The identification is repeated in Einstein (1902), 387; Ashby (1925a), 202.

11. Unfortunately the editor gives no source for this identification. Martin (1969),
xxvi.

12. For the English tourists and wardens lodging at the Hospice, see Foley (1880),
xxxi. The Pilgrim Book does not begin until 29 December 1580. Gasquet (1920),
53–60. For a discussion of English Catholics in Rome, see Einstein (1902), 373–79.

13. Evident already during the Holy Year of 1575. Pollen (1906), 63–65.

14. Frank (1953), 97–98.

15. Parks (1963), ix–xxvii, 23–53; Einstein (1902), 135–37.

16. Munday (1966), 40.

17. "I have gone in their company [the English students] as it is a custome and
an order among them, to goe from Church to Church all the Lent time, to the Stations as they call them, and then each day in Lent, one Church or other hath their
Reliques abroade to be seene. And then they tell the people, this is the Reliques of
such a Saint, and this is such a holy and blessed thing: but they be either covered
with Gold, Silver or Christall, so that we can not tell whether there be anything within or no, except it bee sometime in a broade Christall Tabernacle, and there you
shall see a company of rotten bones, God knowes of what they be" Munday (1966), 51.

18. Moryson (1907), 260. See also Bates (1911), 111.

19. Martin (1969), ix–xxviii.

20. See the diary of Henry Piers who visited Rome in 1595 and used the latest
edition of *Le cose maravigliose*. Frank (1953), 128–29, n. 80.

21. Capgrave (1911).

22. Frank (1953), 103–4. British travellers also had access to Bartolomeo Marliano's
Topographia antiquae Romae which was available in England by mid-century, with an
English translation appearing in 1600. Einstein (1902), 115–47, 386–87.

23. *Harleian Miscellany* (1810), 21. For the author of this late Elizabethan account,
see Frank (1953), 108.

24. Moryson (1907), 284.

25. Montaigne (1929), 131.

26. Moryson (1907), 259. An English tourist of the late sixteenth century also noted
the easy availability of guides in Rome. *Harleian Miscellany* (1810), 16.

27. For commerce in church plans, see the testimony of Nicholas Flute in the 1590s.
Frank (1953), 114.

28. Despite the extra day, Fynes clearly followed the route outlined in *La guida
romana*. He also accompanied his tour of Rome with a city plan "drawn rudely, but
so as to serve the Reader to understand the situation of the monuments." Moryson
(1907), 274–96.

29. *Harleian Miscellany* (1810), 16.

30. The configuration of lodgings and taverns in the city center is discussed by
Romani (1948), 67–69. The inns recommended by the traveller of the *Harleian*

Miscellany (1810, 16) were the "Black Bear" or the "Sword of Monte Gior-dano."

31. Apparently a longstanding tradition as indicated in Flavio Biondo's *Roma In-staurata* (1444-46).

32. *Harleian Miscellany* (1810), 27.

33. Montaigne (1929), 161.

34. For an excellent view of the *vigne* scattered about the Roman landscape, consult the Maggi-Maupin plan of 1625. Frutaz (1962), 2, pl. 307. For the collections of statuary in the *vigne*, see Huelsen (1917), v–xiii; Coffin (1979), vii–viii, 16–22.

Notes to *La guida romana*, Translation

1. The 1563 edition of *Le cose maravigliose* omits the author's introduction and begins with "Of the Borgo. . . ."

2. Clause omitted from the 1563 edition of *Le cose maravigliose*.

3. Otherwise known as the Ponte Neronianus. For the route of the ancient Via Triumphalis, see Valentini/Zucchetti (1953), 1:26, 159.

4. A reference to the depiction of the pine cone, showing its situation in antiquity, on Filarete's doors to San Pietro. Note that Schakerlay does not mention the legendary account reported by Palladio in *Le Chiese* (Trans., 000). The text after "the tomb of the emperor Hadrian" was replaced in the 1563 edition of *Le cose maravigliose*.

5. The collection of ancient statuary displayed in the Vatican Belvedere included the Laocoön (excavated in 1506) and the Cleopatra (installed in a grotto c. 1555).

6. Previous clause omitted in the 1563 edition of *Le cose maravigliose*.

7. Previous clause omitted in the 1563 edition of *Le cose maravigliose*.

8. The "new" bridge resulted from restorations to the Ponte Rotto made by Nanni di Baccio Bigio in 1551. Ruined in the flood of 1557. Dosio (1976), 101–2.

9. Word omitted in the 1563 edition of *Le cose maravigliose*.

10. Near the site of the Jewish ghetto, as it existed in 1555. Du Pérac's map of 1577 shows that the walls and gates extended from the Ponte Fabricio to Piazza Cenci. See Gnoli (1984), 122–23. For a traveller's account, see Martin (1969), 300.

11. The wealthy Cesarini family maintained a city residence and properties in the countryside. Cardinal Giuliano Cesarini (elev. 1493, d. 1510) collected antiquities. Giovanni Giorgio Cesarini maintained a famous collection of sculpture. The family acquired their palace from the Sforza; it had been constructed for Cardinal Rodrigo Borgia, later Alexander VI. Rebuilt in the 1700s. In 1580-81, Montaigne (1929, 169) admired the antique busts but also the modern portraits of Roman women such as Cesarini's wife, Clelia-Fascia Farnese. Schakerlay probably refers to a Giuliano Cesarini, documented in 1531 and 1560, and to the property in the "prati di Testaccio." In 1557, Aldrovandi lists antiquities in the "Casa del S. Giuliano Cesarini, nella strada de' Cesarini," and "nel giardino del S. Giuliano Cesarini che non è molto da la casa lunghi. . . ." Mauro (1557), 221–24.

12. The destruction of the Septizonium was ordered by Sixtus V in 1589. Gnoli (1984), 300.

13. Known as the Baths of Caracalla. First explored under Paul III (1534–49). Nash (1961), 2:434.

14. Word omitted in the 1563 edition of *Le cose maravigliose*.

15. The site of the amphitheater for the army barracks. Marked "Collosseum" on Du Pérac's map of 1577. Parks (1963), 35. The Theatre of Statilius Taurus had been located in the Campo Marzio. Valentini/Zucchetti (1953), 4:280, n. 3.

16. Last clause omitted in the 1563 edition of *Le cose maravigliose*.

17. Once on the site of the present-day Piazza Vittorio Emanuele II. The so-called Trophies of Mars were identified as a monument to Caius Marius' victory, explaining the shields and trophies displayed there. It really served as a fountain for the Acqua Julia, an aqueduct built in 33 B.C. and restored under Augustus, A.D. 11–14. Gnoli (1984), 338; Dosio (1976), 84.

18. Designation of Santa Maria Maggiore omitted in the 1563 edition of *Le cose maravigliose*.

19. Final sentence omitted in the 1563 edition of *Le cose maravigliose*.

20. Heading omitted in the 1563 edition of *Le cose maravigliose*.

21. Last phrase omitted in the 1563 edition of *Le cose maravigliose*.

22. Two previous words omitted in the 1563 text of *Le cose maravigliose*.

23. Previous clause omitted in the 1563 edition of *Le cose maravigliose*.

24. Word omitted in the 1563 edition of *Le cose maravigliose*.

25. The Quirinal was named Monte Cavallo after the statues of Castor and Pollux, or the Dioscuri (the Horse-Tamers) then located between the Baths of Constantine and the Temple of Serapis. Bober/Rubinstein (1986), 159–61; Gnoli (1984), 174; Parks (1963), 28.

26. The Boccaccios, father and son, were among the first to restore the Quirinal during the fifteenth century. They had a collection of antiquities, and their gardens were adjacent to those of the d'Este which Schakerlay already had mentioned. A document of 17 August 1565 cites the *vigna* of the Bertina, formerly belonging to the Boccaccios and then the Cesi. Lanciani (1902–7), 1:139. The Baths of Constantine were still standing. The northern sections were demolished c. 1570, and the remains to the south were destroyed in 1611–12 under Paul V. Nash (1961), 442.

27. Although he undoubtedly exaggerates their length, Schakerlay's account of tunnels below the Baths of Diocletian is not as peculiar as it would first appear. That an extensive substructure remained intact is proven by an unknown French architect who sketched a lower level forming the original system of furnaces for the baths. Such passages extended in front of the Baths at least as far as the middle of the present Piazza Esedra. Salvetti (1970), 462–66. There had long been archaeological interest in the area. Bartolomeo Marliano recorded excavations in 1534, and serious work began in 1542. Lanciani (1902–7), 2:135–44. Construction of Santa Maria degli Angeli, of course, did not start until 1561. It is likely that the author's earlier reference to the king of France resulted from his familiarity with the nearby site of the villa of Cardinal Jean du Bellay (d. 1560).

28. This *vigna* lay on the western slope of the Quirinal, to the north of the "Alta Semita." It was developed by Cardinal Oliviero Carafa whose family rented it to Cardinal Ippolito II d'Este of Ferrara from 1550–55. The *vigna* was acquired and enlarged by d'Este during the 1560s. Coffin (1979), 202–3. Statuary from the Vatican was trans-

ferred from the Belvedere to the Quirinal in 1566, and from the Capitoline in 1568, 1569. Lanciani (1902-7), 1:81-83, 139. The *vigna* of the cardinal of Ferrara appears on Ligorio's map of 1552 as does that of the cardinal of Carpi. Frutaz (1962), vol. 2, pl. 222.

29. The cardinal Rodolfo Pio da Carpi was a renowned collector who divided his antiquities between his palace and *vigna*, the site of his larger pieces. Coffin (1979), 195-99. They attracted the following visitors: c. 1550, Giovanni Antonio Dosio sketched the base of a candelabrum with the inscription: "Alla vignia di Carpi" Huelsen (1933), 16; Lucio Mauro mentions antiquities in the palace and *vigna* in his prologue published in 1557; Aldrovandi, in the same work, lists ancient sculpture in the palace at Campo Marzio and the *vigna* on the Quirinal. Mauro (1557), 201-212, 295-303; Huelsen (1917), 43-84. The cardinal of Carpi sold his *vigna* to Cardinal Giulio Feltrio della Rovere of Urbino in 1565. It was adjacent to the Grimani gardens at the Quattro Fontane. Lanciani (1902-7), 1:139; Bober/Rubinstein (1986), 471-71.

30. The Tomb of Santa Costanza, daughter of Constantine. The church was mistaken frequently as the Temple of Bacchus during the sixteenth century. Dosio (1976), 68-69.

31. Pius IV had given the land around the Baths of Diocletian to the Carthusians of Santa Croce in Gerusalemme in 1561. Michelangelo was named architect on 27 July 1561. The nave of the church was built from 1563-66. Dosio (1976), 40.

32. Word omitted in the 1563 edition of *Le cose maravigliose.*

33. Word omitted in the 1563 edition of *Le cose maravigliose.*

34. Word omitted in the 1563 edition of *Le cose maravigliose.*

35. The Arch of Titus.

36. Word omitted in the 1563 edition of *Le cose maravigliose.*

37. The Basilica of Maxentius and Constantine was called the Temple of Peace by many Renaissance travellers. To name a few: Nicholas Muffel, Andrea Fulvio, Bartolomeo Marliano, Fra Mariano da Firenze. Dosio (1976), 51-52; Valentini/Zucchetti (1953), 4:234, n. 2.

38. Phrase omitted in the 1563 edition of *Le cose maravigliose.*

39. Ranuccio Farnese, Cardinal of Sant'Angelo (d. 1565). The Farnese family first acquired land on the Palatine under Paul III. The *vigna* on the side facing the Via Sacra belonged to the Maddaleni di Capodiferro in 1536. It was sold to the Farnese in 1542. Adjacent was the *vigna* of the Palosci (1500), later the Cesarini (1537); it too passed to the Farnese in 1565. Lanciani (1902-7), 2:34.

40. Phrase omitted in the 1563 edition of *Le cose maravigliose.*

41. The change to the present tense probably reflects the excavation of the Arch of Septimius Severus carried out under Pius IV in 1563. Dosio (1976), 30.

42. Until 1588, the colossal statue was on a street of the same name near the Mamertine Prison. It was moved to Piazza San Marco and, by 1595, to the Capitoline. Bartolomeo Marliano composed an inscription for the original site, now in the Capitoline Museum: "Hic aliqua(n)do insigne / marmoreu(m) simulacru(m) fuit / quodvulgus ob Martis Foru(m) / Marforium / nuncupavit / in Capitoliu(m) ubi nu(n)c est tra(n)slatu(m)" Pietrangeli, *Campitelli* (1967), 1:77-78.

43. Schakerlay notes eight columns, to be corrected in the 1563 edition of *Le cose maravigliose* as three. But the Temple of Concord, situated just below the Capitoline,

had ten columns across the portico. Instead, the three columns belonged to the Temple of Vespasian. Pietrangeli, *Campitelli* (1967), 1:98–100.

44. The Savelli Palace on Piazza Montanara, later known as the Orsini Palace, was built into the ruins of the Theater of Marcellus. It was designed by Baldassare Peruzzi. Cardinal Savelli was appointed Vicar General of Rome in 1564. He had a renowned collection of antiquities, as indicated by artists' sketches and literary descriptions. Huelsen (1917), 39; Mauro (1557), 232–34.

45. The Orsini Palace, located on the Piazza del Biscione near the Campo dei Fiori, was built in the mid-fifteenth century. It rose over the ruins of the Theater of Pompei. Lanciani (1902–7), 1:174–75. The famous collection of statuary and paintings is noted by Albertini (1510), vol. 3, n. pag.

46. The Spada Palace, originally built for Cardinal Girolamo Capodiferro c. 1540. It housed famous antiquities.

47. Thus the 1563 edition of *Le cose maravigliose* corrects Schakerlay's unexplained omission of the Farnese Palace. Construction had already begun, under Paul III, in 1542. An inventory of 1568 demonstrates the scope of the collection of antiquities of which Onofrio Panvinio (d. 1569) was the custodian. Lanciani (1902–7), 2:153–67. The statuary is also described by Aldrovandi in 1557. Mauro (1557), 145–59.

48. Previous two sentences omitted in the 1563 edition of *Le cose maravigliose*.

49. The Column of Marcus Aurelius, often called the Antonine Column by sixteenth-century authors. See Dosio (1976), 77–78. The height and number of steps, of this column and Trajan's, also appear in the *Mirabilia urbis Romae*.

50. The final clause is omitted in the 1563 edition of *Le cose maravigliose*. The "Macel dei Corvi" was located near the foot of the Capitoline, at the head of the former Via di Marforio, marked today by the Clivus Argentarius. Pietrangeli, *Campitelli* (1967), 1:74. Inside the structure, an ancient relief attracted Giovanni Antonio Dosio: "Di marmo antico, murato in un cortile al Macello de' Corvi. . . ." Huelsen (1933), 17.

51. The entrance at the base of the column was discovered in 1536. Dosio (1976), 54.

52. The reference to destruction may reflect the flooding which plagued the area around the Pantheon. A tablet at Santa Maria sopra Minerva records damage from a flood in 1530. Another plaque recalls the disastrous flood of 15 September 1557. Pietrangeli, *Pigna* (1967), 2:56–58. A drawing by Dosio of the Ponte Rotto records damage from the flood. Huelsen (1933), 70.

53. His collection did indeed include fragments of painting as well as sculpture. Some objects reportedly were excavated from the Sette Sale, the Baths of Trajan. Lanciani (1902–7), 2:223–24. Aldrovandi also notes the antiquities "in Monte Citorio nel palazzo de Reverendiss. di Gaddi, e nella Camera di M. Girolamo Garimberto." The courtesy of the collector was exceptional for this author too adds: "Se alcun gentilhuomo si degnerà andar alle sue camere, li sarà mostrato ogni cosa cortesemente dal sudetto M. Girolamo, come'egli ha fatto a me." Mauro (1557), 188, 190.

54. Clause omitted in the 1563 edition of *Le cose maravigliose*.

55. Three previous words omitted in the 1563 edition of *Le cose maravigliose*.

56. Clause omitted in the 1563 edition of *Le cose maravigliose*.

57. No mention was made of the House of the Orsini in the 1563 edition of *Le cose maravigliose*.

58. The Orsini Palace in Agone, commissioned in 1435. Although the excavation

of the statue of Pasquino has been associated with the Orsini family constructions, the popular figure was probably resurrected by Cardinal Oliviero Carafa. Lanciani (1902–7), 1:54.

59. A reference to the nymphaeum at the Villa Giulia designed by Bartolomeo Ammannati and fed by the Acqua Vergine. In 1552, another fountain, designed by Vignola, was built for public use on the corner of the road from Rome. The Villa on Via Flaminia was constructed from May 1551 to March 1555 for Pope Julius III. After his death, the land was sequestered but Pius IV, in 1559, attempted to restore the grounds. The sculpture was not dispersed until 1569. Coffin (1979), 151–74.

60. The text which follows appeared only in the original edition of *Le cose maravigliose*.

61. Probably a reference to the Adonis in the house of the bishop of Aquino which was also singled out by Montaigne (1929), 166.

62. The Palace of San Giorgio was commissioned by Cardinal Raffaele Riario (d. 1521) who was a collector of ancient sculpture. Pietrangeli, *Parione* (1967), 2:74. By 1557, when Aldrovandi compiled his description of these antiquities, the site was called: "Palagio di S. Giorgio, dove la Cancelleria presso a Campo di Fiore." Mauro (1557), 165–67.

63. Cardinal Giovanni Ricci of Montepulciano maintained a distinguished collection. He resided in the Sacchetti Palace on the Via Giulia, which he bought in 1552. See Celio (1967), 97, 129. Construction of his villa on the Pincio, the present Villa Medici, was not underway until 1564. In 1569, Pius V presented the cardinal with antiquities sequestered from the Villa Giulia, the Belvedere and the Casino of Pius IV. Coffin (1979), 174.

64. Schakerlay is unusual in commenting on respectable women in contrast to his countrymen who, like William Thomas in 1549, were preoccupied with Roman prostitutes. Parks (1963), 50.

65. A reference to Santa Costanza. See above, n. 30.

BIBLIOGRAPHY

Alberigo, G. "Daniele Barbaro." In *Dizionario biografico degli Italiani*. Rome, 1964, 6:89–95.

Albertini, Francesco. *Opusculum de mirabilibus novae & veteris urbis Romae*. Rome: Mazochio, 1510.

Armellini, Mariano. *Le chiese di Roma dal secolo IV al XIX*. 2 vols. Edited by Carlo Cecchelli. Rome: Ruffolo, 1942.

Ascarelli, Fernanda. *La tipografia cinquecentina italiana*. Florence: Sansoni, 1953.

———. *Le cinquecentine romana; censimento delle edizioni romani del XVI secolo possedute dalle biblioteche di Roma*. Milan: Etimar, 1972.

Ashby, Thomas, ed. *Topographical Study in Rome in 1581; A Series of Views with Fragmentary Text by Etienne Du Pérac*. London: J. B. Nichols, 1916.

———. "Note sulle varie guide di Roma che contengono xilografie di Girolamo Franzini." *Roma* 1 (1923): 345–52.

———. "Nuove note su varie guide di Roma." *Roma* 2 (1925a): 201–9.

———. "Note sulle 'Cose maravigliose'" *Roma* 3 (1925b): 38–39.

Barberi, Francesco. *Paolo Manuzio e la stamperia del popolo romano (1561–70)*. Rome: Cuggiani, 1942.

———. "I Dorico, tipografi a Roma nel cinquecento." In *La Bibliofilia* 67 (1965): 221–61.

Barbieri, Franco. "Giangiorgio Trissino e Andrea Palladio." In *Convegno di studi su Giangiorgio Trissino*. Edited by Neri Pozza. Vicenza: Accademia Olimpica, 1980, 191–211.

Barbieri, Giuseppe. "La natura discendente: Daniele Barbaro, Andrea Palladio e l'arte della memoria." In *Palladio e Venezia*. Edited by Lionello Puppi. Firenze: Sansoni, 1982, 29–54.

Barichella, Vittorio. *Andrea Palladio e la sua scuola*. Lonigo: Gaspari, 1880.

Bassi, Elena. "Attività del Palladio all'Ospedaletto." *Bollettino del CISA* 20 (1978): 113–28.

Bates, Ernest. *Touring in 1600*. Boston: Houghton Mifflin, 1911.

Bellini, Paolo. "Printmakers and Dealers in Italy during the 16th and 17th Centuries." *Print Collector* 13 (1975): 17–45.

Berger, Ursel. *Palladios Frühwerk; Bauten und Zeichnungen.* Cologne: Bohlau, 1978.

Bernoni, Domenico. *Dei Torresani, Blado e Ragazzoni.* Milan: Hoepli, 1890.

Bertolotti, A. "Speserie segrete e pubbliche di Papa Paolo III." In *Atti e memorie delle RR deputazioni di storia patria per le provincie dell'Emilia.* N.S. 3 (1878), 1:169–212.

Bober, Phyllis and Ruth Rubinstein. *Renaissance Artists and Antique Sculpture.* London: Harvey Miller, 1986.

Borroni, Fabia. "Il Cicognara." In *Bibliografia dell'archeologia classica e dell'arte italiana.* Vol. 2, pt. 4, Florence: Sansoni, 1962.

Boucher, Bruce. "The Last Will of Daniele Barbaro." Journal of the Warburg and Courtauld Institutes 42 (1979): 277–82.

Brewyn, William. *A XVth-Century Guide-book to the Principal Churches of Rome.* Translated by C. E. Woodruff. London: The Marshall Press, 1933.

Bruschi, Arnaldo. "Bramante, Raffaello e Palladio." *Bollettino del CISA* 15 (1973): 69–87.

———. *Bramante.* London: Thames and Hudson, 1977.

Burlington, Richard Boyle, Third Earl of. *The Fabbriche Antiche of Andrea Palladio.* London: 1730; Farnborough: Gregg, 1969.

Burns, Howard. "I disegni di Palladio." *Bollettino del CISA* 15 (1973): 169–91.

Burns, Howard et al. *Andrea Palladio 1508 –80; The Portico and the Farmyard.* London: The Arts Council of Great Britain, 1975.

Capgrave, John. *Ye Solace of Pilgrims.* Edited by C. A. Mills. London: Oxford University Press, 1911.

Castellani, Guiseppe. "La tipografia del Collegio Romano." *Archivum Historicum Societatis Iesu* 2 (1933): 11–16.

Castelli, Pierfilippo. *La vita di Giangiorgio Trissino.* Venice: Giovanni Radici, 1753.

Celio, Gaspare. *Memorie delli nomi dell'artefici delle pitture che sono in alcune chiese, facciate, e palazzi di Roma.* Introduced by Emma Zocca. Milan: Electa, 1967 (facsimile reprint of Naples, 1638 ed.).

Cevese, Renato, ed. *Mostra del Palladio.* Milan/Venice: Electa Editrice, 1973.

Chastel, André and G. Vallet, eds. *Le Palais Farnèse.* 2 vols. Rome: École Francaise de Rome, 1981.

Coffin, David. *The Villa in the Life of Renaissance Rome.* Princeton: Princeton University Press, 1979.

Le cose maravigliose dell'alma città di Roma. Venice: Franzini, 1588; reprinted Rome: Vivarelli e Gulla, 1973.

De Angelis d'Ossat, Guglielmo. "Inedito palladiano e palazzetto romano." *Strenna dei romanisti* 20 (1959): 57–59.

De Beer, E. S. "Francois Schott's *Itinerario d'Italia.*" *The Library* 23 (1942): 57–83.

———. "The Development of the Guide-Book until the Early Nineteenth Century." *Journal of the British Archaeological Association.* 3rd Ser. 15 (1952): 35–46.

De Frede, Carlo. "La stampa nel cinquecento e la diffusione della Riforma in Italia." *Atti della Accademia Pontaniana.* n.s. 13 (1964): 87–91.

Dickinson, G. *Du Bellay in Rome.* Leiden: E. J. Brill, 1969.

Dorez, Léon. *La Cour du Pape Paul III,* 3 vols. Paris: Ernest Leroux, 1932.

Dosio, Giovanni Antonio. *Roma antica e i disegni di architettura agli Uffizi.* Edited by Franco Borsi et al. Rome: Officina Edizioni, 1976.

Egger, Herman. *Römische Veduten: Handzeichnungen aus dem XV -XVIII Jahrhundert.* 2nd ed. 4 vols. Vienna: A. Schroll, 1932.

Einstein, Lewis. *The Italian Renaissance in England.* New York: Columbia University Press, 1902; reprinted 1935.

Ellero, Giuseppe. "Interventi di Palladio sui luoghi pii l'Ospedaletto." In *Palladio e Venezia.* Edited by L. Puppi. Florence: Sansoni, 1982, 121-32.

Ferrari, Giorgio. "La Raccolta Palladiana e collaterale di Guglielmo Cappelletti al C.I.S.A. di Vicenza." *Bollettino del CISA* 28 (1976): 333-574.

Foley, Henry. *Records of the English Province of the Society of Jesus.* Vol. 6. London: Burns & Oates, 1880. reprinted 1966.

Forssman, Erik. *Palladios Lehrgebaude.* Stockholm: Almquist & Wiksell, 1965.

———. "Palladio e Daniele Barbaro." *Bollettino del CISA* 8 (1966): pt.2, 68-81.

Fossi, Mazzino. "Documenti per la storia di Villa Medici e di Palazzo Firenze a Roma." *Antichità viva* 15 (1976): pt.3, 37-44.

Frank, Thomas. "Elizabethan Travellers in Rome." *English Miscellany* 6 (1953): 95-132.

Frommel, Christoph. "Antonio da Sangallos Capella Paolina." *Zeitschrift für Kunstgeschicte* 27 (1964): 1-42.

———. "Palladio e la chiesa di S. Pietro a Roma." *Bollettino del CISA* 19 (1977): 107-124.

Frutaz, Amato. *Le piante de Roma.* 3 vols. Rome: Istituto di studi romani, 1962.

Fumagalli, Giuseppe and Giacomo Belli. *Catalogo delle edizioni romane di Antonio Blado Asolano ed eredi (1516-1593) possedute dalla Biblioteca Nazionale Centrale Vittorio Emanuele di Roma.* Rome: Principali Librai, 1891.

Gasquet, Francis. *A History of the Venerable English College, Rome.* London: Longmans, Green & Co., 1920.

Gnoli, Umberto. *Topografia topomastica di Roma medioevale e moderna.* 2nd ed. Foligno, 1984.

Grendler, Paul. F. *Culture and Censorship in Late Renaissance Italy and France.* London: Variorum Reprints, 1981.

Gualdo, Paolo. "Vita di Andrea Palladio a cura di Giangiorgio Zorzi." *Saggi e memorie di storia dell'arte* 2 (1958-59): 91-104.

Hager, Hellmut. "L'Intervento di Carlo Fontana per le chiese dei monasteri di Santa Marta e Santa Margherita in Trastevere." *Commentari* 25 (1974): 225-42.

Hale, J. R. "Andrea Palladio, Polybius and Julius Caesar." *Journal of the Warburg and Courtauld Institutes* 40 (1977): 240-55.

Harleian Miscellany 5 (1810): 1-41 ("A True Description and Direction of what is most worthy to be seen in all Italy. . .").

Heinz, Marianne. *San Giacomo in Augusta in Rom und der Hospitalbau der Renaissance.* Bonn: Rheinischen Friedrich-Wilhelms-Universitat, 1977.

Howe, Eunice D. *The Hospital of Santo Spirito and Pope Sixtus IV.* New York: Garland Press, 1978.

Huelsen, Christian. *Römische Antikengarten des XVI Jahrhunderts.* Heidelburg: Winter, 1917.

———. *Le chiese di Roma nel medio evo.* Florence: Olschki, 1927.

———. *Das Skizzenbuch des Giovannantonio Dosio im Staatlichen Kupferstichkabinett zu Berlin.* Berlin: Heinrichkeller, 1933.

Hulbert, J. R. "Some Medieval Advertisements of Rome." *Modern Philology* 20 (1922-23): 403-424.

Huse, Norbert. "Palladio und die Villa Barbaro in Maser. Bemerkungen zum Problem der Autorschaft." *Arte Veneta* 38 (1974): 106-122.

Isermeyer, Christian A. "I Commentari di G. Cesare nell'edizione palladiana del 1575 e i suoi precedenti." *Bollettino del CISA* 21 (1979): 253–71.

Johnson, A. F. *The Italian Sixteenth Century.* London: Ernest Benn, 1926.

Krautheimer, Richard. *Rome: Profile of a City, 312 –1308.* Princeton: Princeton University Press, 1980.

Kubelik, Martin. "The Basilica Palladiana and the Loggia del Capitaniato: An Architectural and Socio-Historic Confrontation." In *Palladio: Ein Symposium.* vol. 18, Rome: Bibliotheca Helvetica Romana, 1980, 47–56.

Labacco, Antonio. *Libro appartenente all'architettura.* Rome, 1552.

Lanciani, Rodolfo. "Maps, Plans and Views of the City of Rome with especial Reference to a Drawing of the Sixteenth Century in the Burlington-Devonshire Collection." *Journal of the Royal Institute of British Architects.* 3rd Ser. 2 (1895): 645–50.

———. *Storia degli scavi di Roma.* 3 vols. Rome: Ermanno Loescher, 1902–7.

Lavagnino, Emilio. *La chiesa di Santo Spirito in Sassia.* Rome: Banco di Santo Spirito, 1962.

———. "Una novità palladiana." *Bollettino del CISA* 4 (1962): 52–60.

Lea, Henry Charles. *A History of Auricular Confession and Indulgences in the Latin Church.* 3 vols. Philadelphia: Leo Brothers, 1896.

Lewis, Douglas. *The Drawings of Andrea Palladio.* Washington: International Exhibitions Foundation, 1981.

———. "Palladio, Andrea." *Macmillan Encyclopedia of Architects* 3 New York (1982): 345–62.

Loukomski, G. K. *Vignole.* Paris, 1927.

Lotz, Wolfgang. "Osservazioni intorno ai disegni palladiani." *Bollettino del CISA* 4 (1962): 61–68.

Magrini, Antonio. *Memorie intorno la vita e le opere di Andrea Palladio.* Padua: Tipografia del Seminario, 1845.

Mandowsky, Erna and Charles Mitchell. *Pirro Ligorio's Roman Antiquities.* London: The Warburg Institute, 1963.

Mantese, Giovanni. *I mille libri che si leggevano e vendevano a Vicenza alla fine del secolo XVII.* Vicenza: Accademia Olimpica, 1968.

———. "La famiglia Thiene e la riforma protestante a Vicenza." *Odeo Olimpico* 8 (1969–70): 81–186.

Mantese, Giovanni and Mariano Nardello. *Due processi per eresia.* n.p.: Vicenza, 1974.

Martin, Gregory. *Roma Sancta (1581).* Edited by George B. Parks. Rome: Edizioni di storia e letteratura, 1969.

Masetti-Zannini, Gian Ludovico. *Stampatori e librai a Roma nella seconda metà del cinquecento.* Rome: Palombi, 1980.

Mauro, Lucio. *Le antichità della città di Roma.* Venice: Giordano Ziletti, 1557.

Mola, Giovanni Battista. *Breve racconto delle migliori opere di diversi architetti, pittori, scultori et altri in Roma.* Edited by Karl Noehles. Berlin: Bruno Hessling, 1966 (facsimile reprint of 1663 edition).

Montaigne, Michel de. *The Diary of Montaigne's Journey to Italy in 1580 and 1581.* Translated by E. J. Trechmann. New York: Harcourt and Brace, 1929.

Montini, Renzo. "Palazzo Firenze." *Studi romani* 6 (1958): 422–36.

Morsolin, Bernardo. *Giangiorgio Trissino; monografia d'un gentiluomo letterato nel secolo XVI.* 2nd ed. Florence: Le Monnier, 1894.

Moryson, Fynes. *An Itinerary Containing His Ten Years Travel.* Vol. 1. Glasgow: James MacLehose & Sons, 1907.

Munday, Anthony. *The English Romayne Lyfe 1582.* Edited by G. B. Harrison. Edinburgh: University Press, 1966.

Murray, Peter. Introduction to *Five Early Guides to Rome and Florence.* Farnborough: Gregg, 1972.

Nardelli, Franca. "Torchi, famiglie, libri nella Roma del Seicento." *La Bibliofilia* 86 (1984): 159–72.

Nash, Ernest. *Pictorial Dictionary of Ancient Rome.* 2 vols. London: A. Zwemmer, 1961.

Nichols, Francis Morgan, translator. *Mirabilia Urbis Romae; The Marvels of Rome.* London: Ellis & Elvey, 1889.

Noè, Enrico. "Primo passo per Giambattista Maganza Senior." *Arte Veneta* 30 (1976): 98–105.

Nova, Alessandro. *The Artistic Patronage of Pope Julius III (1550–55): Profane Imagery and Buildings for the Del Monte Family in Rome.* New York: Garland, 1988.

Olivieri, Achille. "Alessandro Trissino e il movimento calvinista vicentino nel cinquecento." *Rivista di storia della chiesa in Italia* 21 (1967): 54–117.

———. "'Microcosmi' familiari e trasmissione 'ereticale': I Trissino." *Convegno su Giangiorgio Trissino.* Edited by Neri Pozza. Vicenza: Accademia Olimpica, 1980, 175–90.

———. *Palladio, le corte e le famiglie.* Vicenza: Istituto per le Richerche di Storia Sociale e di Storia Religiosa, 1981.

Olschki, Cesare. "Francesco Albertini." *Roma* 2 (1924): 483–90.

"Onuphrii Panvinii Veronensis Fratris Eremitae Augustiniani in Ventum Libros Antiquitatum Romanorum Praefatio." *Spicilegium Romanorum.* Vol. 8. Rome: Typis Collegii Urbani, 1842.

Palladio, Andrea. *L'Antichità di Roma.* Rome: Lucrino, 1554; reprinted in Murray, 1972.

———. *I quattro libri dell'architettura.* Venice: Domenico de' Franceschi, 1570.

———. *I commentari di C. Giulio Cesare.* Venice: Pietro de' Franceschi, 1575.

———. *The Four Books of Andrea Palladio's Architecture.* Introduced by Adolf K. Placzek. New York: Dover, 1965; reprint of 1738 English translation.

Pane, Roberto. "Palladio artista e trattista." *Palladio* 6, no.1 (1942): 16–24.

———. *Andrea Palladio.* 2nd ed. Turin: Einaudi, 1961.

Panvinio, Onofrio. *Le sette chiese di Roma.* Rome, 1575.

Parks, George, B. *The English Traveller to Italy.* Vol. 1 of *The Middle Ages (to 1525).* Rome, 1954.

——— ed., *The History of Italy (1549) by William Thomas.* Ithaca, N.Y.: Cornell University Press, 1963.

Paschini, Pio. "Daniele Barbaro letterato e prelato Veneziano nel cinquecento." *Rivista di storia della chiesa in Italia* 16 (1962): 73–107.

Pastor, Ludwig von. *The History of the Popes.* Vol. 16. Edited by F. I. Antrobus et al, 7th ed., London, 1949.

Peddie, R. A. *Subject Index of Books Published up to and including 1880.* London: Grafton & Co., 1948.

Pescarzoli, Antonio. *I libri di viaggio e le guide della Raccolta Luigi Vittorio Fossati Bellani.* 3 vols. Rome: Edizioni di storia e letteratura, 1957.

Pietrangeli, Carlo, ed. *Guide rionali di Roma.* Rome: Assessorato Antichità, 1971–82.

Pollen, J. H. "The Memoirs of Father Robert Persons." *Miscellanea Catholic Record Society* 2 (1906): 12–218.

Puppi, Lionello. *Scrittori vicentini di architettura del secolo XVI.* Vicenza: Accademia Olimpica, 1973.

————. *Andrea Palladio.* Translated by P. Sanders. 2nd ed. Boston: New York Graphic Society, 1975.

————, ed. *Andrea Palladio; Il testo, l'immagine, la città.* Vicenza: Electa Editrice, 1980.

Rigon, Fernando. *Palladio.* Bologna: Capitol, 1980.

Rinaldi, Ernesto. *La fondazione del Collegio Romano.* Arezzo: Cooperativa Tipografica, 1914.

Romani, Mario. *Pellegrini e viaggiatori nell'economia di Roma dal XIV al XVII secolo.* Milan: Societa Editrice Vita e Pensiero, 1948.

Salvetti, Caterina Bernardi. "Il sottosuolo delle terme di Diocleziano nel secolo XVI nei disegni della Biblioteca d'Arte nel Museo di Stato di Berlino." *Studi romani* 28, no. 1 (1970): 462–66.

Scaglia, Giustina. "The Origin of an Archaeological Plan of Rome by Alessandro Strozzi." *Journal of the Warburg and Courtauld Institutes* 27 (1964): 137–63.

Schmarsow, August, ed. *Opusculum de mirabilibus novae urbis Romae* by Francesco Albertini. Heilbronn: Henninger, 1886.

Schroeder, Henry J. *Canons and Decrees of the Council of Trent.* St. Louis: Herder, 1941.

Schudt, Ludwig. *Le Guide di Roma; Materialien zu einer Geschichte der römischen Topographie.* Vienna: Filser, 1930; reprint: Farnborough: Gregg, 1971.

Short-title Catalogue of Books Printed in Italy and of Italian Books Printed in Other Countries from 1465 to 1600 now in the British Museum. London, 1958.

"A Sixteenth Century Guidebook." *Connoisseur* 2 (1902): 204.

Temenza, Tommaso. *Vita di Andrea Palladio.* Venice: G. Pasquali, 1762.

Tiepolo, Maria Francesca. *Testimonianze veneziane di interesse palladiano; mostra documentaria.* Venice: Archivio di Stato, 1980.

Titi, Filippo. *Studio di pittura, scultura ed architettura nelle chiese di Roma.* Rome, 1674.

Trenkler, Ernst. *Le guide di Rome in der Österreichischen Nationalbibliothek.* Vienna: Österreichische Institut für Bibliotheksforschung, 1976.

Trettenero, Vittorio. *Andrea Palladio scrittore.* Milan: EST, 1938.

Valentini, Roberto and Giuseppe Zucchetti. *Codice topografico della città di Roma.* 4 vols. Rome: Istituto storico italiano per il medio evo (Fonti per la storia d'Italia), 1953.

Waetzoldt, Stephan. Introduction to *Trattato nuovo delle cose meravigliose* by Pietro Martire Felini. Rome: Zannetti, 1610; reprint: Berlin: Bruno Hessling, 1969.

Wittkower, Rudolf. *Architectural Principles in the Age of Humanism.* New York: Norton, 1971.

Zaccaria, Francescantonio. *Storia polemica delle proibizioni de' libri.* Rome: Generoso Salomoni, 1777.

Zander, Giuseppe. "Il Vasari, gli studiosi del suo temp e l'architettura antica." *Il Vasari stori ografo e artista; Atti del Congresso internazionale nel IV centenario della morte.* Florence, 1974, 333–50.

Zanella, Giacomo. *Vita di Andrea Palladio.* Milan: Ulrico Hoepli, 1880.

Zorzi, Giangiorgio. *La vera origine e la giovenezza di Andrea Palladio.* Venice: Estratto dell'Archivio Veneto-Tridentino, 1922.

————. *I disegni delle antichità di Andrea Palladio.* Venice: Neri Pozza, 1959.

————. "La famiglia Palladio secondo nuovi documenti." *Archivio veneto.* 5th ser. 70 (1962): 14–51.

————. *Le chiese e i ponti di Andrea Palladio.* Venice: Neri Pozza, 1967.

Le cose maravigliose: List of Editions Consulted

Date	Publisher	Place of Publication
1557	Dorico	Rome
1558	Dorico	Rome
1561	Dorico	Rome
1562	Blado	Rome
1563	Dorico	Rome
1565	Amador	Venice
1565	Varisco	Venice
1566	Varisco	Venice
1566	Accolto	Rome
1568	Accolto	Rome
1569	Toso	Rome
1571	Osmarino-Gigliotto	Rome
1572	Osmarino-Gigliotto	Rome
1573	Osmarino	Rome
1574	Accolto	Rome
1575	Degli Angeli	Rome
1575	Blado	Rome

1575	Rampazetto	Venice
1575	-?-	Venice
1576	Accolto	Rome
1579	Osmarino	Rome
1584	Osmarino-Gigliotto	Rome
1585	Osmarino-Gigliotto	Rome
1587	Zoppini	Venice
1587	Martinelli-Diani	Rome
1587	Osmarino-Gigliotto	Rome
1588	Francini	Venice
1589	Martinelli	Rome
1589	Diani	Rome
1589	Francini	Rome
1591	Accolto-Facchetti	Rome
1594	Zannetti-Facchetti	Rome
1595	Facciotto-Francini	Rome
1596	Mutii-Franceschini	Rome
1600	Zannetti-Francini	Rome
1600	Francini	Rome
1600	Zannetti	Rome
1600	Fei-Facchetti	Rome
1609	Mascardi-Giuliani	Rome
1610	Zannetti-Francini	Rome

Index

INDEX OF HISTORICAL NAMES AND PLACES

Andrea Palladio: The Churches of Rome presents the first translation into English of Andrea Palladio's *Descritione delle chiese* (1554), the most popular account of Roman churches in the sixteenth century. Palladio's short book, about fifty unnumbered folios, became the basis of all subsequent editions of the guidebook, published under the title *Le cose maravigliose di Roma*. Palladio's text is here collated with an English translation of the next important edition of the guidebook (1563). In addition, Professor Howe includes an English translation of a contemporary guide to Roman antiquities (*La guida romana*) composed for the foreign tourist and published for the first time with Palladio's *Descritione* in 1557. This too has been collated with the revised version appearing in *Le cose maravigliose* of 1563.

Professor Howe's introductory essay examines issues which had an impact on the genesis and dissemination of the guidebook, including Palladio's motives for composing the *Descritione*, his practical and scholarly concerns, the debt he felt to his patrons, and the religious climate of mid-sixteenth-century Italy. In her final chapter, she proposes sources for Palladio's guidebook and traces the manner in which it was transformed into successive editions of *Le cose maravigliose*.

Eunice D. Howe is Associate Professor of Art History in the School of Fine Arts of the University of Southern California. She has received grants from the American Association of University Women and the American Philosophical Society. Her publications include *The Hospital of Santo Spiritu and Pope Sixtus IV* (1978) and articles in *Gazette des Beaux Arts* and *The Dictionary of Art*.

mRts

medieval & renaissance texts & studies
is the publishing program of the
Center for Medieval and Early Renaissance Studies
at the State University of New York at Binghamton.

mRts emphasizes books that are needed —
texts, translations, and major research tools.

mRts aims to publish the highest quality scholarship
in attractive and durable format at modest cost.